Outperform

T0328376

Outperform

Inside the Investment Strategy of Billion Dollar Endowments

John Baschab and Jon Piot

WILEY

John Wiley & Sons, Inc.

Copyright © 2010 by John Baschab and Jon Piot. All rights reserved.

Published by John Wiley & Sons, Inc., Hoboken, New Jersey.
Published simultaneously in Canada.

No part of this publication may be reproduced, stored in a retrieval system, or transmitted in any form or by any means, electronic, mechanical, photocopying, recording, scanning, or otherwise, except as permitted under Section 107 or 108 of the 1976 United States Copyright Act, without either the prior written permission of the Publisher, or authorization through payment of the appropriate per-copy fee to the Copyright Clearance Center, Inc., 222 Rosewood Drive, Danvers, MA 01923, (978) 750-8400, fax (978) 646-8600, or on the Web at www.copyright.com. Requests to the Publisher for permission should be addressed to the Permissions Department, John Wiley & Sons, Inc., 111 River Street, Hoboken, NJ 07030, (201) 748-6011, fax (201) 748-6008, or online at http://www.wiley.com/go/permissions.

Limit of Liability/Disclaimer of Warranty: While the publisher and author have used their best efforts in preparing this book, they make no representations or warranties with respect to the accuracy or completeness of the contents of this book and specifically disclaim any implied warranties of merchantability or fitness for a particular purpose. No warranty may be created or extended by sales representatives or written sales materials. The advice and strategies contained herein may not be suitable for your situation. You should consult with a professional where appropriate. Neither the publisher nor author shall be liable for any loss of profit or any other commercial damages, including but not limited to special, incidental, consequential, or other damages.

For general information on our other products and services or for technical support, please contact our Customer Care Department within the United States at (800) 762-2974, outside the United States at (317) 572-3993, or fax (317) 572-4002.

Wiley also publishes its books in a variety of electronic formats. Some content that appears in print may not be available in electronic books. For more information about Wiley products, visit our web site at www.wiley.com.

Library of Congress Cataloging-in-Publication Data:

Baschab, John, 1968–
  Outperform : inside the investment strategy of billion dollar endowments / John Baschab and Jon Piot.
      p. cm.
  Includes bibliographical references and index.
  ISBN 978-1-118-96184-1 (pbk); ISBN 978-0-470-44213-5 (cloth);
  ISBN 978-0-470-65101-8 (ebk); ISBN 978-0-470-65129-2 (ebk).
  ISBN 978-0-470-65130-8 (ebk).
  1. Endowments–United States–Finance.   2. Investments–United States.
3. Institutional investments–United States.   I. Piot, Jon, 1966–   II. Title.
  HV91.B28 2010
  332.67′253–dc22
                                                        2010006831

10 9 8 7 6 5 4 3 2 1

Contents

Preface

The idea for this book came to us in late 2007. After spending several years researching the money management business, we were intrigued by the continual stellar performance of university endowments as it pertained to their investment returns. While these endowments would report double-digit returns year in and year out, the individual investors we knew were hardly earning middle single digits. Take out fees and taxes and the individual investor was lucky to earn a couple of points.

We had just sold our second company and were searching for a home for the proceeds. We interviewed personal wealth advisors, but after a while, all the presentations started to sound the same. There was not much differentiating investment management between providers.

What we figured out is that the average retail and so-called high-net-worth or private wealth management professionals are often simply "asset gatherers" for investment banks. The management approach is frequently simplistic: after you sign on they help you determine a risk profile that fits you, and build an asset allocation model. Unfortunately, in this arrangement, oftentimes at best, you'll begin to earn market returns less fees or at worst, you sign up with a dishonest manager and lose your life savings (a la Bernie Madoff).

We could have taken another route, that of the highly active self-managed account of the individual investor. This is typically the individual who avidly watches the business news channels hoping to spot the next Google or Apple early on. This person has a standard 60 percent/40 percent equity bond portfolio. In the equity portfolio, they've selected 20 diverse stocks and try to keep up with those 20. Some of these investors do great while others fail miserably.

We found the endowment model intriguing. In June 2007, Harvard reported their endowment returned 23 percent that year. Yale returned 28 percent while minimizing risk. We wondered how are these endowments earning such exceptional returns? The more we read, the more interested we became, and we decided to figure out the puzzle once and for all. What is there to be learned from endowment investing? How can the individual learn from endowments and achieve superior returns?

We have written three previous books, and we felt the best way to understand the topic was to research it and document our findings, and in early 2008, we established the concept for the book.

In mid-2008 we had interviewed several chief investment officers from endowments and foundations. We were convinced that key learnings from the endowment investment model existed for individuals, and we were on track to publish the book in late 2008 or early 2009. The fiscal year end for most endowments is June 30, and the results for the period ended June 30, 2008, for most of the top endowments were respectable: Harvard 8.6 percent, Yale 4.5 percent, Stanford 6.2 percent. During the same period, the S&P had a negative double digit return (not including dividends). However, things changed rapidly beginning in the second quarter of 2008. In March 2008, the Federal Reserve Bank of New York provided an emergency loan to Bear Stearns to avert the collapse of the bank. On Monday, March 17, 2008, the *New York Times* reported that JPMorgan had offered to purchase Bear for just $2 per share ("Could Bear Stearns Do Better," *New York Times*, March 17, 2008). The company had traded for $30 per share on Friday and was off its 52-week high of $133. This shocking sequence of events was the prelude to one of the worst bear markets in U.S. history.

On September 15, 2008, Lehman Brothers filed for bankruptcy, and by the time we reached our anticipated publication date, the United States and the world were in a full-scale economic disaster. We knew that our work would not be complete without the results of endowment performance during the 2008–2009 fiscal year.

The seriousness of the situation caused many college presidents to publish emergency letters to the community. On November 10, 2008, President Drew Faust sent a letter to the Harvard University faculty, students, staff and alumni detailing the significance of the recent events. The letter by President Faust detailed the implications of the global economic crisis for the University.

He wrote, "We all know of the extraordinary turbulence still roiling the world's financial markets and the broader economy. The downturn is widely seen as the most serious in decades, and each day's headlines remind us that heightened volatility and persisting uncertainty have become our new economic reality."

President Faust explained how the university had weathered numerous other difficult times over centuries and that this event was similar but would take extraordinary efforts to adapt to change and manage resources.

Faust stated that revenue would be affected and the need to plan was important in order to preserve priorities such as teaching, research, and service. The effect would be felt in the income received from the endowment, from donors and foundations who are less able to give, and from federal grants from "stressed federal budgets."

He wrote, "Consider, first, the endowment. As a result of strong returns and the generosity of our alumni and friends, endowment income has come to fund more than a third of the University's annual operating budget. Our investments have often outperformed familiar market indexes, thanks to skillful management and broad diversification across asset classes. But given the breadth and the depth of the present downturn, even well-diversified portfolios are experiencing major losses. Moody's, a leading financial research and ratings service, recently projected a 30 percent decline in the value of college and university endowments in the current fiscal year. While we can hope that markets will improve, we need to be prepared to absorb unprecedented endowment losses and plan for a period of greater financial constraint."

He went on to assure the community that Harvard would press on with important programs such as financial aid, scholarships, research and other critical programs that allow the university to attract and educate the best and brightest people in the world during this difficult time. The economic crisis was far from over and multi-hundred point swings in the Dow Jones Industrial Average were shocking but nevertheless still occurring.

On June 30, 2009, endowments reported dismal numbers. For many it was the worst drawdown in modern times. Returns of negative 30 percent were seen.

However, a broader view of endowment performance showed that the model still produces superior returns over long periods. The endowment model still handily beats the S&P index for the 10-year period ending June 2009.

We believe there is tremendous value for individual investors to understand how endowments manage their money. This book is important for several reasons. First, we have directly interviewed a significant number of the top investment professionals in the endowment business. Second, concepts that you will read can be put to use in developing your own investment philosophy. Third, the trends identified by the CIOs we have interviewed will certainly be important for years to come.

We are excited to share these insights and to provide an updated, first-hand look at the architecture of an exceptional investment approach. As always, we invite and welcome your feedback. We can be reached at:

JOHN BASCHAB
jbaschab@chicagobooth.edu
JON PIOT
jpiot@mba1995.hbs.edu

Acknowledgments

This project began as a quest to improve our own understanding of superior investment management and to understand the workings of a great investment model. It is the result of countless contributions by mentors, colleagues, friends, family, and teachers. We thank all of them for helping us along the way.

We would like to thank Pamela Van Giessen, Emilie Herman, Melissa Lopez, and the team at John Wiley & Sons for their invaluable assistance and advice as we completed this work. Thanks also to Rafe Sagalyn and his team at the Sagalyn Literary Agency.

We would also like to acknowledge the interviewees and contributors for their invaluable time and effort. This includes Bob Boldt, Mary Cahill, Jeremy Crigler, Celia Dallas, Rafe de la Gueronniere, James Hille, Jonathan Hook, Anjum Hussain, Lyn Hutton, Don Lindsey, Thruston Morton, Guy Patton, Sally Staley, Sandy Urie, James H. C. Walsh, Scott Wise, Mark W. Yusko, and Bruce Zimmerman.

Several people were instrumental in assisting us with contacts in the industry. Kim Davis, Tom Gale, Bob Rowling, Mike Smith, and Elizabeth Williams were especially helpful here.

Thanks to the team at NACUBO and the Commonfund for providing such valuable annual research to the endowment business, and for permission to utilize their research in this book.

Last, and most important, we thank our families, Mary, Emily, and Will Baschab; and Susan, Lauren, Allison, and Will Piot, and close friend John Martin. Without their patience, support, and sacrifices of time, this book would not be possible.

Part I

ACADEMIC ENDOWMENTS

Chapter 1

Academic Endowments Overview

"Investment in knowledge pays the best interest."
—Benjamin Franklin

Each year over 800 of the United States' best-known academic institutions take part in the National Association of College and University Business Officers (NACUBO)-Commonfund study of endowments. The much anticipated survey ranks the university investment pools on performance and assets for the prior fiscal year. The most powerful and influential universities are perennial entrants in the top 10 percent of the list, with the cutoff being nearly a billion dollars under management. The size and performance of a university's investments has a tremendous impact on its ability to carry out a mission of teaching, research and service. It is no surprise that the NACUBO-Commonfund study commands the attention of a wide variety of constituencies, from professional money managers to university administrators.

Until 2009, the investment performance of academic endowments has been exceptional, and positive. In 2007, academic endowments returned on average 17.2 percent, compared to a considerably more modest 8.88 percent Dow and 5.49 percent S&P 500 index return that year. 2007 was no exception—in the last 15 years, large endowments have outperformed the broad market indexes eleven times. This extended long-term performance is a remarkable testament to the effectiveness of the endowment investment model and to the professionals managing the investment pools.

3

More recently, the credit crisis and market dislocation of 2008–2009 tested the very foundations of the endowment investment model. Did the model hold up? What are these investment managers doing today based on what they learned? These are important questions and are particularly relevant to individual investors. The S&P 500 index, which is a reasonable proxy for the returns a typical small investor might expect, returned negative 2.2 percent annualized over the 10-year period ending June 2009. During that same period, endowments returned 6.6 percent annualized. To avoid a repeat of this "lost decade," individual investors can look to the endowment model to better understand how endowments so consistently outperform and to inform their own decisions.

The World of Endowments

Academic endowments are a long-term, carefully managed pool of funds used to support the operating budget and long-term goals of the institution. The endowments in the 2009 NACUBO-Commonfund study represent over $306 billion in combined assets. The smallest endowments are under $25 million in assets while the largest have over $1 billion in endowment assets. Even after the losses of the 2009 fiscal year, over 50 academic endowments had over $1 billion under management. Endowment management complexity ranges from part-time investment committee oversight to sophisticated offices with dozens of investment professionals and activities rivaling the largest hedge funds. Large endowments will employ a Chief Investment Officer (CIO) to oversee the investment decisions and operations of the endowment.

Endowments have enjoyed a remarkably durable and consistent track record of performance over the past 20 years. Even with the global economic crisis of 2008–2009, the large endowment returns still surpassed almost any measuring stick or competitive benchmark. There is much to learn from studying endowment fund management for the individual investor, and in this book we have documented how endowment CIOs are thinking about investing in the coming years.

At over $26 billion, the Harvard endowment takes top ranking for endowment size. It was hard to foresee that the establishment of the fund in 1669 would grow over the next 340 years to a peak of

$36.9 billion in 2008. Harvard represents one of the most powerful elements of endowment returns—a perpetual time horizon for investing. Sixty pounds, the initial amount in the Harvard endowments and a considerable sum of money at that time, compounded at 6 percent over a 340-year period would yield $36 billion today, not accounting for withdrawals or additional contributions. Endowments are the ultimate long-term investor, created to last in perpetuity, and to provide a steady income to the institutions. While only spending a portion of the earnings they generate, they compound their principal to keep up with inflation and preserve purchasing power.

For almost 300 years of U.S. endowment investing, since the inception of the Harvard endowment and until the early 1970s, endowment investment management followed a fairly staid approach—employing a standard investment mix of bonds and stocks. In the 1970s endowment investment philosophy began to change, primarily based on a new set of standards reflected in the Uniform Management of Institutional Funds Act (UMIFA). These changes provided dramatically increased flexibility in portfolio management, risk evaluation, spending policy and use of outside managers. The implementation of UMIFA provided the avenue for endowments to begin transformating into the sophisticated investment engines they are today. To support their institution, most endowments employ complex techniques to achieve a relatively simple set of objectives, which can be broken down into three pieces:

1. Maintain the corpus in perpetuity—preserve the principal over time. This is the primary objective.
2. Grow the corpus at or faster than the inflation rate—this is to maintain the "real" value of the corpus so that it can be invested the following year with the same purchasing power.
3. Distribute excess earnings (over the inflation rate) to the institution in support of its objectives; this is often in support of the operating budget or can be specific projects undertaken by the institution.

Although endowments are intended as perpetual entities, their mandate to provide annual income for the institution requires careful planning to ensure an appropriate level of liquidity on an annual basis.

History of Endowments

Endowments at U.S. institutions have early roots. In 1649, Harvard received its first gift from alumni by members of the Harvard Class of 1642 (John Bulkeley and George Downing, the college's first teaching fellows) and the Class of 1646 (Samuel Winthrop and John Alcock). According to the *Harvard Guide*, this initial gift was real estate, "a once upon a time cowyard." The gift was granted the name Fellows' Orchard after alumni planted apple trees on it. "Widener Library now occupies part of the site," according to the *Guide*.[1]

In 1669, 10 merchants from Portsmouth, New Hampshire, pledged £60 per year for seven years to Harvard. Harvard endowment lore also holds that the lumber merchants sometimes paid the school in lumber, which the treasurer sold to convert to cash.[2]

Harvard has managed its endowment well. It has maintained the value of its fund in real terms while providing a strong support for the university operating budget. In addition, the university is one of the top fund-raising schools in the world and receives new gifts which increase the size of the endowment so that income keeps up with the growth in university expenses that exceed inflation.[3] In the fiscal year ended 2008, Harvard ranked second behind Stanford in raising funds from private donors with $690 million raised.[4]

Endowments are important to schools for many reasons. Primarily, they provide a stable mechanism for predictable long-term annual income to support the projects and goals of the institution, such as instruction, research, new facilities, technology and capital improvements. This predictability allows the institution to engage in planning over extended timelines. A well-managed endowment is a critical component of an effective and successful educational institution.

While endowments may appear to be an undifferentiated pool of money, this is not the case. A typical endowment consists of dozens or even hundreds of multiple funds that that may be managed as one or more pools of assets. The source of funds is usually private donors who gift restricted and unrestricted funds. Restrictions may influence spending and investment policy and hinder the investment officer's ability to maximize returns across asset pools.[5]

Academic Endowments in the Context of the Investment World

Endowments are just one type of investment vehicle, and it is useful to place them in context of other institutional investments as well as the broader markets. Academic endowments are surprisingly small relative to other investment pools in terms of assets. The net asset value of sovereign wealth funds is almost eight times larger than the net asset value of all U.S. college endowments combined. (See Table 1.1.)

While endowments are comparatively small, their exceptional performance over the past two decades warrants outsized attention to their techniques and philosophies.

Large Academic Endowments

This book is focused on endowments and investment managers with over $1 billion in assets. The focus is intentional. Not only have endowments

Table 1.1 Investment Entities by Total Assets Managed (Q3, 2007)

Investment Entity Type	Net Asset Value (Billions)
U.S. College Endowments	$411
Private Foundations	$485
Private Equity	$686
Hedge Funds	$2,680
Sovereign Wealth Funds	$3,200
Pension Funds	$20,000
Mutual Funds	$26,000
Total U.S. Equities Market	$60,874

SOURCES: 2007 NACUBO Study (Endowments); International Financial Services London, Private Equity 2008, August 2008 (Private Equity); Investment Company Institute, *2009 Investment Company Factbook*, Section 7, Worldwide Mutual Fund Totals (Mutual Funds); World Federation of Exchanges, Statistics, 2007 Equities Market Capitalization (Equities); *The Economist*, January 27, 2008 (Pension Funds); *Alternative Investment Management Association's Roadmap to Hedge Funds*, November 2008, Alexander Ineichen (Hedge funds); *Sovereign Wealth Funds*, Bryan Balin, March 27, 2008 (Sovereign wealth funds) in aggregate performed well, but the largest endowments have traditionally outperformed their smaller peers. When evaluating the performance data, an interesting fact appears: The larger the endowment, generally speaking, the better the return. The two largest endowments, those of Harvard University and Yale University, have significantly outperformed the average endowment. Following is a sampling of the largest endowments in the United States and their assets under management.[6]

Top 12 Largest Endowments (Net Asset Value—Fiscal YE 2009)
1. Harvard University ($25.7B)
2. Yale University ($16.3B)
3. Stanford University ($12.6B)
4. Princeton University ($12.6B)
5. University of Texas System ($12.2B)
6. MIT ($8B)
7. University of Michigan ($6B)
8. Columbia University ($5.9B)
9. Northwestern University ($5.5B)
10. University of Pennsylvania ($5.2B)
11. University of Chicago ($5.1B)
12. The Texas A&M University System and Foundations ($5.1B)

The following is a brief overview of the top five endowments in the United States, ranked by net asset value.

Harvard University: Harvard Management Company

Harvard University was established in 1636 and is the oldest higher education institution in the United States. There are approximately 7,100 undergraduate and 12,870 graduate students at Harvard. The President and Fellows of Harvard College, a governing board, oversees financial affairs. Harvard was one of the first universities to separate its endowment into a separate investment group. Harvard Management Company (HMC), a wholly owned subsidiary, was founded in 1974 to manage the university's investment assets. The endowment consists of over 11,000 separate funds established over many years. Over the past 10 years, endowment income has grown to support roughly one-third of Harvard's annual operating budget. As a result, HMC views its work as integrally linked to the work of Harvard's faculty, students, and staff. The Harvard endowment had a net asset value of $25.7 billion as of fiscal June 30, 2009.[7]

From 1974 to mid-2009 (academic endowment typically ends their fiscal year in June), under HMC, the endowment has grown from $2 billion to $25.7 billion. The endowment's aggregate payout rate is approximately 4.8 percent with a target rate of 5–5.5 percent. The payout rate when multiplied by the aggregate size of the endowment equals approximately a third of Harvard's operating income. HMC employs approximately 150 staff. Figure 1.1 shows the reporting structure relative to the university. HMC has most recently been managed by Jane Mendillo. Prior to Ms. Mendillo, Mohamed El-Erian, now CEO and

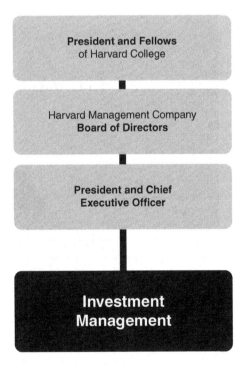

Figure 1.1 Reporting Structure of Harvard Management Company
SOURCE: Harvard Management Company

co-CIO of PIMCO, presided over the endowment. Jack Myer, who with David Swensen is widely credited with creating the modern endowment investment model, was president and CEO of HMC in the 1990s.

Figure 1.2 shows the overall growth of the Harvard endowment for the past 20 years.

Table 1.2 shows the impressive annual returns the Harvard endowment has achieved in various time periods.

Although the returns weren't reported in the 2009 annual report, at the end of fiscal 2008 Harvard's endowment returns were 13.2 percent since inception and 14.6 percent annualized over 30 years. Table 1.3 shows the evolution of the Harvard endowment asset allocation and policy portfolio. You will find a dramatic reduction in equities and an increase in real assets and absolute return.

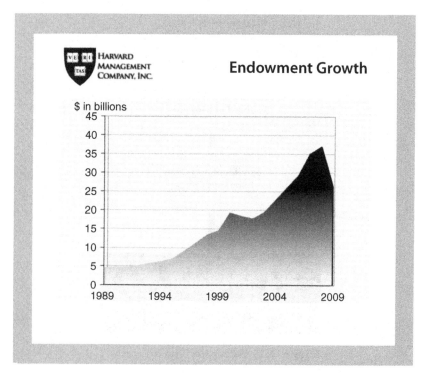

Figure 1.2 Harvard Endowment Growth
SOURCE: Harvard Management Company

Table 1.2   Harvard Average Returns
for the Periods Ended June 30, 2009

Period	Total Return
1 year	−27.3%
5 years	6.2%
10 years	8.9%
20 years	11.7%

SOURCE: Harvard Annual Report, June 30, 2009
*Total return is net of all fees and expenses

Yale University: Yale Corporation Investment Office

Yale is the third oldest university in the United States, established in 1701. There are over 11,500 undergraduate and graduate students at Yale.[8] The Yale Corporation Investment Office (YCIO) manages the endowment and other university financial assets. The Investment Office was created in 1975, and the Investment Committee is responsible for

Table 1.3   Harvard Asset Allocation

	Fiscal Year		
	1995	2005	2010
Domestic Equities	38%	15%	11%
Foreign Equities	15	10	11
Emerging Markets	5	5	11
Private Equities	12	13	13
Total Equities	*70*	*43*	*46*
Commodities	6	13	14
Real Estate	7	10	9
Total Real Assets	*13*	*23*	*23*
Domestic Bonds	15	11	4
Foreign Bonds	5	5	2
High-Yield	2	5	2
Inflation-indexed Bonds	0	6	5
Total Fixed Income	*22*	*27*	*13*
Absolute Return	0	12	16
Cash	−5	−5	2
TOTAL	**100%**	**100%**	**100%**

SOURCE: Harvard Annual Report, June 30, 2009

oversight of the endowment. The YCIO is led by the chief investment officer, David Swensen, who is perhaps one of the most well-known investment professionals in the United States. He created the modern endowment investment model, also known as the Yale model, and published two bestselling books on the topic: *Pioneering Portfolio Management* in 2000, and *Unconventional Success: A Fundamental Approach to Personal Investment* in 2005. Prior to joining Yale in 1985, Swensen spent six years on Wall Street at Lehman Brothers and Salomon Brothers. In addition to managing the endowment, he is also a professor at Yale College and Yale School of Management.

Over the past 10 years, endowment income has grown to support roughly 36 percent of Yale's $2.3 billion annual operating revenue.[9] The Yale endowment had a net asset value of $16.3 billion as of June 30, 2009.[10]

Over the past 10 years, the endowment grew from $5.8 billion to $16.3 billion with annual net investment returns of 11.8 percent. The endowment outpaced its benchmark and outpaced institutional fund indexes. The Yale endowment's 20-year record of 13.4 percent per annum produced a 2007 endowment value more than seven times that of 1989. See Figure 1.3 for the growth in the Yale endowment.

Yale attributes its success to:

- Disciplined, diversified asset allocation policies
- Superior active management results
- Strong capital market returns

Spending from endowment grew during the last decade from $191 million to approximately $850 million, an annual growth rate of approximately 16 percent. The endowment consists of thousands of funds with a variety of purposes and restrictions. Funds are commingled in an investment pool and tracked with unit accounting much like a large mutual fund.

The Yale Investment Company employs 19 full-time professionals. Several notable ex-Yale professionals have gone on to manage other large academic endowments, notably MIT (Seth Alexander), Harvard (Jane Mendillo) and Princeton (Andrew K. Golden). As at Harvard, Yale's investment philosophy has directed a large percentage of the endowment

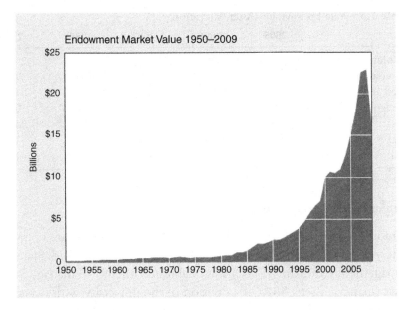

Figure 1.3 Yale Endowment
SOURCE: Yale University

toward investment in assets expected to produce equity-like returns. Both institutions were leaders in the industry move toward alternative and real assets and non-U.S. public equities relative to historic levels.[11]

Table 1.4 shows the returns for the past five years for the Yale endowment.

Table 1.5 shows the evolution of the Yale endowment asset allocation and policy portfolio. You will find a reduction in equities and an increase in real assets and absolute return.

Table 1.4 Yale Endowment Returns

	Fiscal Year				
	2009	**2008**	**2007**	**2006**	**2005**
Market Value (in millions)	16,326.6	$22,869.7	$22,530.2	$18,030.6	$15,224.9
Return	−24.6%	4.5%	28.0%	22.9%	22.3%

SOURCE: Yale University

Table 1.5 Yale Endowment Asset Allocation

	2005	2006	2007	2008	2009
Absolute Return	25.7%	23.3%	23.3%	25.1%	24.3%
Domestic Equity	14.1%	11.6%	11.0%	10.1%	7.5%
Fixed Income	4.9%	3.8%	4.0%	4.0%	4.0%
Foreign Equity	13.7%	14.6%	14.1%	15.2%	9.8%
Private Equity	14.8%	16.4%	18.7%	20.2%	24.3%
Real Assets	25.0%	27.8%	27.1%	29.3%	32.0%
Cash	1.9%	2.5%	1.9%	−3.9%	−1.9%

SOURCE: Yale University

Stanford University Endowment

Stanford was founded in 1891 by Leland Stanford. There are approximately 15,300 graduate and undergraduate students at Stanford. Stanford Management Company (SMC) was established in 1991 to manage Stanford's financial assets. SMC is a division of the university with oversight by the board of directors appointed by the university board of trustees. SMC manages $15 billion of endowment and trust assets.[12] The endowment consists of over 6,000 funds.

Over past 10 years, the endowment has achieved an 8.9 percent annualized rate of return, growing from $4.3 billion to $15 billion. SMC manages the assets to optimize long-term returns, provide stable annual payouts, and preserve purchasing power. The endowment provided 29 percent of Stanford's 2009 operating revenue. Table 1.6 shows the long-term policy targets set by Stanford.

Stanford has achieved over 15 percent annual returns for the previous 10 years as shown in Table 1.7.

Table 1.6 Stanford Long-Term Policy Targets

	Target
Absolute Return	18%
Public Equity	37%
Fixed Income	10%
Private Equity	12%
Real Estate	16%
Natural Resources	7%

SOURCE: Report from the Stanford Management Company, 2009, http://www.stanfordmanage.org/Annual_Report.pdf

Table 1.7 Stanford Average Returns for
the Period Ended June 30, 2009

	Total Return
1 year	−25.9%
3 years	−1.0%
5 years	6.8%
10 years	8.9%

SOURCE: Report from the Stanford Management
Company, 2009,
http://www.stanfordmanage.org/Annual_Report.pdf

University of Texas System Endowment: University of Texas Investment Management Company

The University of Texas System comprises 15 education institutions and approximately 195,000 students. The largest school in the system, the University of Texas at Austin, is a public education institution located in Austin, Texas. The university was established in 1883. There are approximately 50,000 undergraduate and graduate students at the main campus.

The University of Texas Investment Management Company (UTIMCO) was established in 1996. The University of Texas was the first public educational institution to create an external investment management corporation. UTIMCO reports to the UT System board of regents and is governed by a nine-member board. It is led by Bruce Zimmerman, CEO and chief investment officer. UTIMCO employs about 48 professionals.

The combined net asset value of UTIMCO funds equaled $15.2 billion as of August 31, 2009.[13] UTIMCO expects the long-term rate of inflation to equal 3.0 percent. Fund distributions range from 3.5 percent to 5.5 percent using a smoothing formula (e.g., three-year average net asset value). We estimate that the endowment provides approximately 6 percent of the UT System operating revenue, which was $8.5 billion in fiscal 2009.[14] The UTIMCO asset allocation targets, which are consistent with other university ranges, are shown in Table 1.8.

UTIMCO has achieved a 4.97 percent annual return for the past 10 years as shown in Table 1.9.

Table 1.8   UTIMCO Allocation Targets

	Peer Group	UTIMCO Target
Equity	25.0%	24.4%
Hedge Funds	25.1%	29.2%
Private Investments	34.5%	22.8%
Real Estate / Other	0.1%	4.5%
Fixed Income	13.3%	14.5%
Natural Resources	2.0%	4.6%

Source: UTIMCO Annual Report 2009

Princeton University: Princeton University Investment Company

Princeton University is a private research university located in Princeton, New Jersey and was established in 1746. There are approximately 7,300 graduate and undergraduate students at Princeton.

The Princeton endowment is managed by Princeton University Investment Company (PRINCO). PRINCO is structured as a university office but maintains its own board of directors and operates under final authority of the university's board of trustees. In 1745, according to "A Princeton Companion," 10 men pledged £185 to help create a liberal arts college for New Jersey. The money was to be invested, not spent, and the interest used for salaries and other expenses. The Princeton endowment stood at $12.6 billion as of June 30, 2009. Because the endowment is so large relative to the Princeton operating budget, the endowment typically funds almost half of the university's $1.3 billion budget.[15]

The Princeton endowment has the largest ratio of endowment assets-to-student-enrollment in the United States.

Andrew K. Golden is president of Princeton University Investment. Before joining Princeton in 1995, Golden worked with David Swensen

Table 1.9   UTIMCO General Endowment Fund Investment Returns

Period	Total Return
1 year	−12.98%
3 years	1%
5 years	5.08%
10 years	4.97%

Source: UTIMCO Annual Report 2009

Table 1.10 Princeton Policy Portfolio, June 30, 2009

	Policy	Actual
Cash	0%	3.2%
Domestic Equity	7.5%	5.5%
International Equity Developed	6.5%	4.9%
International Equity Emerging	9.0%	5.8%
Independent Return	25.0%	22.0%
Fixed Income	6.0%	2.1%
Private Equity	23.0%	33.4%
Real Assets	23.0%	23.1%

SOURCE: Princeton Annual Report 2009

as an intern and then as portfolio manager at Yale's Investment Office from 1988 to 1993. Golden earned his bachelor's degree from Duke University and his master's degree from Yale School of Management in 1989.

Princeton's asset allocation model, shown in Table 1.10, is similar to those of both Harvard and Yale. The Princeton endowment achieved a 14.9 percent return over the 10-year period ended June 30, 2008, as shown in Table 1.11.

Implications for Individual Investors

Although endowments manage considerable assets, their techniques, organization, strategy, and philosophy are relatively unknown outside the

Table 1.11 Princeton Average Returns for Periods Ended June 30, 2009

	Total Return	Policy Portfolio	Median University Endowment	Lehman 65/35*
1 year	−23.5%	−16.0%	−19.9%	−15.2%
10 years	9.7%	7.1%	4.1%	1.0%

SOURCE: Princeton University, PRINCO, Report on Investments, 2008–2009. Policy Portfolio returns represent a weighted average of individual benchmark returns by asset class. The median college and university endowment returns represent data compiled by Cambridge Associates for 129 college and university endowments and provided in the Princeton Report of the Treasurer. *65/35 is a passive blend of 65% S&P 500 and 35% Barclays Government/Credit Index

industry. Year in and year out new investment strategies surface and disappear with varied success. Meanwhile endowment managers have continued to score consistent gains year after year until the crisis of 2008 and 2009. The fiscal year ended June 30, 2009 marked only the 4th year in 20 in which endowments posted a negative return. In the worst investing year since the Great Depression, billion dollar endowments posted a 6.1 percent annualized gain over the 10 years from June 30, 1999 to June 30, 2009, compared to the S&P 500 index, which posted a loss of 2.22 percent, or the typical 60 percent equity/40 percent bond portfolio, which posted a gain of 1.4 percent.

Initially we set out to determine what, if anything, individual investors could learn from endowment investing. Our hypothesis was that at least some of the techniques that endowments utilize to realize exceptional returns were instructive to the individual investor. The extent to which individuals can replicate specific techniques of endowments is a matter of some controversy in the endowment world. We believe the reader will benefit from understanding how some of the best minds in the investment management field think about their job and the future. We also think that the endowment approach can inform how an individual makes strategic investment decisions, particularly in defining broad asset classes that will compose their portfolio. There are several pieces to the endowment investing model that, if not easily replicable, are interesting and noteworthy and can improve the investment prowess of the average investor. These components of investing traverse many topics including:

- Investment goals
- Diversification
- Asset allocation
- Rebalancing
- Asset class selection
- Securities selection
- Manager selection
- Tax implications
- Alpha
- Beta
- Risks (fees, currency risk, inflation risk, tail risk)

- Organization
- Tools
- Trends and themes
- ETFs

The interviews presented in the book will help the reader improve their understanding of how endowments succeed and enable the reader to evaluate how this knowledge can benefit their investment strategy. We explore questions such as:

- How did the events of Fall 2008 change things?
- What are endowment managers doing differently today because of the financial crisis of 2008–2009?
- What investment trends are anticipated for the coming years?
- What are the unique investment philosophies of leading institutional investors?
- In what ways can investment management be best organized?
- What investment model do institutions find most effective?
- How much leverage do they employ?
- How do institutional investors select hedge funds or private equity fund investments and managers?
- What strategies are they using to reduce risk?
- Is there a way to mitigate tail risk?
- How comfortable are investors with the current state of the public markets?
- What can individual investors learn from endowment investing models?

We have interviewed some of the top investment professionals in the endowment management field, including current and former chief investment officers. They will share their thoughts on the above questions and more in the chapters of this book.

Summary

The techniques of endowment investing have developed over several centuries. Most of the large endowments have developed sophisticated investment operations, accelerating dramatically in the past 35 years, and have experienced spectacular growth in assets over that period. There is much to learn from how these endowments manage their money and consistently beat U.S. equity benchmark performance. The principles they employ are of benefit to the average investor who wishes to better understand money management and evaluate their own portfolio. Our direct interviews with top professionals in the business provide insight into a high-performing corner of the investment universe.

Notes

1. *The Harvard Guide*, 2007 President and Fellows of Harvard College.
2. *The Harvard Guide*, 2007 President and Fellows of Harvard College.
3. *The Harvard Guide*, 2007 President and Fellows of Harvard College.
4. "Stanford Named Top Fundraiser," *Stanford Report*, February 25, 2009.
5. NACUBO 2007 Endowment Study.
6. NACUBO-Commonfund 2009 Study of Endowments, Public Tables Endowment Market Values.
7. Harvard Annual Report, June 30, 2008.
8. *Yale Facts* (http://www.yale.edu/about/facts.html). Retrieved January 16, 2010.
9. Yale Finance Office Annual Report 2008, http://www.yale.edu/finance/controller/resources/docs/finrep07-08.pdf.
10. http://opa.yale.edu/news/article.aspx?id=6924.
11. Yale Endowment Annual Report, 2008, http://www.yale.edu/investments/Yale_Endowment_08.pdf.
12. http://www.stanford.edu/about/facts/finances.html.
13. http://www.utimco.org/funds/allfunds/2009annual/index.asp.
14. University of Texas System Annual Financial Statements, November 2009, page 16, http://www.utsystem.edu/cont/Reports_Publications/CONAFR/Consolidated_AFR09.pdf.
15. http://www.princeton.edu/pr/pub/ph/08/h and Karen W. Arenson, "Big Spender," *New York Times*, April 20, 2008.

Chapter 2

Historical Endowment Performance

"If past history was all there was to the game, the richest people would be librarians."

—Warren Buffett, "Despite Setbacks, Drexel Still
Calls Shots," *Washington Post*, April 17, 1988

"Over the past 200 years, the stock market's steady upward march occasionally has been disrupted for long stretches, most recently during the Great Depression and the inflation-plagued 1970s. The current market turmoil suggests that we may be in another lost decade.

The stock market is trading right where it was nine years ago. Stocks, long touted as the best investment for the long term, have been one of the worst investments over the nine-year period, trounced even by lowly Treasury bonds."

—E.S. Browning, "The Lost Decade,"
Wall Street Journal, March 26, 2008

Academic endowments received substantial publicity during the past decade. Through early 2008, this attention focused on the consistently superior investment returns endowments achieved. In the summer of 2008, just after the conclusion of most universities' fiscal year, it was common to see business press headlines praising an endowment for double-digit returns, a return with a large lead over market indexes. Meanwhile, the average individual investor had to be satisfied with perhaps half the return achieved by the largest endowments.

On August 7, 2008, the *Wall Street Journal* published an article titled "Harvard Aces a Brutal Year," observing that Harvard ended the recent fiscal year up 7 to 9 percent. Meanwhile the S&P 500 was down about 13 percent during the same period.

The flattering press clippings came to an abrupt end soon after August 2008. By September 2008, the global financial crisis was fully underway. As of December that year, the press had turned negative and endowment articles were distinctly unflattering. A sampling of *Wall Street Journal* endowment headlines post September 2008 indicates how the tide had turned in business media:

12/17/2008: "Yale to Trim Budget as Its Endowment Falls 25%"

1/09/2009: "Princeton Cuts Budget as Endowment Slides"

1/27/2009: "College Endowments Plunge"

2/07/2009: "Harvard's Endowment, Beset by Losses, to Pare Its Staff"

2/12/2009: "Harvard Endowment Cut Stock Holdings"

6/06/2009: "The Age of Diminishing Endowments"

6/30/2009: "Ivy League Endowments Finally Dumb"

8/24/2009: "Harvard Endowment Regroups"

9/10/2009: "Yale Endowment Down 30%"

9/12/2009: "Columbia Endowment Falls 21%"

9/16/2009: "MIT Endowment Off by 21%"

9/23/2009: "Yale Endowment Posts a 25% Loss"

9/30/2009: "Princeton Endowment Fell 23%"

10/10/2009: "Endowment Drops 23% at Dartmouth"

The question was being asked in the institutional money management business: Are endowments the superior investors they had been perceived to be for the previous two decades? Or had the crash of 2008–2009 exposed material flaws in the endowment investing model? Was a new management model in order for endowments?

Investment Returns

During 2008 and 2009 U.S. equity markets, the primary province of individual investors, suffered historical declines. From July 1 to

November 30, 2008, the S&P 500 fell 29.3 percent. During the twelve months ended June 2009, the S&P 500 index declined 26.2 percent.[1] College and university endowments did not escape this downdraft, not only in the markets, but across real estate, private investments, hedge funds, and other asset classes. The U.S. GDP decline for 2009 was the most severe since 1946. The worst recession in recent memory began to ease midway through 2009 as the effects from an unprecedented liquidity and stimulus program by the U.S. Federal Reserve and Treasury Department began to take hold. The market reached its bottom on March 6, 2009 roughly a 53 percent drop in the Dow Jones Industrial Average from its top in 2007. From the March low, the markets rallied and performed well through the end of fiscal year on June 30. (On a side note, since June 30, 2009 and through the completion of this manuscript in April 2010, the Dow Jones Industrial Average increased another 28 percent. The figures and returns in this book do not include this subsequent rally in the markets and corresponding asset values. The inclusion of the subsequent rally would further enhance the endowment returns reported in this book.)

The results from the 2008 NACUBO-Commonfund Endowment Study Follow-Up (shown in Table 2.1) indicate that the billion-dollar endowment investments fell about 20.5 percent during that five-month period. They outperformed the S&P but underperformed relative to expectations regarding diversification and asset allocation.

As the market got worse in fiscal year 2009, so did the endowment returns. At the conclusion of the 2009 fiscal year, billion dollar endowments would see their 10 year net returns averages decline from 9.5 percent to 6.1 percent as shown in Table 2.2.

Table 2.1 Average Endowment Investment Returns FY 2008

Endowment assets (as of June 30, 2008)	FY 2008	July 1 to Nov 30, 2008	5 Years	10 Years
Greater than $1 Billion	0.6%	−20.5%	13.3	9.5
$501 Million–$1 Billion	−1.9%	−22.2%	11.4	7.6
$101–$500 Million	−2.9%	−23.5%	10.1	6.4
$51–$100 Million	−3.2%	−22.1%	9.3	5.8
$25–$50 Million	−4.3%	−23.1%	8.4	5.1
Full Sample	−3.0%	−22.5%	9.7	6.3

SOURCE: 2008 NACUBO-Commonfund Endowment Study Follow-Up

Table 2.2 Average Endowment Investment Returns FY 2009

Endowment assets (as of June 30, 2009)	FY 2009	3 Year Return	5 Year Return	10 Year Return
Greater than $1 Billion	−20.5%	−0.8%	5.1%	6.1%
$501 Million–$1 Billion	−19.8%	−2.0%	3.5%	4.3%
$101–$500 Million	−19.7%	−2.5%	2.6%	3.7%
$51–$100 Million	−18.6%	−2.7%	2.7%	3.7%
$25–$50 Million	−18.5%	−3.2%	2.1%	3.4%
Full Sample	−18.7%	−2.5%	2.7%	4.0%

Source: 2009 NACUBO-Commonfund Endowment Study

For fiscal year 2009, endowments suffered substantial losses. While endowments typically had highly diverse asset allocations, the breadth and severity of the crisis spared no asset with the exception of U.S. treasuries and cash. Typically large endowments do not hold significant cash positions due to low returns and the erosion effect from inflation.

To make matters worse, many large endowments were heavily invested in illiquid assets, which made it difficult to produce the cash necessary to meet their obligation to the university operating budget. In some cases this necessitated selling near-liquid assets, such as U.S. public equities, at a low point. Figure 2.1 details Yale's asset allocation changes from 1985 to 2005.

The chart in Figure 2.1 demonstrates how Yale moved from highly liquid U.S. equities to higher allocations in real assets and absolute return to achieve less volatile and higher returns. In the market crash of 2008, most all asset classes declined in unison and illiquid, non-bond-oriented portfolios did not perform well.

While the liquidity issues at some endowments were problematic, in general we do not believe the FY2009 endowment performance indicts the model. Endowments have perpetual time horizons and typically do not make investments with near-term performance in mind. While it is interesting to look at a five-month period of returns, it doesn't really make sense for endowments. The 5-year, 10-year, or longer time frame is a much better evaluation period.

For example, note the Stanford endowment track record shown in Figure 2.2. Accounting for the period through June 30, 2009, Stanford achieved a 10-year return rate of 8.9 percent while the 60/40 portfolio

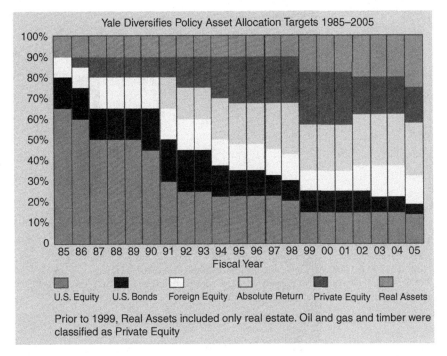

Figure 2.1 Yale Asset Allocation Targets 1985–2005
Source: Yale Endowment Annual Report 2005

benchmark achieved only a 1.3 percent annual return over the same period.

As illustrated in Figure 2.3, the Harvard and Yale endowments over the past 16 years have consistently overachieved the benchmarks. When you total up the overachievement and subtract the decline in 2009, the endowments are still far ahead.

Table 2.3 shows the returns for the Harvard endowment for the fiscal year ended 2009. Even accounting for the 1-year dismal performance, the 5-year, 10-year, and 20-year annualized returns for the endowment investments dramatically outpaced a 60/40 portfolio typical of the individual investor. Although there seemed to be a rush-to-judgment on the endowment model based on the short-cycle performance in 2009, a longer term look vindicates the model. The private and alternative investments that declined and the risk they entail produced the outsized returns of the past.

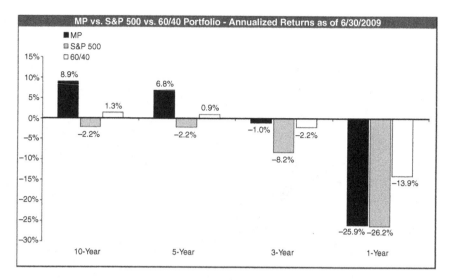

Figure 2.2   Historical Investment Returns for Stanford

SOURCE: Stanford Annual Report 2009

NOTE: The Merged Pool (MP) represents the primary investment vehicle of Standard's endowment. The 60/40 Portfolio represents a passively managed index portfolio consisting of 60 percent S&P 500 and 40 percent Barclays Capital Aggregate Bond Index.

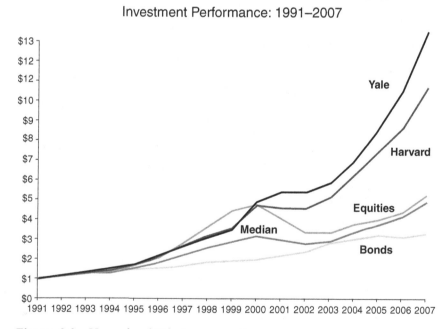

Figure 2.3   Harvard and Yale Investment Returns

SOURCE: Harvard University

Table 2.3 Harvard Historical Investment Return—Annualized

	Harvard	60/40 Stock/ Bond Portfolio*	TUCS Median**
1 Year	−27.3%	−13.5%	−18.2%
5 Years	6.2	1.0	2.5
10 Years	8.9	1.4	3.2
20 Years	11.7	7.8	8.0

*S&P 500/CITI US BIG
** Trust Universe Comparison as compiled by Wilshire Associates
SOURCE: Harvard Management Company Annual Report 2009

Evaluating the 10 years of data from NACUBO-Commonfund (Figure 2.4) highlights a similar point. Large endowments have outperformed the S&P 500 in 9 out of 14 years. And they have achieved this with less volatility.

Over the long term larger endowments have typically outperformed their smaller counterparts, and the most recent study from

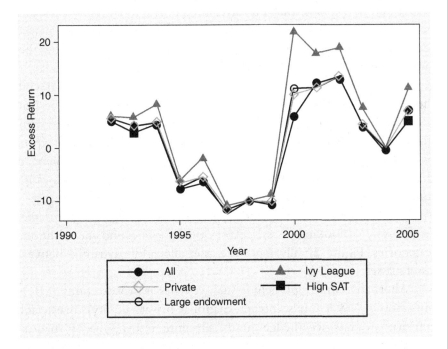

Figure 2.4 Excess Returns by School Type
SOURCE: NACUBO
NOTE: Endowment return minus the Standard & Poor's 500 in same year.

NACUBO-Commonfund highlights this fact. Table 2.2 illustrates how the large endowments have performed 2.7 percent per year better than small endowments over the prior 10-year period. However, smaller institutions outperformed larger ones in FY2009, likely due to their more conservative asset allocation mix.

Asset Allocation

It has been widely published that asset allocation is responsible for 90 percent of investment returns. Endowment managers spend considerable time developing an asset allocation policy. Finding uncorrelated asset classes helps build portfolio diversification and subsequently reduces the variability of the returns. Managers get a double benefit when they can simultaneously reduce the variability and maintain or increase the return. Highly diversified endowments delivered superior returns in the 1990s and mid-2000s. But, this diversified portfolio couldn't reasonably save the endowments from a deep recession and a broad based market decline. The CIOs we spoke to discuss in individual chapters how they are responding to 2008–2009 in updating asset allocation policies.

Table 2.4 illustrates the difference in asset allocation between the billion dollar endowments and their smaller counterparts. Of note, institutions under $25 million had allocated 25 percent to fixed income while the $1 billion endowments allocated only 10 percent. This would explain why the smaller endowments outperformed the larger endowments in FY2009. Over the long term that fixed-income-oriented asset allocation underperformed the allocation model of the $1 billion endowments.

Lyn Hutton, Commonfund's Chief Investment Officer, presented a new way of looking at asset classes that goes beyond the traditional categories. Figure 2.5 illustrates the asset allocation dynamics between asset classes.

Alternative strategies include such vehicles as private equity (LBOs, mezzanine, M&A funds and international private equity), marketable alternative strategies (hedge funds, absolute return, market neutral, long/short, event-driven, and derivatives), venture capital, private equity real estate, energy and natural resources, and distressed debt.

Table 2.4 Asset Allocations for Fiscal Years 2008 and 2009

(%) Asset Class	Greater than $1 Billion		$501 Million–$1 Billion		$101–$500 Million		$51–$100 Million		$25–$50 Million		Under $25 Million	
	2008	2009	2008	2009	2008	2009	2008	2009	2008	2009	2008	2009
Domestic Equities	20	14	24	20	30	26	39	34	42	37	46	38
Fixed Income	10	10	13	14	16	17	18	21	22	23	25	27
International Equities	17	12	19	17	19	17	17	17	15	15	10	13
Alternative Strategies	52	61	42	43	32	33	23	22	17	18	11	13
Short-term Securities/ Cash/Other	1	3	2	6	3	7	3	6	4	7	8	9

Source: NACUBO-Commonfund Study of Endowments 2009

	Risk Assets/Growth	Inflation Hedges	Deflation Hedges	Diversification
Most Liquid	• Public equities (large)	• Commodities	• Cash	• Commodities
		• TIPs	• U.S. treasuries	• Fixed income
	• Public equities (small)			• Currency (non-U.S. $ investments)
	• Long/short equities	• CTAs	• Short equity bias funds	• Trend following hedge funds
	• Activist funds			• Glogal macro hedge fund strategies
	• Event funds			
	• Opportunistic credit			• Relative value strategies
	• Distressed debt			• Distressed debt
	• Venture capital	• Core real estate		• Real estate
	• Private equity	• Natural resources		• Natural resources
	• Opportunistic real estate	• Infrastructure		
Least Liquid	• Value-add real estate			

Figure 2.5   Evolving Asset Classes and Portfolio Dynamics
Source: NACUBO-Commonfund Study of Endowments

Summary

The endowment model, while needing some minor adjustments, held up through the events of 2008–2009, and, evaluated over longer time frames, produces superior results.

We believe that endowments will continue to adhere to their historical asset allocation and rebalancing strategies, with perhaps a renewed emphasis on liquidity management and pursuit of some opportunistic or theme-driven investing. Those principles helped large billion-dollar endowments grow in excess of 11.5 percent over the past 20 years. David Swensen grew Yale's endowment from $1 billion in 1985 to $16.3 billion on June 30, 2009. In a recent article, Swensen said periodic losses are inevitable in a portfolio tilted toward stocks and built to grow over many years.[2]

"When you have a market in which any type of equity exposure is being punished, it's going to hurt long-term investors," he said.[3] "There isn't an investment strategy that can produce the kind of long-term results we've generated at Yale that isn't going to post the occasional negative return," and, "we're not even done with the current fiscal year. Judging a long-term investment strategy based on the results of a five- to six-month period is foolish beyond words."[4]

Notes

1. https://pgnet22.stanford.edu/get/file/g2sdoc/InvestmentPerformance
   .pdf.
2. Oliver Staley, "Yale's Swensen Sees Extraordinary Opportunity to Snap
   Up Debt," *Bloomberg News*, January 2, 2009, http://www.bloomberg
   .com/apps/news?sid=ab08HlxLZ5FY&pid=20601087.
3. Ibid.
4. Ibid.

Chapter 3

A Look Inside Endowments

"Everyone is a genius at least once a year. The real geniuses simply have their bright ideas closer together."
—Georg Christoph Lichtenberg

T
hrough our research and interviews with investment professionals we learned a number of useful and interesting things about
this relatively undocumented corner of the investing world. A
number of these findings were counter to expectations or conventional
wisdom. Some are of general interest to those dealing with endowments,
typically private investment general partners. Others have implications
for how endowments will make decisions in the future. Finally, individual investors can take away several key points to use in developing their
own approach and for context throughout the remainder of the book.
We have highlighted eight relevant learnings in this chapter.

Endowments Are Different

From outside the industry, the approach for managing large pools of
institutional money seems homogeneous. After all, they have a number
of things in common: large sums of money, typically organized as a
nonprofit, supporting a large and often well-known institution. Given
that there is probably a convergence of thinking on what makes for
prudent money management, it stands to reason that the technique

for doing that would be the same across these apparently very similar groups.

As it happens, endowments are much different in nature from other institutional funds. The two most frequent funds that are mentioned at the same time as endowments are foundations and pension funds. Sovereign wealth funds are another oft-mentioned institutional asset pool.

Foundations differ from endowments on a few key points. First, they are typically static in terms of additional funds coming in. A foundation will be established with an initial sum from a donor or donors, and then will typically not have any additional contributions. Academic endowments, by contrast, most often have additional funds on an ongoing basis from alumni and other sources. This makes managing liquidity and operating budgets easier for endowments. Foundations also have, by virtue of the tax code governing nonprofits, an annual distribution requirement of 5% of the previous 12-month average fair-market value of the investment assets. This means that foundations have narrow latitude in a given year on how much money to distribute. An endowment can work with the institution in a bad or good year and adjust the distributions accordingly.

Likewise, pension funds have different constraints. Pension funds are often larger than endowments. The assets in the largest pension fund are nearly 10 times the size of the largest endowment. Pension funds, however, are more conservative than endowments in their investing. This is the result of two factors. First, pension funds have target liabilities that they can calculate based on the demographics of the retired or retiring population they support. There is no flexibility in their distributions, and therefore they must keep higher liquidity and lower-risk, lower-return assets on average than an endowment. Second, the governing boards of pensions are often more conservative and focused on asset preservation rather than growth. These factors mean that pension funds, while larger, may not generate the same returns that endowments can.

We also found that not only are academic endowments clearly different from pension funds and foundations, they are also quite different from each other. There are obvious differences, such as size and whether the institution is public or private. Other differences include things such as the percentage of the operating budget that the institution asks the endowment to provide. The culture of the institution, the composition of the investment committee, whether the endowment manages university working capital, the amount of new funds coming in from the donor base, the CIO's philosophy on outsourcing or use of consultants, the vintage of the investments in the endowment pool, even the geography of the endowment may influence liquidity needs—for example, Tulane and its commitment to ensuring appropriate cash available during hurricane season. In all, we found that endowments are quite different from each other and this means that there is no consolidated "endowment model" for investing to be identified and documented. There are, however, basic principles that CIOs adhere to and fundamentals that they know will lead to good investing decisions. These are the things we focused on in our interviews.

Endowments Define Asset Classes Broadly

Endowments think about asset classes in the broadest possible way. As outlined in Chapter 2, endowments invest in a wide variety of asset types with a significant portion of their funds going to private or alternative investments.

This differs significantly from the approach typical of the individual investor, which considers an allocation to fixed income and a variety of large-cap, mid-cap and small-cap U.S. equity growth and value stocks to be a diversified portfolio. The CIOs we interviewed were nearly unanimous in their thinking that most individual investors have too much of a "home bias" and therefore an overallocation to U.S. public equity markets.

A look at the type of investments that endowments will typically have indicates how broadly they define this area. A fund will of course include allocations to fixed income and U.S. public equities but will also include other carefully researched and selected public equity investments in emerging and frontier markets. The alternative/private portion of the portfolio typically includes allocations to private equity, venture capital, real estate, real assets (land, precious metals, timber), and hedge funds of all types.

Endowment CIOs believe that a considerable amount of the return (and year-to-year consistency) is derived from asset allocation and diversification. This is conventional wisdom for individual investors as well. However, there is a wide gap between the asset classes typically used by endowments versus individuals, which we believe accounts for a significant portion of the performance difference between the two.

Endowments Achieved a One-time Sophistication Improvement

As we discussed the unique outperformance of the endowment model, CIOs were quick to point out that endowment portfolios prior to the 1970s looked like, and performed like, the typical individual investor portfolio. They believed that a number of factors contributed to the rise of endowment performance in the past 35 years, primarily due to increased sophistication of the method and the definition of asset classes as outlined above.

The implementation of UMIFA and UPMIFA standards which gave endowments considerably improved investment flexibility produced a ramping up of sophistication in the endowment approach. This, combined with investment committees populated by members with strong investment backgrounds (often hedge fund managers themselves) accelerated the move to the endowment model used today.

Endowment CIOs are cautious in forecasting the ability for endowments to produce some of the exceptional performance improvements seen in the first few decades after UMIFA. As one CIO put it, "you can move to a sophisticated model only once."

We believe this is not a discouragement to the individual investor who wants to learn from endowments. Whether or not the outperformance of endowments in past decades is due to a one-time adoption of sophistication, the model has proven to produce durable consistent returns.

Endowments Are Nimble

There are two theories of management in the endowment world. The first model consists of building clear asset class definitions, identifying target allocations by asset class, performing rigorous manager selection, investing with managers, and then periodically rebalancing the portfolio to the target allocations. The second model adds more flexibility and less strict definition of target allocations within asset classes. For a certain portion of the portfolio—somewhere between 10 and 40 percent—this model will invest in what the CIO sees as a mid-term trend (or theme) in the global markets. This model has wide latitude for the investment management team, and the team may, in addition to investing with managers, take direct positions in the market using a variety of instruments. They will do this in pursuit of specific opportunities they identify or to hedge risks they perceive. This process is generally called "thematic investing."

We found that endowments aren't necessarily wed to one model or the other, but instead see themselves somewhere on a continuum between the two models. They will take varying amounts of flexibility in their investing approach, depending on their unique situation and what they see happening in the economy and marketplace overall. We found that what CIOs had in common was wide latitude from the investment committee to determine where on the continuum to take their endowment. What emerged from our research and our interviews was a picture of endowments that was much more dynamic, nimble, and proactive in decision making and execution than is apparent from outside the industry. Endowments will make opportunistic investments, use direct investing to hedge risk, and have considerable room to maneuver when they need it.

This also means that endowments pay close attention to the global macroeconomic environment. They want to understand what factors will influence the threats and opportunities they face. In our interviews, we asked them what trends they were following in the near- to mid-term. The answers are in the interview chapters, as well as aggregated in the final chapter.

Endowments are Evaluating Approaches to Managing Tail Risk

After the extreme events of 2008–2009 there was much discussion in the investment management world of insuring against "tail risk"—the highly unlikely, but potentially highly-damaging event, similar to the financial chaos of late 2008 and early 2009. In our interviews, we asked

CIOs how they were approaching tail risk and if they believed that the tail risk profile had changed.

We received a variety of responses to this. Some believe that the tails are "fatter"—that is, that the possibility of a tail event is higher now. Others instead believe that the tail-risk probability remains the same, but that rapidity of events and interconnectedness of the financial world means that the low probability events will happen with more frequency.

In both cases CIOs seem to agree that the probability of tail events is higher now, and they are taking steps to anticipate and reduce risk, and there is an ongoing discussion on how best to insure against tail-risk. In some cases endowments will use the discretionary portion of their portfolio to purchase inexpensive insurance against potential events, for example, buying puts for an industry sector in which they have a material investment. For others this means building portfolios that will perform well in most conditions, at a potentially reduced return. Instead of trying to anticipate the direction and magnitude of inflation, they will simply incorporate deflationary elements—fixed income—and inflationary elements—real assets—into their portfolio to ensure that they are balanced.

CIOs are working through how to manage tail risk while satisfying their return objectives. Although tail risk insurance by definition should be inexpensive (the event is unlikely) it can be difficult to determine what form it should take, given the high complexity of the endowment portfolio and the overall global economy. CIOs also expressed concern that investment committees may grow weary of paying an insurance premium over time, and as the events of 2008–2009 fade in memory, may elect to eliminate tail-risk insurance just in time for the next catastrophic event. How endowments ultimately decide to hedge these risks over the long term will be something important to watch.

Endowments also Manage Working Capital

In the past decade, universities became increasingly interested in how to most effectively manage the non-endowment portion of their assets. Most universities have considerable working capital of various durations—short term items such as tuition funds that come in at the beginning of the semester, but are consumed over the following few months, and longer-term funds such as donations to support a long-term building project and numerous things in between.

These working capital funds are distinct from the long-term endowment funds of a university. The size of the working capital fund can be large—in some cases as large as the long-term endowment itself. A number of universities determined that with some coordination and planning, working capital could produce better returns through being managed by the endowment office instead of being placed in short term vehicles such as bank accounts or treasuries.

This model has generally been successful and produced additional income for universities. However, it requires careful management due to the need to accurately forecast the short and mid-term liquidity needs of the university. Aggressive management of working capital was likely a contributor to the liquidity crisis experienced by some endowments in 2009.

Endowments Manage Liquidity Carefully

The most important event in the endowment management world in the past few years was the 2008–2009 market crash and the ensuing liquidity problems experienced by some institutions.

Endowments have enjoyed for some years an "illiquidity premium." Due to the size of their asset pool and their perpetual time horizon, endowments can set aside a material amount of money that they will not need to access for a considerable time—as much as a decade or more. Their willingness to invest and lock up funds for long periods allows them to participate in a variety of higher-return private investments.

Endowments also have to carefully manage liquidity, because the institution they support will be counting on the endowment for a distribution for some portion of its budget in a given year. This is typically 5 to 10 percent, but can be as much as 30 to 40 percent. Any shortfall in endowment support for the institution budget is felt immediately and profoundly. This means that endowments need to be sure that appropriate amounts of cash (liquidity) are available on the appropriate budget cycle for distribution.

In the 4–6 years leading up to the financial crisis of 2008–2009, a set of conditions emerged that hindered endowment liquidity. First, the private investments (private equity or hedge funds) that endowments were using had been consistently returning cash to the endowment. When an investor puts money to work in a private investment, the terms usually provide for periodic optional distribution. However, there are no guarantees of the distribution, and furthermore, the private investment usually reserves the right to take more capital from investors depending on their overall commitment to the fund. In some private investments the fund can even ask for a return of capital that was previously paid out.

When the market crashed in 2008, the return of cash from private investments not only dried up, but furthermore the private funds began making capital calls. Endowments needed a source of cash. Because all investments, regardless of asset class, were correlated in this crash, there were no easy-to-access sources of cash. Raising money often meant selling equities at the bottom.

Exacerbating the situation were the conditions being experienced by the institutions. Large new donations to the school endowments were naturally trending downward, reducing an important source of liquidity. Credit markets were troubled, meaning that student loan providers were either slowly funding or refusing to fund student loans. This meant that the university was holding the receivables on student loans, and that source of cash was missing.

Finally, credit markets freezing meant that raising liquidity through institutional debt was difficult or impossible. Normally an institution could resort to the debt market in order to find temporary liquidity, but this was often not an option during the crash. The liquidity challenge for some universities was furthered by their use of working capital invested in longer-term assets, as outlined in the previous section.

This situation led to some difficult choices for some institutions, manifesting in budget cutbacks and spending freezes that will likely continue for a number of years. The powerful market performance of mid-to-late 2009 provided a timely bailout of sorts for many endowments. Now the endowment management business is changing how liquidity is managed. The institutions that we interviewed fared well during this time, but out of caution are reviewing their approach to liquidity. The industry as a whole is evaluating this topic carefully and making changes to the amount of cash or near-cash securities they hold as well as changing the terms on private investments.

Endowments are Changing their Approach to Performance Measurement

The final trend we have identified in the endowment management business is performance measurement. We believe there will be a declining emphasis on relative peer-group performance going forward. In the past decade, the performance of endowments received considerable publicity. Investment committees began incorporating relative peer group rankings into their evaluations. In some cases this was also made part of the compensation of the investment management team. Often the target would be to appear consistently in the upper quartile of peer group performance each year. This became known as the "benchmark derby."

Overemphasizing the derby seems to have produced some unintended negative consequences for the industry. As we pointed out earlier in this chapter, individual endowments each have a unique situation. This makes comparing their results in a given year difficult. For instance, endowments with higher operating budget obligations need higher liquidity and therefore structurally they will have lower returns.

The performance derby meant that endowments with very different situations were being measured by the same yardstick. Tying this to compensation distorted the incentives for investment staff and encouraged short-term (annual) risk taking in order to achieve the objectives. We believe that the aggressive investment allocations dictated by the performance derby, combined with a trend towards endowment working capital management, accentuated the damage done to endowment assets in the events of 2008–2009.

Summary

- Endowments have unique characteristics separating them from individuals and also from other institutional funds.
- Endowments invest in a wide variety of asset classes and have a much broader approach than the typical individual investor.

- The endowment investment performance over the past two decades has likely been enhanced by a one-time move to management sophistication and alternative investments.
- Endowments are more nimble investors than most would think. They spend considerable time and resources to spot global macroeconomic trends and act on them.
- Endowments are increasingly looking at tail risk management strategies.
- The conventional wisdom among large endowments is being challenged and some will hold more cash to take advantage of periodic distressed opportunities.
- Over emphasizing peer group comparisons could likely hinder long-term investment decision making.

Part II

PUBLIC
UNIVERSITIES

Chapter 4

Jonathan Hook

Chief Investment Officer

The Ohio State University

"Looking at themes and understanding the types of risks you both do and don't want in the portfolio makes more sense than looking at a style box and saying you have to have a certain percent in large-cap growth and another percent in small-cap value."

The Ohio State University and the Endowment

The Ohio State University (OSU) is a public university in Columbus, Ohio. The school was established in 1870 and has an enrollment of over 60,000 students across all campuses.

In 2008, the university established an Office of Investments to manage the long-term endowment pool of over $2 billion. The endowment provides support for Ohio State initiatives, including student scholarships, academic and research programs, professorships, and libraries. The investment office is responsible for developing investment policies, strategic asset allocation targets, policy and performance benchmarks, and risk management practices.

The Ohio State University presently ranks 30th among all universities based on asset size and 8th for public universities in the NACUBO 2009 National Endowment Study. Jonathan Hook

45

is the chief investment officer for Ohio State. He took this role in August 2008, when Ohio State established the position in order to move to a more professional money management approach like many of its peer institutions. At that time, OSU had the second largest university endowment that was not managed by a CIO and investment staff. At OSU the CIO is responsible for managing the university's long-term investment pool.

Prior to OSU, Jonathan was the chief investment officer at Baylor University. There he managed a $1.1 billion endowment. In 2005, *Endowment and Foundation Money Management* magazine named him the Endowment Officer of the Year with the best performing portfolio (25.2 percent) of all universities in the annual survey conducted by the National Association of College and University Business Officers (NACUBO).

Prior to his role at Baylor University, Hook had a 20-year career in financial services, most recently serving as senior vice president for First Union Securities in Atlanta. He received his bachelor of science from Willamette University and an MBA from Baylor University.

Q: What do you think are some of the most important issues faced in the institutional money management business in general and the endowment world in particular over the past few years?

The issue of the last year or so has been the "liquidity issue." That has been most interesting to watch, and I think that it may have exposed complacency in some investment pools, where effective liquidity management was either forgotten or ignored. Some of this occurred because for the prior six or seven years we had a nice virtuous circle. You funded managers with your left hand and cash distributions or dividends came in from the right. You would get about two-thirds through funding a manager, the cash would start coming back, and you could use it to fund a new manager. In effect you could get the illiquidity premium without the illiquidity. There really wasn't illiquidity in the market per se. There still is an illiquidity premium, and now there will be a bit of a catch-up while you pay that back.

Now there will be a reevaluation of how much cash you need to hold. The performance of the market and the virtuous circle of cash coming back so rapidly led to very little cash being held in institutional portfolios. In addition, some endowments had arranged credit facilities to meet their liquidity needs, which could let them hold no cash if they wanted. They could use the credit line with their local bank, or their custodian bank, wherever they had established it, in case they needed cash.

Fixed income allocations also went lower during this time, even as far down as 3 percent to 5 percent. Just a few years ago fixed income could have been as much as half of one's corpus. When the market crashed, holding such a low level of cash and short-term debt came to an abrupt halt.

At OSU, I was fortunate to be starting as CIO just when all this was happening, because it gave us a chance to look at things almost from square one. We were able to avoid some of the traps that this situation created. Part of this was due to timing. Some of the advantage OSU had came from being a little on the heavy side on liquidity. We were beginning to move in the direction of less liquidity, so we were able to adjust more rapidly to what was happening in the market. Clearly this helped us during the last two years.

As the year has gone on and the equity markets have seen a large rebound, institutions and their boards are revisiting the liquidity issue. How one decides this is clearly different for each institution. We have been holding more liquidity than we necessarily needed, but during this time felt that it would be an appropriate trade-off against the potential of a higher return accompanied by higher risk.

Do you think the "performance derby" has been harmful to endowment management over the past few years?

Over the next several years there will be some changes in how the industry measures endowment portfolio performance. Most recently boards have wanted to evaluate performance relative to peer institutions. I think now people will want to understand what risks they are incurring when they try to achieve top-quartile returns every year, and incorporate that into how they benchmark themselves. Foundations and endowments will also want to think about their specific situation, which will differ from those of any peer institution. A number of things go into this—how much of the operating budget do you support, what is the culture of the institution, the composition and goals of the board, and what kind of institution it is. For instance, a hospital may need to keep more cash than a typical foundation or endowment.

Institutions where the endowment provides a large portion of the operating budget had a tough time over the past two years. Many are able to handle a 10 percent cut for a year or two, but a 40 percent cut really hurts. Putting more emphasis on what your institution needs to do relative to its own goals and budget, and less on comparing performance to other schools, which have different situations, will be healthy. There will also be more interest in understanding the risks that are being undertaken to achieve the returns.

It seems that performance measurement and endowment staff compensation are intertwined, so to get compensation right the performance measurement needs to be right as well.

Yes, in today's environment, compensation issues can be problematic. There are a number of schools where investment staff compensation is based on the performance derby. Every school should want to set its compensation policy differently to fit its particular situation. This is an area in which to be careful because you want to have the right incentives in place to attract and retain the investing team. They should balance risk and return to the advantage of the institution and be congruent with its goals. One thing that helps with compensation setting is that there are ways to quantitatively measure success in the investment business. Public schools and public pension funds have an additional issue that they must deal with, which is the public scrutiny over publicly disclosed salaries.

For academic institutions, one appropriate place for relative comparison across schools is the investment staff jobs. Periodically there are comparisons made of investment staff compensation to other jobs on campus, when a more relevant comparison is against the same job at another school. It can be tempting to compare the job to similar positions on Wall Street, but there are some important differences. Nevertheless, you do live in both worlds—the money management and Wall Street finance community and the university community—simultaneously.

Working in a university environment has an element of qualitative compensation, and you have a chance to make a real difference to an important institution.

In all, the good that came from this year is that investment committees are taking a closer look at this question—how the endowment goals should be set and how investment staff compensation should work. There is an interrelationship between risk, return, liquidity requirements, performance measurement, and staff compensation that will be rebalanced now.

How should academic endowment CIOs be involved in institution working capital management?

I think there have to be very clear and candid conversations between the investment office and the treasurer or CFO's office. These might also include another person or two on campus—perhaps the president or provost—to make these types of decisions. The discussion will try to set policy and process for what you should do when you have extra operating cash. In the past, some universities have put extra operating cash into the endowment. At OSU we have done this when we believed that the cash could be designated as a long-term operating fund. When this happened, detailed conversations occurred with the CFO's office to make sure we had adequate liquidity and the university operating budget was still firmly supported. We wanted to evaluate the risk of another potential market dip and make sure that, if it happened, the university would still be in a comfortable position with sufficient liquidity.

After we evaluated the situation, we decided there was room to invest some money for the long term and moved a portion of operating cash over to the long-term pool. We had to make it clear that there would be a long lock-up on the money so that everyone could plan appropriately. The ability to get additional return from extra operating cash is attractive, but it is not a given that the markets will continue to provide that extra boost. In 2008–2009, it fell the opposite way. You need a good process to be as sure as you can that you have done your contingency planning before you transfer the funds. It is worse to take liquid funds, put them to work in the long–term pool, and then need to give them back in a relatively short period of time.

The other thing we look at in evaluating cash needs and working capital requirements is the state budget cycle. For public universities, especially right now, there can be uncertainty about what the impact will be from annual or biennial changes in state higher-education budgets.

Did the improvement in the market in 2009 provide a "bailout" for endowments that were having liquidity concerns?

There have been several stories this year highlighting universities that had to take draconian cuts to their budget in the current year. Some announced cuts of 15 percent for the next two years or so. Others have dealt with the shortfalls by cutting the budget a smaller amount but over a much longer time period. It is hard to say at this point which strategy will be better, but it is clear that the bounce back helped ease some of this, especially for endowments that were at the margin.

It is not something that is going to be a one-year phenomenon. Most spending policies are based on three- to five-year rolling averages, and so if you have a big down year, then it is going to be with you for several years. At OSU, we changed our formula to a seven-year rolling average, and so the past two years are going to be influencing our spending for some time. The operating budget is not heavily reliant on endowment returns here, so we won't be as negatively impacted by the downturn as some of our private school peers.

What are your thoughts on selecting managers and how you want to see them use leverage?

We are not mandating that managers can't use leverage, but we prefer nonleveraged strategies. Clearly some strategies like LBOs are reliant on leverage and so that is a strategy that might be less attractive now. Hedge funds may or may not have some embedded leverage. On the real asset side, we are more inclined toward managers that aren't using leverage. If we do engage with them, then we want transparency about how much.

On the fund side, we are not leveraging our portfolio. This was something that some endowments had done in the past and it worked well for them. If you had fund leverage in the past 18 months, however, it was probably pretty painful. It is certainly something one needs to be thinking of. If you use it, it will amplify returns, both gains and losses. It is not necessarily right or wrong to use leverage, but you need to know what your risks are with it.

Good manager transparency is helpful here—knowing how the manager will use leverage and how much they use. In the end, it falls to the endowment to walk away from managers where they lack adequate information they need on this front. It can be hard to exit a good manager but the money management industry is competitive. Each plan sponsor has many options, so if a manager will not provide enough information, another can be found.

Periodically you may have a chance to invest with a manager that you believe is the best in his space. You would work hard to align all aspects so you can invest with that firm. However, if you can't get what you need in transparency, terms, or any other important area, then you may have to move on to whom you believe to be the next-best manager in that area. The process is important because you hope to be with a manager for several years and so satisfaction with the communication and transparency is critical.

Are the limited partners (endowments) getting an improvement in the fees and terms that managers are asking for now?

This is hard to say, because the top managers are still often oversubscribed. They don't have difficulty attracting capital and are still in high demand. This means that they can still drive fees and terms, although I don't think they are being overly aggressive on it.

What managers have done, though, is become more flexible on some things. For instance, some hedge funds with a lock-up have allowed the limited partners to access some small portion (up to 5 percent) of their capital if they need it. On the whole, I haven't seen too many managers cut their fees. In cases where they have, it has been to trade on other terms—a longer duration lock-up in exchange for a lower fee or carry.

We look at fees as a test of reasonableness and a test of where the market is at the time. There has been some industry momentum to take managers to task on fees. However, one's ability to make much change probably has a lot to do with the size of one's asset base. A large pension fund with tens of billions can influence the market, but a smaller endowment has less ability to change things. If we don't like a fee structure we see, we have the ability to look for another manager rather than fight about it. We really just look for reasonableness here.

The biggest benefit has been improvement in transparency, as we discussed. This is moving in the right direction today, and my hope is that the fund managers will take the offensive on this. There is a concern that if transparency doesn't improve, then there may be an effort by the government to step in to sort things out. This could have unpredictable effects and therefore is probably not in the industry's best interest. It makes the most sense for LPs and GPs to work together to a joint solution.

Are there other places the government might get involved in the business?

I think any action by the government was pushed back by the events of last year, but one thing I could see happening would be the imposition of required payout levels for endowments, similar to what is mandated for foundations. Research shows that this is not helpful for the long-term viability of the endowments, because over a long time period the corpus of the fund will be depleted. This would put added pressure on university fund-raising efforts. If legislation is enacted forcing a higher mandatory payout, especially before endowments have a chance to recover from the past few years, it will increase the difficulty for the industry.

What is your position on a thematic versus a style box approach to investing?

We were an early adopter of thematic investing and continue to like it as a model. This was something that we did at Baylor and have also adopted at OSU. This meant that we changed our asset allocation in the middle of 2009. In some ways the market conditions made it easier to do, because there was high interest in making sure we were carefully and actively managing our risk and return.

Looking at themes and understanding the types of risks you both do and don't want in the portfolio makes more sense to me than looking at a style box and saying you have to have a certain percent in large-cap growth, and another percent in small-cap value. I think that many had the belief that if you had your style boxes covered and all nine boxes filled, then it meant that you were diversified. In last year's environment, style box saturation did not provide positive help since all correlations went to one. I think moving beyond style boxes and overlaying themes on your allocation process makes more sense.

What specific trends are you watching?

As we discussed, liquidity management in the investment pool is an important topic. We spend time on this right now and are watching it carefully.

We believe that inflation will come back, and when it does it may be significant. We aren't certain of the timing but we have moved in the direction of inflation-protecting assets. Here we like real assets such as energy, commodities, and timber. Real estate often gets put in this category, but we do not think it is a good play at the moment. Eventually there will be some good opportunities in real estate for undervalued assets. Many of these assets also add a level of protection against dollar depreciation as well. We like that aspect and believe it lowers overall portfolio risk.

The march toward emerging markets and the emerging market middle-class demographic growth is another trend. We are looking at different ways to be invested here. The BRIC countries may move in fits and starts, but they are clearly running on a higher growth rate now than is the United States. Their balances of payments are positive. Many of the individual countries are now net creditors, not net borrowers.

We are looking at how to make the portfolio more global. I think you often see a home bias in investing, especially by individual investors. In the past this may not have mattered as much as it does today, because the U.S. economy was such a large component of the worldwide picture. Now, as global GDP grows, the U.S. portion will continue to shrink as a percentage of the whole, and so it will be important to be in front of this and be invested in places with higher-than-average GDP increases.

For us, the focus will be directed toward how to be surgical about it—we don't believe in a shotgun-style approach to increasing our global diversification. We want to be clear about what we are trying to address and the process of how to get there. For example, a growing middle class may mean good opportunities over the next five to 10 years in areas like energy, water, agriculture, and consumer goods.

Is it sometimes difficult to find an investable asset, even if you have found a specific trend or investment theme that you like?

Yes. We saw this in agriculture. We also have seen it in water. It can take a lot of time to find something that meets your criteria. For instance, last year we entered a fund that consolidates sheep and cattle ranches in Australia. We had been looking for something like this for several years before we found the particular investment.

We have found very few attractive ways to invest in water. What complicates the matter are various policies on water rights. We believe water will become more scarce over time, and so we have to keep our eye on it, but good places to invest are rare here.

Green energy is another example. This has been hard, not because there aren't funds investing in the space, but because it is difficult to determine which things will become commercially viable. At an early stage it is a challenge to determine the likely winners. For instance, I don't think there will need to be 50 solar panel manufacturers. Also I think the green energy area has been fashionable, which increases the competition and drives valuations too high.

What can individuals learn?

Individuals may be succumbing to the style box fallacy I mentioned earlier. Individuals may think that by scattering their investments across a wide variety of U.S. public equity subclasses that they have successfully diversified. This is a notion that you want to avoid. As you put together a personal portfolio one needs to understand what asset classes are available, what is owned, and how the pieces fit together.

On the fixed income front, some variety of government bonds— TIPS and others—can be a good counterweight to an equity allocation. There are also some ways that individuals can play real assets like energy, timber, or real estate through indexes, or MLPs, REIT funds, or ETFs. Some individuals use these to sculpt their portfolio.

I am not in favor of an individual entering hedge funds at minimal levels. There should be a high bar here—the individual who might only be able to put a small amount of money to work in a hedge fund probably should not be in it to begin with. On the other hand, if one can afford to invest $1 million of risk capital, then he can probably also afford the pain of losing it all. Most individuals shouldn't go in this direction, and I don't think the industry should be looking for ways to be complicit.

Individuals also don't usually have the capacity or expertise to evaluate alternative investments well. The due diligence required to pick a good manager or even a good fund of funds is something they just aren't equipped to do. Endowments can live with the adage of "buyer beware" and are equipped to go through the selection process in a way that an individual either can't or won't replicate. This means that the chance of the individual losing all their money in an alternative investment is greater.

I also think that individuals should avoid trying to overdiversify within an asset class. If they decide they want a certain percentage in equities, they often pick too many mutual funds or too many stocks. Again, this may make them think they have more diversification than they actually do. Last year the difference between large- and small-cap stocks didn't make much difference.

Finally, there is the well-established tendency for the individual investor to chase performance. Invariably people want to invest in funds with the best previous three-year return. Investing in a fund right after a good run often means buying at the top. Endowments can afford to hire a manager and hang on longer to wait for the returns. Endowments can be patient because they have much longer time horizons. We are also talking with the managers frequently in a way that individuals can't. This also goes back to alternative asset classes, which require long time horizons. Private equity investments can take many years to wind up and the retail investor may not have the tolerance for it.

Any other lessons for the individual from 2008–2009?

It is hard to say what an individual could have done differently last year. Unless you were in all cash or Treasuries in 2008 you probably were seriously hurt in the market. If one was overly aggressive in his asset allocation in 2008, then a large share of pain was felt.

One thing to carry forward is to not forget what just happened. I think there is a tendency, as the equity markets march upward, to lose sight of what happened and to not take the right steps to hedge your portfolio risks. Most people will remember for a while, but it is easy to lose track of it. In the endowment world, those who had the most liquidity problems will also have the issue front and center with them for some time.

Inevitably, though, there will be those who start stretching for more yield. It won't hurt to be reminded of this periodically. Also, the more tenure that someone has in the business or as an investor, the more of these lessons they can hopefully incorporate into their decision making. It is understandable to get burned by this once, but not twice.

Chapter 5

Guy Patton

President and Chief Executive Officer

The University of Oklahoma Foundation

"This notion of large cap, small cap, a sliver of international, and a slug of fixed income is an extraordinarily incomplete asset allocation strategy."

"One of the skills that investment professionals develop is seeking out contrarian viewpoints, because it helps drive some of their thinking and investment professionals aren't that worried about what they know. They're constantly worried about what they don't know."

University of Oklahoma and the University of Oklahoma Foundation

The University of Oklahoma (OU) is a co-educational university located in Norman, Oklahoma. It was founded in 1890, and has an enrollment of over 29,500 undergraduate and graduate students. Today, at nearly $850 million, the endowment is ranked number 72 in the 2009 NACUBO study. The endowment has a ratio of over $28,000 per student. As shown in Figure 5.1, during the period of 1999–2008, the Oklahoma foundation asset base has, through a combination of investment returns and new funds, grown from over $400 million to over $1 billion before settling back to $850 million in 2009.

Established in 1944, the University of Oklahoma Foundation manages the OU endowment, and seeks to maximize benefits to the university from its private donor support. It was started with a $160 gift

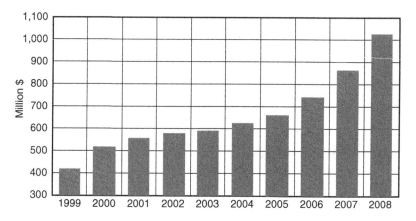

Figure 5.1   The University of Oklahoma Foundation Assets
Source: University of Oklahoma Foundation, 1/22/09 https://www.oufoundation.org/ouf/
charts.aspx

from the three original trustees. Its formation was "in response to private
donors who were concerned that money given directly to a state public
institution might be used for unintended purposes or in other areas of
state need." The foundation is an independent organization that receives,
administers, invests, and expends private funds solely for the benefit of
the University of Oklahoma.

The foundation has added staff as its growth has required, and
currently has a full-time staff of over 20. The foundation is governed
by a board of trustees from varying professional and philanthropic
backgrounds.

G uy L. Patton is the president and chief executive officer of
the University of Oklahoma Foundation, which he joined in
2007. Patton is a Tulsa native and was an executive with Fidelity
Investments for nearly 23 years prior to coming to the Foundation.

*Q: What is changing in endowment investment theory as the result of
the financial crisis? Are endowments rethinking how they invest?*

I do not think we are questioning the basics of diversified asset allocation
and the theories that support it. I've seen nothing that would suggest

that those concepts aren't still critical, especially in an endowed portfolio with a perpetual time horizon. I think what was wrong was in the implementation of asset allocation. There was some complacency in the industry, a notion that you can just plug in the allocation and let it ride with a little periodic rebalancing. I don't think that worked before and it definitely doesn't now. You can't run asset allocation on autopilot.

However, even good asset allocation wasn't much help in 2008–2009. Returns correlate to 1 in a global catastrophe. There's no place to hide. If a bomb hits, it doesn't matter whether your house was made of matchsticks or concrete blocks. This means that you don't spend too much time worrying about the 100-year flood line. You just accept that if it happens during your 100 years, then you're going to get wet and you keep moving. That is just part of the risk and return equation. There is no avoiding it.

We still very much believe in a diversified asset allocation strategy. We think the points of diversification matter. That is to say, this notion of large cap, small cap, a sliver of international, and a slug of fixed income is an extraordinarily incomplete asset allocation strategy. The weights and balances among those various classes matter a lot, and they are determined by what role they play in the overall portfolio. Different asset classes, hedge funds as an example, are not a replacement for long-only equity. They have different risk return characteristics, or at least they should have. The endowment should also know what it is trying to get out of its fixed income portfolio. Is it diversification? I think some institutions were trying to get alpha out of their fixed income portfolio.

This means that sophisticated asset allocation entails being mindful of what role each asset class plays in the portfolio vis-a-vis their performance and volatility in a variety of market environments. Good management doesn't mean simply plugging each asset class, hiring appropriate managers, walking off, and raking in the money. You have to frequently evaluate if each fund you are using is working within the portfolio as you predicted. That is why we have fairly wide tolerances in our allocation targets, and that is why we periodically rebalance and evaluate themes that we believe will be important.

A final point is that you have to be effective in translating theory into practice on this topic. You must pay attention to allocation at the strategic level, but there is a great deal of important activity at the tactical level. The operational aspect matters. The idea that you can get to some level of assets and quit paying attention to the details is simply not going to be the case. In fact, most investment professionals would say, "I never want that to be the case. I like being in those details."

As you look for broad asset classes, how do you think about alternative or private investments?

One thing that distorted returns in the business in the past few years was a large move to private investments. I think that the illiquidity premium started to look like easy money. What made this more dangerous was that many endowments had relatively immature systems and processes for managing, forecasting, evaluating, or measuring liquidity. I found this surprising, because it is standard operating procedure in other parts of the money management industry.

We have an explicit allocation to hedge funds, private equity, and venture capital. We are extraordinarily selective on private equity and venture capital funds because of concerns about valuations, lack of illiquidity. However, there are lots of deals currently that look attractive.

From a hedge fund standpoint, right now, we are at 18 investment managers. We will probably get to 19 or 20, with much smaller allocations, and very much focused on good stock picking in various parts of the world, geographies or industries or absolute return or long-short. There will be little to no leverage outside of the long-short using the short proceeds. In our view, long-short hedge funds are not a replacement to long only. It is to deliver a lot less volatility in your returns. And so, we expect lower return profiles from them, but we still expect good stock picking underneath all that. My sense is that hedge funds got overdone in the past few years. In part they became popular because that is what everybody was doing. There were people who made private equity investments because that is what everybody was doing. And in certain cases, unfortunately, the corporate-level due diligence was overlooked. They really didn't understand who they were doing business with nor did they understand why. It is important to know why those funds are in the portfolio and what role they play. I think the rapid move to adopt hedge funds may in hindsight have had elements of a fad. That is changing now.

In vetting managers, we do use consultants because our team is still relatively small. I worked at Fidelity, and one of the things that Peter Lynch has always said that was both simple and profound was, "When buying stocks, know what it is that you own and know exactly why you own it." The same thing goes for managers you pick and the funds they manage.

Do you think the liquidity issues in endowments were problematic in 2008–2009?

Yes. In some cases it was ruinous. If you don't manage liquidity correctly, you can wind up selling all your commitments at a discount, which happened among many of our peers. Again, I'm afraid that for some institutions, it looked like easy money. At OU we spent time looking for inexpensive ways to buy some of these distressed commitments, in fact.

You see good discipline on this topic in the pension world. In my view, it is as important as managing portfolio construction. You can't say, "Well, we had a bad year, so we're not going to distribute anything." At Fidelity I spent time with pension funds, and they used a liability-driven approach to ensure they could meet their annual cash commitments.

How should endowments evaluate performance? There has been a lot of discussion about what is an appropriate benchmark and should relative peer group rankings be used.

It is hard to compare endowments because they are so different. They have different internal staffing levels, different goals, and mean different things to the institutions they serve. You can look at investment performance overall, but it doesn't have much meaning without also understanding what is going on at a more granular level.

One area that has received a lot of attention in recent years is the relative performance measuring stick. Most of us have been forced into discussing relative returns this year as either being good or not good. I think many of our peers didn't spend a lot of time talking about relative returns in the past because the overall return was positive. They could say, "We didn't really beat our weighted market benchmark or target but we still made 12 percent or 13 percent. We're covering our spending policy."

This year, however, you have to look at benchmarks. You had to say, "We outperformed on a relative basis against our benchmark," and hope that you had a thoughtful benchmark established in advance. This topic is really important as it relates to how staff and the investment committee work together. I believe that there should be clear performance benchmarks in place that are owned by both staff and the investment committee that establish the basis for running the portfolio. If you are doing that well, then there is not as much pressure on the short-term performance indicators. They will understand what you did, why you did it, what information you were using at the time to make the decisions. This avoids hindsight bias and is just a good practice in working with the board. You must have process discipline in your investment decisions and clear board communications, which I believe start with clear performance goals and benchmarks.

Looking ahead, it seems that the industry is being reasonable by looking at three-year and five-year moving averages. This means there is probably another year before we will really start seeing the first real data points on what philosophical changes have occurred as a result of the events of 2008 and 2009.

Will you take direct positions in the market for opportunistic investments or to manage specific risks you see?

We haven't done this in the long-term endowment portfolio. I think you can see many applications for doing direct investing, and we've actually done some of it in our nonendowment, working capital portfolio. It's just a fast easy way to either hedge a position that you think is at risk or to hedge out some of the gains and lock them in. Clearly these are more short-term moves and are not part of the strategic asset allocation. This gets back to my earlier point regarding auto-pilot for the endowment. We just believe that there are opportunities to add value by active, tactical management of the portfolio.

Periodically you may also have to do this based on a specific initiative the university is going to do. For instance, if you are looking at a university project overseas that has a material expense in a foreign currency, then you may need to start hedging currency risk to eliminate any downside surprises as you start down the spending path.

As you were changing the sophistication in the OU endowment, did you make policy, operating, or organization changes to support the new approach?

I came here two years ago (2007) after a 23-year career in the investment industry. The University of Oklahoma Foundation had historically been a relatively conservative investor. Part of the reason I was brought aboard was to take a look at the existing process for investing and change it if necessary. The foundation board wanted to be sure that we were evaluating and implementing appropriate investment management techniques given the current size of the endowment. The endowment had grown significantly in the past 10–15 years and it had been hard for the investment process to keep pace with the level of change that had occurred with the size of the portfolio.

One of the most important things we did was recalibrate our strategic asset allocation. We increased the number of asset classes that we allocated to and we expanded the tolerances among the asset classes, which allowed us to be more nimble in the execution of the long term strategy. This was something new for OU.

This move, together with a great working relationship with the investment committee, improved the dynamism of the foundation. These were important changes, and changes that were appropriate, given the size of the OU foundation and the pace of change in the economy and markets. There had been a historically static view on asset allocation. There was also historically a lag time between generating a theme, having it approved, and then implementing it. This meant that we would periodically miss an opportunity, or miss part of the opportunity because it might take a year to implement. Becoming more nimble has been good for the foundation, which of course is good for OU.

The other important change we made was in the staff area. Before I arrived, there had never been a professional investment staff at the foundation. We now have two investment professionals, a director of investments, and a staff analyst. We think that for an organization our size that the process should be like a three legged stool. The investment consultant made recommendations and the investment committee made decisions in the Foundation's legacy process, but there wasn't anyone who was accountable every single day to make sure those decisions were implemented in a timely fashion. Adding a third leg to the stool, a dedicated investment staff, to manage the process, help inform strategy setting, and implement recommendations, has been a big improvement for us.

There's a big step change in sophistication required on the part of the investment organization that starts happening when you go from $500 million and start getting close to $1 billion in assets.

Yes. We were in the process of making some of the changes I outlined to our process and staff model when the crisis began. This turned out to be fortunate because we had done a lot of thinking about how we should operate, and the agenda was set. I believe this allowed us to react more quickly to events as they transpired.

Are there unique aspects to operating an endowment in a public university?

At OU we have a real connection to the university and to the state's political process because we are a state institution. I suspect that is the case at every state school.

Further, a new dynamic is emerging with respect to public university fund-raising and funding models. There has been a lot of success at universities in private fund-raising. In public universities private funding has begun to come closer to and in some cases exceed state appropriations. That dynamic is present here at OU. Twenty years ago, private funding, while important, was very small relative to the state's explicit appropriation to the university. Today, nearly all significant change on campus has a sizable private funding component to it.

Do academic endowments get a one-time performance improvement as they adopt sophisticated investing techniques and move beyond simple U.S. equity and fixed income portfolios?

I can at least speak to our experience at OU. We have certainly seen a pickup in terms of relative performance of our portfolio since we started to implement some of these new, more sophisticated approaches. We believe that applying these techniques puts you on a different long-term trajectory, one with higher average returns. The compounding effect means that the **angle** (emphasis) of the line has changed, as opposed to a one-time lift. Is it 400 basis points a year of higher performance? It is not likely to be that much. I feel strongly that it is something greater than zero, and 100 basis points over 50 years or 60 years is clearly material in terms of outcome.

What trends are you following currently? What are you thinking about from a macroeconomic standpoint for the coming three to five years?

I'd say we're thinking of not just the next three to five years but actually a little longer. Also, I would mark the start of this particular time frame as the beginning of 2009. The emergence from the trough of '08/'09 has shaped what we're worrying about materially. In many cases the themes we are following were driven by the response to the events of the fall of 2008.

We are certainly concerned about a weakening dollar and inflation. It's kind of an odd thing given the deflationary environment we have experienced in this economic downturn. What we worry about is a "whipsaw" from deflation to inflation driven by the monetary and fiscal policy response to the downturn. So, people are asking is now a good time to sell dollars and buy euros. The answer is probably "no," at least in the short term, but it may be "yes" in the intermediate term. The United States has created a lot of dollars to buy treasuries and the U.S. debt levels are rising pretty quickly. That cannot help but have a negative impact on the dollar in the intermediate term.

Some sovereign wealth funds have been accumulating gold. Is this related?

Yes, absolutely. But that too has its own disturbing trend. If investors are in effect shorting the dollar by going long gold, it has a significant impact on the price of gold. So you have seen a significant run-up in the price of gold and our question now is "are you actually getting future inflation protection with gold at these prices? We are not so sure . . . We are worried about the dollar. Again, this is not unique, we are worried about inflation. It is an odd thing because we believe we're still largely in a deflationary situation inside the United States or at least we are at the risk of falling back into one. We think that could change very quickly once the economy gets its footing.

Have you estimated the timing of the end of deflation?

It certainly is not tomorrow but it is not three years from now either. You can estimate a range but being more precise is very difficult. It could be as soon as the middle of next year, which would be a fairly rapid escalation of inflation. A lot of it is dependent upon a combination of U.S. and global economic growth.

When we start seeing declines in unemployment here in the United States, that will be our bellwether. So, it may not be as soon as next summer, but it could be by the end of 2010 when I would imagine we would start having increased jobs, consumer spending will start to increase, and retail sales will pick up. Then again, we worry about the current trend of converting currency, a lot of it dollars, to hard assets. It is inflating hard asset prices without any job growth.

The other thing that we're worried about is the U.S. economy. We are very bullish on America. I certainly am extraordinarily optimistic about the vibrancy and strength of this economy in the long term. Having said that, there's an enormous amount of political and policy uncertainty, and that is getting layered on top of a lot of economic uncertainty. Markets hate uncertainty and this environment of uncertainty can be very stifling in terms of businesses' willingness to invest capital, willingness to add people to their payrolls, and that will continue until the smoke clears. In the long term, we are certainly bullish. But in the intermediate term, it is not clear to us that this regulatory policy and political uncertainty isn't going to cause a fair amount of indecision in the markets and in business in general. That's not good. I think most businesses can deal with whatever the rules are as long as they know them.

Does the investment office at OU also manage university working capital?

Yes. The velocity of the funds is quite different in this area. Often a dollar comes in and then immediately goes back out. A few things can be somewhat longer term—a building project, for instance, where we will raise the private monies as much as four or five years before the money actually gets spent on the project itself. We have put in a system to take pretty detailed snapshots of the liability structure of our working capital and we "bucket" the money into various time frames. We see one bucket as less than 60-day money. We see another as less than 6-month money. We see another as less than 12-month money. We see yet another as less than 2-year money, and so forth. Then, on the investing side of the equation, we've got an asset configuration that lines up well with that time oriented liability structure.

You've got to build a liquidity ladder that allows you to fund every one of those commitments as they come. I would argue, nonendowment money requires a different but nearly comparable level of sophistication if you want to optimize the returns on that cash. We do this, and most state university foundations do as well because the return on those monies, call it "float," is a material source of flexible funding that you can give back to the university. It could be a large amount of money in aggregate. So, you're definitely leaving a lot of money on the table if you don't manage it.

What kind of tools do you use for reporting? Do you have anything special or anything you think is unique?

We developed some internal portfolio analytic tools that we use for reporting. This is an area that has become sophisticated in the past few years even for individual investors, if you look at what brokerage web sites like Fidelity or Schwab are doing for their customers.

We rely a lot upon our custody bank for, not so much analytics, but for data. That's one of the things that we re-architected into a new custody arrangement. We are expecting more and more timely information. We are also evaluating some additional tools that have been implemented at some of the larger endowments to see if they would benefit us.

Our consultant is Cambridge, who also provides not only regular analytics, but they're also very responsive to the custom things that we want to look at.

What sort of inputs do you take to help you think about big trends?

We spend a lot of time making sure we have good relationships with industry partners, which includes not only the obvious suspects, but also with the folks on the sell side of the street who we may not have a direct relationship with. The typical institutional investor is mostly doing business with the buy side—money managers that support the investment, institutional investment management area. Most of the players, whether it's large institutions like Fidelity or small institutions like a small hedge fund, live almost exclusively on the buy side. The large investment banks and brokerage houses bring a very different perspective to any given discussion. We find that to be very helpful when trying to develop a specific theme or strategy.

Of course our consultant, Cambridge brings many ideas to us. The more that we can relate those ideas to those we are learning from the other relationships the more interesting the dialogue. In the end, we believe that creates a more robust decision making process.

If we see a theme that will be important, we try to gather up as many diverse points of view on the topic as possible, read them ourselves, and we will present that material to the investment committee. The notion is to try to find as many diverse views on a topic as you can. Inevitably those come from all different kinds of sources.

One of the skills that investment professionals develop is seeking out contrarian viewpoints. It helps drive some of their thinking. Investment professionals aren't that worried about what they know. They're constantly worried about what they don't know.

I also still pay a fair amount of attention to what's going on in the pension world. That business has its own interesting parallels to what we do even though the goal set may be quite different. Obviously I read the standard things every day that anyone would—*Financial Times* and the *Wall Street Journal,* etc.

Chapter 6

Bruce Zimmerman

Chief Investment Officer

University of Texas Investment Management Company

"No one enters an investment thinking they are going to lose money . . . you need to be able to properly evaluate risks and calculate their probabilities in order to succeed as an institutional or individual investor."

The University of Texas System and UTIMCO

The University of Texas System is comprised of nine university campuses and six health science centers or hospitals. The campuses are located throughout Texas. It is one of the largest university systems in the United States, with enrollment at the flagship university in Austin exceeding 50,000 graduate and undergraduate students. Total enrollment in all locations is over 200,000.

The work to establish a university system in Texas began in 1839 with the set-aside of land by the Congress of Texas. This act predated the annexation of Texas into the United States in 1846. In 1883 the flagship University of Texas in Austin began classes.

The University of Texas Investment Management Company (UTIMCO) manages the endowment and operating capital for the 15 institutions comprising the University of Texas System. In November 2009 the total amount managed by UTIMCO was over $21 billion

69

dollars, making it one of the top three largest academic endowment pools in the United States. Nearly \$16 billion of the funds are part of the permanent and long-term endowment. The target annual rate of return to support current and future institutional objectives is 8.2 percent. UTIMCO was founded in 1996 and initiated a trend in the public university endowment business of creating an external entity to manage university endowment and operating funds. A number of leading universities now use this model. The group has nearly 60 full-time staff in investment management, operations, and administrative roles.

A look at the structure (Figure 6.1) of the UTIMCO assets demonstrates the high complexity and multiple components of large institutional pools. UTIMCO manages both the endowment and operating (working capital) funds for the system, and has several subfunds that have different goals, sizes, and time horizons. Table 6.1 shows the UTIMCO

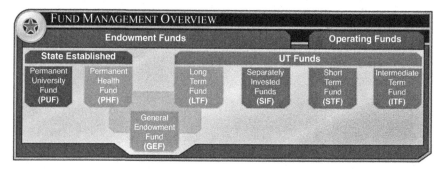

Figure 6.1   UTIMCO—Categories of Funds under Management
SOURCE: UTIMCO Annual Report

Table 6.1   UTIMCO Permanent University Fund
(PUF)—Asset Allocation as of June 30, 2009

Asset Class	June 30, 2009
Investment Grade Fixed Income	14.1%
Credit-Related Fixed Income	16.1%
Real Estate	5.6%
Natural Resources	6.5%
Developed Country Equity	44.4%
Emerging Markets Equity	13.3%
TOTAL	*100%*

SOURCE: UTIMCO Annual Report

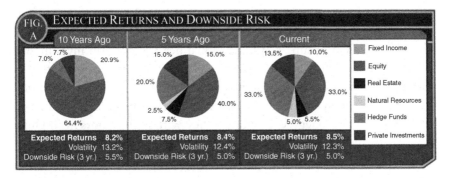

Figure 6.2   UTIMCO Goals by Asset Category over Time
SOURCE: UTIMCO Annual Report

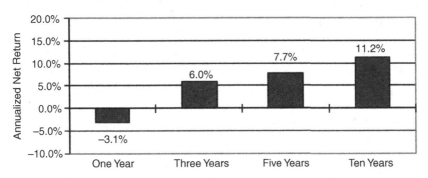

Figure 6.3   UTIMCO—Permanent Endowment Fund Performance for Years Ended August 31, 2008
SOURCE: UTIMCO Annual Report

allocations across asset classes. Figure 6.2 shows how these' allocations have changed over time. The performance return UTIMCO has enjoyed is shown in Figure 6.3.

UTIMCO is led by Bruce Zimmerman, chief executive officer and chief investment officer. Bruce joined UTIMCO in May 2007 from Citigroup, where he joined as chief investment officer of Citigroup Alternative Investments (CAI), established by the company to serve as the home for all alternative investments offered to clients. While at Citigroup, Bruce managed over $80 billion in assets as well as the finance, operations, and technology platforms for CAI. Bruce also served as Citigroup's CIO and global head of pension investments, where he managed over $30 billion in U.S. and international assets. His group achieved a 14.75 percent investment return in 2006 and averaged 12 percent in the prior three years, exceeding comparable benchmarks. He has a bachelor's degree in public policy with high honors from Duke University and an MBA with distinction from Harvard University.

Q: What are some of the basics that moderate net worth investors should be thinking about and what can they learn from the endowment investing methodology?

It is helpful to start with first principles. I am a believer in diversification. There are three basic asset classes: stocks, bonds, and real assets. Some groups also consider splitting bonds between real bonds and nominal bonds. There is a fairly constant relationship across asset classes in terms of unit of return vs. unit of risk, if you back out leverage, and that is about 0.25.

Eliminating correlation through diversification can allow you to construct portfolios that can get that up to about 0.5. But correlations don't stay constant—you have to continually "pressure test" your portfolio to understand correlations in the face of change. As I think about moderate net worth investors I would start with those basics: Be diversified and realize what you are going to get from each asset class in terms of risk and return. I'd also say that for the individual, they should err on the side of conservatism.

Is this barbelling?

I would call it a safety net. You need to determine how far off the ground feels safe for you in terms of a safety net and keep that much money in very conservative assets. The less money you have, the more conservative you need to be. When I look at the portfolios of ultra-high-net-worth individuals, they have nothing but private equity and hedge fund investments—except for the large amount of money they have tucked away in Treasuries and municipal bonds as a safety net, which assures that they will always have a certain amount of wealth.

Bottom line, this is an individual choice that people have to make for themselves and it really depends on their specific situation.

Beyond these basics, what else can individual investors learn from endowment management?

I think the endowment model, beyond this basic notion of diversification, is misunderstood. It is not "let's pour a lot of money into private equity and hedge funds." Instead it says if you are really a long-term investor, then equities will do better than bonds. If you are long term and you can afford some illiquidity, then you can take some of that risk so long as you were comfortable that you were getting an appropriate return for it. Now, recently, this may have been overdone and it caused some problems.

However, it would be wrong for the pendulum to swing back too far in favor of liquidity. Endowments are in-perpetuity investors, presumably with new money coming in, and have the longest of long-term horizons. Individuals don't have this perpetual viewpoint and, accordingly, will have a different appetite and tolerance for illiquidity. As a long-term investor, however, illiquidity risk and return is something that has to be managed. You can take some illiquidity risk if you believe you will be rewarded.

What endowments do is, first, look for asset classes or capital market opportunities that are mispriced—places where they think the risk-return ratio imbalanced. This is often where there is a large need for capital and a small supply of capital. This is very hard to do. It takes a lot of smart people and a lot of time and effort. An example of this is the timber investing done by endowments a decade or so ago. This is going to be hard for the individual to replicate.

Second, endowments believe that skill does matter. You should try to partner with the best talent you can find, while ensuring that there is a good alignment of interest. These principles manifested themselves in this move to private equity and hedge funds. Those vehicles had the important characteristics—such as the ability to identify market opportunities and payment of an illiquidity premium. Mostly, however, they succeeded because that's where the talent was, driven by, in large part, compensation.

Nonetheless, there is nothing magic about using financial instruments such as short or long public equity plays, derivatives or leverage. The instruments are like a power tool—in the hands of a skilled carpenter they can produce great results and be constructive. On the other hand, if you give them to your unskilled teenage child you may have a disaster.

Can investors learn at least philosophically from endowments? What are some of the key differences between endowments and individuals?

Bandwidth is some of it. Access is a large part of it as well. Having large sums of money to invest lowers fees and increases the number of managers that you can evaluate and that will allow you into their funds. Managers also like institutional investors with name brands because an investment from an institution can help them later with their marketing. Larger investments also reduce the sales effort for the manager per dollar acquired, which reduces their costs. Managers also know that endowments have long time horizons and may not need to access the money near-term.

Furthermore, we talk to our managers all the time. They know that we also are thinking about what the trends are and that we are taking in a lot of information from a variety of sources, and so we can provide them with insights as well—an endowment staff conversation with fund managers is a two-way street.

In combination these factors allow a large endowment a different level of access and fees than the individual can achieve. Individuals with only $10–$20 million to invest just can't get into the kind of funds that an endowment can. The top funds are simply out of reach. Recently we have gone into a few new funds that we have been considering for a period of years. These are funds that have been closed for a long time—they pick their investors and rarely take anyone new. They just wouldn't take an individual's money.

There is another approach that ultra-high-net-worth investors, people with a billion in net worth, can implement. It goes back to the notion that skill in investing really is a differentiator. If you believe that investment talent is the key and that there are maybe 50 or 100 virtuoso investors in the world, then the optimal thing is to go out and identify them and invest with them, not worrying about asset classes or diversification at that level. Then, adding it all up at a portfolio level, if you feel that you have too much bias in any direction or you have exposures you don't want, at that point you could use ETFs, indexes, derivatives, or other tools to balance things out and manage the portfolio. Finding the best managers is hard, however, as Howard Marks of Oaktree once said: "There aren't that many people out there that deserve 2 and 20."

What do you think about funds of funds? Are they moving out of favor due to fee structures?

It depends. You can't paint all fund-of-funds or endowments with the same brush—every endowment is in a different part of its lifecycle and growth. For instance, I am on the board of a foundation that has a little over a billion under management. It is hard for these groups to have enough staff, but they have to get the work done anyway. At UTIMCO we have 5–6 people focused on a given asset class, which is just not possible for smaller institutions or foundations. Fund of funds can make good sense for smaller endowments, and then as they gain experience and size they can consider direct hedge fund investing. Going back to the individual, at the smaller range of net worth, I don't think an individual with, say, $2 million should be in private equity or hedge funds. They wouldn't be able to access them directly—they would have to go through a fund of funds. Maybe as you get to $10 or $20 million you could consider putting some money into a fund of private equity firms or fund of hedge funds. One of the problems you run into with limited amounts of money is the vintage year of the investment. You really want to be able to diversify across the inception year of the investment. This increases considerably the amount that you need to be able to put to work in private equity.

How should individual investors think about asset class choices and manager selection?

Going back to first principles, individuals should be sure they clearly understand what they are buying and what risks they are taking. No one enters an investment thinking they are going to lose money. Everyone thinks they are going to make money or they wouldn't do it. However, when things don't work out it is often because the investor didn't fully appreciate how complicated the instrument was—what were the water-fall effects, for example—and therefore also didn't realize the risks they were taking on.

You will have investments that don't work out. If it happens because of scenarios that came along that you envisioned and predicted at low likelihood, that is okay. If it doesn't work out because of things you never even considered, then you didn't do your job. I have yet to come across an investment that was riskless and also generates any sort of reasonable return. This means you need to be able to properly evaluate risks and assess their probabilities in order to succeed as an institutional or individual investor.

Endowments seem more nimble than one might expect of institutional investors; this includes things like direct investing and thematic investing. What do you think?

Endowments fall on a continuum of flexibility. An ultra-high-net-worth family office may be more nimble than an endowment, which in turn is more so than a large state public pension plan. In our case, we try to be nimble by being a bit matrixed across asset classes and across trends and opportunities. For example, UTIMCO is organized primarily by investment type, but a few years ago we thought there would be a lot of opportunities in credit-related fixed income and built a cross-group task force to understand what our response should be.

What are the trends and opportunities that you are thinking about for the coming few years?

There are a number of things we are looking at in the coming years. First, there is still too much debt in the developed world and an overall imbalance between creditors and debtors. In Texas we have seen that before and it entails either a short and painful or a long and more painful workout process. We may have stopped the dire emergency, but there is still a lot to do to fix the underlying credit imbalances.

I also think that globally we will see more government involvement in marketplaces. In some cases this may be helpful where regulations need to be more highly enforced, but as with many cycles, the pendulum will likely swing too far. The political process in a country influences regulation in a cyclical way as well and during the upcoming election year financial regulation and retribution is likely to be part of any national campaign platform.

Endowments became more sophisticated over time and incorporated a much greater allocation to alternative investments. What will happen in this area in the future?

I think that the term "alternative investments" is too broad if it encompasses private equity and hedge funds. Even within hedge funds, knowing someone is in that business tells me nearly nothing about what the investment is like. It is a phrase that doesn't bring clarity to the business and in fact may further obscure what the industry is about.

As far as the future for endowments, I don't see us returning to our caves. Now that we have "discovered fire" I don't think there is any going back, even if some in the industry have gotten burned recently. I do think there will be a little pullback in the coming years, especially for those who may have gotten overbalanced in complex investments. There is a lot that finance theory and science can teach managers, and to ignore it is not a good way to approach investing. I think this will prompt introspection in the industry for institutional money and managers in the alternatives business where they will make sure that they have learned and incorporated the lessons of the past two years.

Looking at some of the events of 2008 and 2009, what are you thinking about tail risk now and what are you doing differently, if anything, as a result?

We have been working on it. We think about tail risk in terms of portfolio insurance—how much money can you and should you be willing to pay in insurance premiums and what are the catastrophic risks.

Going back to the macro trends on the debtor/creditor imbalance, I think there is a large inflation risk in debtor countries. We are nowhere near that right now, but over time, if you are creating a lot of money, inflation is likely. In theory you can pull the money out at the right time, but that is much harder to do than it was to put the money in. This will in turn elongate the workout process—the sooner you take your medicine, the less medicine there is to take—but it is unpleasant when you are taking it. This also goes back to the political influences over investing because there is a tendency to want to postpone the pain.

We have been blessed with a period of global growth over the last few decades, as more people around the world have been able to participate in freer markets. They have been able produce and earn and then have been able to spend their earnings on things they want. This has been the catalyst for a lot of growth. As we try to work our way out of these large imbalances there will be real pressures on the open global framework. This used to be called trade wars but I think it will manifest as currency wars in the coming years.

Does this retrenchment mean that investors should be expecting lower-than-historical returns in the coming decade?

Yes. If there is less growth, then returns are impacted. The flip side of that is that we will also have more volatility, and investors who understand that, can spot the opportunities, and be on the right side of those moves will do very well.

Several funds have been created for private investors that replicate the endowment model and are operated by former endowment chief investment officers. Are those funds getting to the size and point where they can mimic the features of the large academic endowments?

Yes. There are a half-dozen or so of them. They all have different investment strategies, but their common theme is that they are headed by a former endowment CIO. It is an evolving business model and one that can make sense, and there are some that are having success with it.

Part III

PRIVATE UNIVERSITIES

Chapter 7

James H.C. Walsh
Chief Investment Officer

Cornell University

"Our industry is not good at having patience with people who are contrarians and don't make money for a number of years, even though they make a lot of money for us when things go badly wrong."

Cornell University and the Endowment

Cornell University is located in Ithaca, New York. The university was established in 1865 by Senator Ezra Cornell and Andrew Dickson White. Senator Cornell provided an initial endowment for the university composed of land for the campus and an initial sum of $500,000. Ezra Cornell founded the university as "an institution where any person can find instruction in any study." White was the first president of the university.

Cornell has a total enrollment of more than 20,000 students and is a member of the Ivy League.

Cornell's endowment currently has a market value of approximately $4 billion, putting it in the top 20 college endowments in the United States by market value. The 2009 NACUBO study ranks Cornell number 19 among U.S. university endowments.

J ames H.C. Walsh joined Cornell as chief investment officer in 2006.[1] He earned his bachelor's degree with honors in economics from Brunel University, London, and his master's degree in economics from Birkbeck College, University of London. Prior to joining Cornell, James was manager of the BT Pension Scheme (BTPS), executive director of strategy and alternatives for Hermes Pensions Management in London, the United Kingdom's largest fund. Walsh has been awarded *The Independent* newspaper's Golden Guru award for his work forecasting the British economy.

Q: What are you seeing change in the endowment investing business? Liquidity has been a big topic.

I'll start with what are we thinking about now, and it's linked to what has changed. It comes to your question, philosophically, how much premium do we need from illiquid assets? I think a misstep that many endowments made over the last few years was assuming that they didn't need that much liquidity. I think from the bigger endowment perspective, we have seen a very tight balance between the endowment performance and liquidity requirements and the operating budget needs of the university.

It seems that institution budget needs can be hard to predict because so many things like enrollment, grants, and new gifts have an impact. The endowment needs to maximize return while still providing liquidity.

Yes, this is a balancing act. It is a long-term decision because when we lock up our liquidity, we're often sending it out for 7 to 12 years. We found that with private equity and real estate, we might not see a chunk of that money back for the best part of the decade. It is not a decision you can quickly change. I suspect that through the coming years, endowments will be more liquid than they have been in the past. This will take some time, because they haven't got back the capital from private investments quite yet. The things you mention are impacting most endowments—a slowdown in gifts, a shrinking of the endowment size, and increasing demands from university budgets. Also, spending policies are often calculated on a long historical tail. For instance, we use the previous 12 quarters to calculate. From the perspective of early 2010, clearly the market was higher 12 quarters ago, and so we are paying out a much higher percentage of the current size of our endowment these days.

The amount of the operating budget that an endowment provides varies a lot across institutions—as little as 2 to 3 percent and as much as 30 or 40 percent or more. How does this affect how endowments will operate going forward?

If the payout is going up as the market declines, then you are selling low. You need to think about what that means to the endowment going forward in terms of recouping the losses of the last couple years.

This is the thing universities have realized. If they are all going to be long-term investors and they are going to be the providers of liquidity when liquidity has dried up everywhere else, then they really need to change their policy to support that liquidity. My background is in the pension world. My previous employer for 11 years was the biggest pension fund in the United Kingdom, and we spent a lot of time worrying about our liabilities each quarter and how to be sure we had appropriate liquidity to meet them.

Do you think the endowment model will migrate toward something that looks closer to the pension model?

Pensions are different, of course, but I think that there will be more attention paid to liquidity. Over the last 18 months endowments have learned a significant lesson, and it's a good lesson. In that sense, endowments will look more like pension schemes. I don't think that they will be maturity matching in the way that pension schemes do. I don't think endowments will necessarily be moving down the risk/return curve dramatically, but they will be taking risks in more liquid ways. I believe that endowments will start holding more cash.

Do you think CIO views on cash will change? Will cash be viewed more positively, and holding it will allow CIOs to be opportunistic when chance arises?

That's exactly the thing you would hear if you talked to the most skilled portfolio managers. Whether it is an equity manager or a multistrategy manager, that is what they will tell you. CIOs and endowment managers must act more like this, so I believe that they will hold more cash in the portfolio.

What is your view on thematic investing versus strict asset allocation? Do you try to look for macroeconomic trends?

One of the strengths of the perceived endowment model is that money is managed externally. That does two things: One is we get great insights into the economy and the market by talking to our managers. We invest considerable time in gathering this intelligence. Second, it means that we can reallocate painlessly by redeeming a little from one manager and putting it somewhere else, but not necessarily redeeming completely from managers.

Does mid-term portfolio maneuvering mean sometimes taking direct positions?

Opportunities are usually better sourced and invested by people that are able to do it all the time, so we would select a manager for that. However, occasionally we can add value by taking on hedges, and especially hedging tail-risk events.

The next step is trying to institutionalize tail risk hedging in the form of policy. It can be expensive to insure tail risk, and so endowments will need to evaluate this themselves and then work with the investment committees to determine what they are willing to pay for insurance.

How did endowments that had tail risk insurance in place the past 18 months do?

It is hard to tell from what gets disclosed. If you look at the list of who did well the last fiscal year, the ones at the top probably did some of this. However, no one managed away the total risk, not by a long shot, but I think it is something that endowments will be looking at going forward.

Aside from tail risk hedging, what other changes do you think institutional money managers will make?

I think CIOs will spend a bit more time thinking about how you get other people, such as your managers, to hedge in the future.

I think that will be another trend, not just what you do yourself, but actually add managers who have an asymmetric payoff. The portfolio has to allow them to be boring in the good times and expect them to shoot the lights out when things go bad. Our industry is not good at having patience with people who are contrarians and don't make money for a number of years, even though they make a lot of money for us when things go badly wrong. It requires patience.

What about the relative performance derby going on between endowments?

I think it's a tough thing to try and follow. Each institution is different. The amount of risk you are going to take must be driven by your obligations to the university.

Another problem with relative comparisons is the time frame. A single year's numbers are not going to be useful. It provides an incentive to follow fads or to take a short-run view, or to add more risk than is warranted.

At the same time, it is inevitable that endowments will be compared to one another. The important thing is to try to make the evaluation truly comparable by looking at a longer period of time and trying to highlight some of the big differences that affect the amount of risk the endowment can and should take. Endowments should be long-term investors, yet we expect them to "win" on an annual basis as if they were the school's sports team.

What would be a good way to compare endowments—what time frame would be better—perhaps three years?

It's better than one year, but it's probably still too short. It's probably five years minimum. I also think it varies a good bit by asset class. Think about how long it takes to put a private equity portfolio together. Two to three years is actually the investment period. You don't know how good your private equity portfolio is until the end of the cycle, which is much longer than three years. The same can be said for real estate—four or five years minimum there.

You could say three years is effective for the liquid side of the portfolio. But even then there are problems.

What are your thoughts on private equity now? How much do you like it and have you changed how you thought about it over the past year or two?

If you look at the returns over 10 or 20 years they still stack up. I think that what's changed is too many people bought into it, from an investor standpoint. Too much money came in, which inevitably reduces the return. Too much leverage got involved as well. And people should have been thinking about it more tactically. I think, ironically, the next two to three years will probably be very good times to invest new money in new private equity deals. The biggest danger at the moment is that a lot of this new investment will be follow-up money, rescuing deals which shouldn't have been done in the first place.

Some institutional money managers are against highly leverage-oriented private equity. There is a belief that leverage-based returns can be had cheaper.

There are private equity managers who have made their money out of leverage, which is a lot less interesting to us. And there are private equity managers who made their money out of going in and restructuring businesses. That will always be something that pays off and it's worth doing. It comes back to picking your managers—picking good managers and diversifying your managers. You also have to realize that even some of the good ones get caught in a bad cycle.

Do you look for manager transparency on leverage?

Absolutely. On the liquid side of things, we watch the leverage very carefully. We, of course, don't use leverage at the endowment level. We look very carefully at our hedge fund managers to understand how much leverage they are taking on so we can do something about that. We carefully examine what leverage goes into the deals with our illiquid managers. It does come into the equation in terms of where we see the risks and how we might hedge. We spend a lot of time thinking about the maturity of the debt and structure of the debt in our portfolios.

How do you look for visibility to what leverage managers are using?

Again you have to evaluate it by asset class. In private equity funds, you have to evaluate it on a deal-by-deal basis. You have to go to your managers and say, "Give us the information; tell us the maturity of the debt, tell us what the covenants are and tell us how much head room you have against these covenants." On the hedge fund side, it's more difficult, because they are usually moving quickly. There is more interest from institutions now, and the hedge fund managers are responding to that. It comes down to having people in the investment office that understand leverage and ask the right questions.

How many investment professionals do you have in the endowment? How do you organize the team?

The total organization is 25 people; 16 of those are investment people. We do organize by asset class, but I am a big proponent of collaboration, so there is a lot of crossover. For instance, we have individuals who will deal with illiquid asset classes who will also look at liquid assets because the links are really quite substantial. They meet frequently and compare notes. We are making sure that this is happening across the organization, and it has proven to be helpful.

What is your manager selection process?

We go into great detail when looking at managers, which makes it a lengthy process. We spend a lot of time talking to managers and to industry participants that can source managers. When we identify candidates, we then spend a lot of time getting to know them before we invest with them. We don't put RFPs out like the pension world does. We go proactively looking for the managers. It is unusual that anyone who comes to us directly happens to be what we are looking for. Normally, we have to go seek them out. Our predisposition is toward managers who are off the beaten path or from a slightly different analytical bent. There is inevitably a clustering of endowments around the same managers. We want to make sure we are doing our own research and coming to our own conclusions.

What sorts of things have you found effective in manager sourcing?

As I mentioned, we spend considerable time talking to people in the industry. We also use our network of alumni, and we look for referrals. It also helps to have an experienced investment staff.

Does having a large asset base to work from help with manager access?

It does help, but you have to put it in context. We are not huge—compared to a CalPERS, which will have nearly $200 billion. We're four and a half billion. That said, we can put money to work that would be useful to a manager. I think endowments may have lost some of their perceived benefits as investors over the last year, but we are still seen as long-term investors and a good brand to have; these are important attributes to a manager.

Do you employ funds of funds?

We don't invest through funds of funds. We did at first when the investment office was expanded. They serve a perfectly good purpose for the smaller investor. They don't serve a great purpose to us. We don't need to pay a second layer of fees.

For larger endowments, is there a trade-off of fund-of-fund fees versus being able to fund an internal staff?

That's fair. An internal staff gives you more flexibility. We can more precisely target what we are looking for. We can have an asset allocation portfolio which matches what we're looking for as opposed to what the average of other investors are looking for. I think we get better access than a fund of funds might. Because a fund of funds will typically have multiple smaller investors, they may be more subject to redemptions during a downturn, something that managers clearly want to avoid, since it is disruptive and can affect their other investors.

In manager selection, besides the things you quantify, how much do soft skills matter?

The difficulty about investing is that you don't necessarily know if someone is a skilled investor until long after they have been skillful. A big mistake that you see endowments make, collectively, is we tend to hire people at the top and sell people at the bottom.

We're trying to avoid that. Sometimes you can't go to people who performed well recently because of this. What you may be looking for is a contrarian manager, or a manager who has not had a great track record recently. Those are often the managers who are good, but currently underrated.

As far as the qualitative part goes, I think the old adage is that a person's character tends not to change. This also seems to apply in the investment world. If they've misbehaved in the past, they will likely do it in the future. I try to avoid cynicism, but you have to be clinical about these things. In the end, you have to trust people with your money or your university's money. It comes down to: Do you like their strategy and their process? Do you think they have an edge? Do you think they have structured the fund correctly? And do you trust them with the money? Of course, there are a considerable number of quantitative things that you have to check off as well, such as compliance, audit, and reporting.

If you don't want to wind up chasing performance, does it put a lot more pressure on the nonquantitative parts of the manager's selection process?

You're going to find, unfortunately, in this business that there are quite a lot of people who got one-time peaks in performance. There is also a sense that there are only a few really good managers. I don't agree with that. There may only be a handful of really good managers that are also popular, but often there are good managers that are off the headlines. Those are the ones we don't want to overlook.

What do you think are the big differences between what an individual can do as an investor versus what an endowment can do?

It is hard to get access and to properly diversify. As an individual, for example, it is difficult to get into private equity. It's difficult to get the diversification you might want from real assets like real estate. You can solve some of the problem. For instance, it is a lot easier these days to get a country, regional, sector–type exposure that you couldn't easily do before, because there are new instruments. The nice thing with ETFs is that that you can do your own allocation in a way you couldn't before. The tough thing is getting the alpha. Inevitably the alpha is directed much more toward the institutional investor. Even if you could get access to the best managers, picking the managers and monitoring them is a significant job and not something an individual can likely do.

What advice do you have for the individual investor?

First, don't try to time the market in a way that some investors think they can. You've got to stick to an asset allocation that makes sense, and you have to tinker with it a little bit, and try to be a long-term investor. You have to realize that you haven't got the edge. Buying asset classes and being diversified makes a great deal of sense. Diversification is usually the one thing that saves you. It didn't save us a lot in 2008, but it usually does. Try not to follow fads. The strategy of endowments is diversify and be patient. Those are both things individuals can do.

Endowments became sophisticated during the 1980s and 1990s. Can individuals repeat this one-time sophistication improvement in their own investing?

I think that it's always a danger to look back at what anyone has done historically, because what worked in that particular world and what worked in the last 10 years almost certainly won't work over the next 10 years. For instance, we just had a decade which was driven by leverage and the growth of leverage. More money has come in to the strategies that endowments have been following. We know in the last few years that the pension schemes and other institutional money and private wealth are going into alternatives.

Also, endowments are changing what they are doing going forward. It may well be that they actually will be targeting lower returns and going back to basics. There is more concern with liquidity, which will lower returns. Endowments are not likely to be targeting the returns they saw in the past few years. It just happened that until recently things turned out very well for that period.

You also have to worry about the investments that a lot of people are piling into. These can be the start of the next bubble.

You've got to be desperately careful about those and particularly as an individual investor, because you also find that the institutional investors will be getting out ahead of the peak of these markets, whether it's emerging markets, whether it's gold, whether it's other commodities, or any other asset. The individual can get left in the investment until too late.

What absolute return strategies do you like the best?

For today's environment, I like macro strategies. I like managers who have the ability to go in and out of different areas through liquid instruments, can follow trends where they want to, or be contrarian if they want to. The contrarian piece is great because not only do they add value in the long term but also act as a downside buffer. You've got to have things in the portfolio that do well when everything else crashes out.

It was just as much true in 2009 as it was in 2008 that everything is correlated. The difference in 2009 was that everything correlated up in the second half of the year. And one of the things that we pay attention to is what's driving equities, what's driving credit, what's driving the dollar, what's driving commodities is basically the same thing—it is liquidity. And if that starts turning off, everything goes down at the same time.

What are the 6- to 36-month trends you're thinking of?

Inflation concerns us for the moment. Interest rates are a concern. That is one of the long-term things. We're more focused on interest rates than inflation because there is a significant risk, both for the long and the short term, that we will get a spike up in interest rates and everyone is going to be heavily exposed to that. I think the difficult thing today is that some of the best inflation hedges like real estate are not good places to be. Also, traditional hedges like real estate may not be as effective as they have previously been. Endowments will have to be more creative on hedging interest rates and inflation.

We work to identify tail risk hedges or at least try to add strategies that would do better in a different environment. We are a little bit more focused on stock pickers because we had a year or two where the fundamentals haven't really mattered. Everything has just gone down. Our view is that's going to change over the next 18–24 months. So those people who have underperformed the indexes or benchmarks will actually do really quite well. There's some great opportunities in that area.

What are some examples of frontier markets?

Africa and Eastern Europe, the ones that look like what emerging markets looked like a decade ago. Usually not the most healthy in terms of their fiscal policy, or monetary policy, but also priced appropriately. Our current emerging markets, the big ones, in some cases actually look better than the developed world in terms of their fiscal monetary policy.

We're looking at ways to diversify outside of the United States because we are concerned about the direction of the U.S. economy. Not that we necessarily think it's going to be bad, but you have to argue there was a greater risk surrounding U.S. growth now than there was 10 years ago.

In the short term, distressed and credit investments have done spectacularly well in the second half of 2009. We're going into a potentially very interesting distressed cycle. I think we're in a lull today because of the slide in liquidity. That lull will probably come to an end at some point, but nobody knows when. And then, it will be really messy again. So we actually have to be able to deploy more capital to some of the interesting illiquid asset classes in a year or two.

Where do you think distress will show up? Will it be in private equity–backed small company assets or will it be real estate, land, or something else?

Probably all of the above. Certainly in real estate. Securitized debt is hard to come by. I think there's a lot of denial at the moment because interest rates are historically low and real estate owners can pay the interest on their loan.

At some point, interest rates have to go up and then it will become nasty. There is a huge amount of debt that would need to be refinanced. Much of the debt put in place in the boom was 5–7-year debt. It will come due in the coming few years—2012, 2013, and 2014. If the securitized debt business hasn't recovered by then, it is going to be very painful.

It seems that you believe that distressed opportunities will be linked to interest rates.

Yes, I think that will be the trigger. At the moment, the consensus is interest rates in the United States won't go up until 2011 or thereabout. Some are saying after 2011. If that consensus proves to be wrong I think we could see a lot of distressed and bankrupt real estate, which will then have secondary impacts.

What do you read or what kind of information do you consume that helps you in your job and in your decision-making process?

You have to read all the normal things that the investment and business community reads. It is also helpful to try to read those things off the beaten path. Some of the more long-term things, it's keeping an eye out for those things which other people aren't reading that is crucial. This is consistent with our desire to take in contrarian points of view.

Note

1. James H.C. Walsh is now chief executive officer and chief investment officer of Cayuga Capital Partners, LLP, a London-based investment manager focused on Global Macro.

Chapter 8

Sally J. Staley
Chief Investment Officer
Anjum Hussain
Director of Risk Management

Case Western Reserve University

"Risk is the cost of return."

Case Western Reserve University and the Case Western Reserve University Endowment

Case Western Reserve University is located in Cleveland, Ohio. It has an enrollment of over 9,700 undergraduate and graduate students. The university in its current state was formed in 1967 by the combination of the Case Institute of Technology (founded in 1881) and Western Reserve University (founded in 1826).

Today, at nearly $1.5 billion, the endowment is ranked number 37 in the 2009 NACUBO study. During the period of 1989 to 2009, the Case Western Reserve endowment grew from about $435 million to over $1.4 billion, reflecting an annualized growth rate of 6 percent net of investment return, gifts, distributions and expenses (see Table 8.1).

The endowment is managed by the chief investment officer, who has an investment staff of five, including the director of marketable investments, director of private investments, and director of risk management.

Table 8.1   Case Western Reserve University Endowment Performance

Fiscal Year	Pool Return	Benchmark Return	Outperformance
2009	(19.01%)	(24.54%)	5.53%
2008	0.59%	0.81%	(0.22%)
2007	20.06%	15.53%	4.53%
2006	14.28%	13.75%	0.53%
2005	15.59%	11.09%	4.50%
2004	17.81%	17.50%	0.31%
2003	2.98%	3.25%	(0.27%)
2002	(2.19%)	(6.50%)	4.31%
2001	(3.75%)	(5.45%)	1.70%
2000	13.13%	11.74%	1.39%
Fiscal Year	**Pool Return**	**Benchmark Return**	**Outperformance**
3-year	(0.74%)	(4.21%)	3.47%
5-year	5.07%	2.12%	2.95%
10-year	5.17%	2.90%	2.27%

SOURCE: Sally Staley, 10/26/2009

Sally Staley became chief investment officer of Case Western Reserve University in March 2006. Immediately prior, she served the university as associate treasurer since 2002 and participated in manager and fund selection, asset allocation, risk assessment, rebalancing, and spending, and directed the endowment's allocations.

Sally began her career in international bond market research and institutional sales with Salomon Brothers and Merrill Lynch. She moved to investment management at the State of Wisconsin Investment Board where she established the public pension fund's international fixed income program and managed an international bond portfolio. Sally later worked as senior consultant with the investment management consulting practice of PricewaterhouseCoopers. She holds a master of international affairs degree from Columbia University and a bachelor of arts degree from The College of Wooster where she currently serves as a trustee and member of the Investment Committee. She is also a board member for the Great Lakes Theater Festival and Saint Luke's Foundation of Cleveland.

Anjum Hussain joined the Office of Investments in April 2006. He oversees risk management functions including: synthetic derivative exposures, investments, operations, technology systems, data management, and reporting. He is responsible for the asset allocation/risk budgeting process (building and deploying various quantitative models) and for identifying, researching, and implementing hedging and tail risk management strategies, alpha overlay strategies, and using derivative and structured products. He develops in-house proprietary systems to facilitate risk management and measurement, stress testing, and endowment reporting. He is also actively involved in manager reviews, performance and style tracking, determining the manager fit within the context of the overall portfolio, and in decisions to hire/terminate managers.

He has prior experience as an investment analyst with Oberlin College, financial consultant with Smith Barney, portfolio manager associate/equity research analyst with Victory Capital Management (Key Bank), managing director technology and operations with Victory Capital Management (Key Bank), and various other technology-related roles with the trust divisions of Key Bank and its predecessors, Society and Ameritrust. Anjum holds an MBA in finance from the Weatherhead School of Management at Case Western Reserve, an MA in economics from the University of Akron, and a BA in economics from the University of Bombay, India. In addition, he is a Chartered Financial Analyst (CFA) and a Chartered Alternative Investment Analyst (CAIA) Holder.

Q: Given the events of the past 24 months, what has changed in the world of endowment investing or investing in general?

Sally: I think everyone is paying more careful attention to risk management and looking at additional ways to monitor and reduce tail risk. We started looking at this carefully during the downturn to satisfy ourselves that we were doing everything we could, and we did identify some things we wanted to add.

Getting in front of things rapidly was a difference maker for us. In our liquidity and in our return outcome relative to our benchmarks and relative to our peers, we came through much better than our forecasts in the midst of the crisis. A lot of that really comes from getting busy and being proactive in a quickly changing environment.

You decided to get aggressive and sophisticated in response to what was happening. Where did you look for models about how to update what you were doing? Did you look to the alternative investment industry, to other endowments, or foundations, or to advisors?

Sally: A couple of things had been on our radar screen, and all of a sudden they made sense to move on. Anjum had been talking with some of the derivative and structure people at a major broker we work with. They had been showing us some of their approaches to thinking about sophisticated transactions that manage risks.

We'd been looking at that for a while, but mostly just thinking, and then the environment demanded some abrupt changes. At the same time, through my board duties at The College of Wooster, we saw an excellent, risk-controlled transaction implemented. Wooster has a small $250 million endowment with a very sophisticated investment program. One of the ideas that came from their advisory firm was a structured note with embedded options that created an asymmetric risk profile (i.e., more upside than downside). And I looked at that on behalf of Wooster and immediately turned it around and said, "That's an idea that we can change a little bit and adapt very well to what we're thinking for the Case Western Reserve endowment."

So, in our own work, I saw a live, very opportunistic example of leveraged upside and one-for-one downside that took advantage of the very high volatilities that existed a year ago and gave us a risk-adjusted exposure profile that we wanted.

Could you elaborate on that in particular in terms of the applicability of that approach to an individual investor and/or how could other people could use it to their benefit?

Sally: We implemented several synthetic strategies with leveraged upside, while maintaining a significant underweight in equities (which we

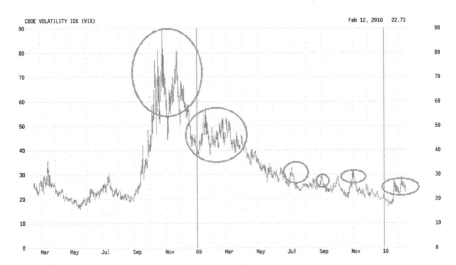

Figure 8.1   Short Volatility Strategy

initiated in June 2008). This was a significant contributor to our relative success during the last fiscal year. This is a short volatility strategy. It is only attractive when volatility levels (as implied by the VIX) are at elevated levels. We sold volatility at the height of the market crisis in order to generate significant upside leverage. Figure 8.1 references the VIX and the circles are the points where we deployed a series of levered option strategies. It is not a strategy that would be accessible to most individual investors.

What are some other strategies you've implemented because of the financial crisis of 2008–2009?

Anjum: We are approaching a number of things differently since the fall of 2008.

It is critical to be aware of every risk factor and market opportunity and constantly look for cheap ways to hedge the risk or capitalize on opportunities. Conflicting objectives necessitate creative thinking. As we've discussed, successfully eliminating tail risk can lead to lower volatility and higher returns over time, but this has to be done intelligently or it will be expensive. Traditional asset allocation has been used as the tool to diversify risk and it's still critical. However, the allocation of capital does not necessarily translate into allocation of risk in extreme market environments. Prudent defensive risk management allows us to engage in offensive risk management when it is most appropriate to do so.

Risk management is not only about managing downside risk but includes upside risk and the risk of missing opportunities. Risk management (upside, downside, and opportunity cost) is woven into the fabric of everything we do here at the Case endowment. In addition to asset allocation and the allocation of capital to managers, there has to exist another dimension of asset management, which allows us to "de-risk" or "re-risk" the portfolio when attractive opportunities with asymmetric payoffs present themselves. So, diversification is still important. However, there needs to be another view, which assumes that there are tail risk events where correlations can go to 1, and thus an investment in strategies which protect against these events is not a "should" but a "must."

We often hear others say that hedge funds are the risk-reducing piece of their total portfolio. However, hedge fund manager incentives are often at odds with principal protection due to their compensation structures and investment time horizon. Engaging in long-term hedges may not be in the best interest of a manager seeking to maximize short-term revenue. Thus it is imperative that the endowment take on the responsibility of protection against extreme events. Traditional asset class diversification should be viewed in the following way:

- Diversify sources of return.
- Diversify sources of alpha.
- Diversify risk.
- Reduce volatility in normal environments.

While we believe that the traditional breakdown of asset classes provides a reference framework for benchmarking and peer group comparisons, we are more concerned with the exposure to macro risk factors. The portfolio risk/return profile has to be consistent with the funding needs of the organization. The higher the uncalled commitments, the more difficult it is to recover from deep drawdowns. Liquidity means the ability to raise cash without suffering a significant loss in the process.

This is not to be confused with the ability to liquidate marketable instruments assets at distressed levels.

We were hoping that individuals could replicate a lot of this, but it may be that individuals are going to be able to think about investing differently, but not necessarily do investing differently.

Anjum: The individual investor can find somebody else to manage their money for them. It can be done. I don't think an individual can go out all by herself or himself because I feel they don't have the knowledge or the background.

Sally: If it is someone trying to save within the context of their corporate 401k plan, then these things are not possible. But if it's someone with enough savings or wealth that they're thinking of investing rather than just saving, then I think the perspective becomes more likely. You do have to take some risks here. Risk is the cost of return.

I think for someone with $2 to $50 million or more of assets, you could do it with some of this advice or maybe most of it, but with the assistance of somebody who thinks like an endowment thinks to bring that perspective to managing for an individual.

Advisors tend to be focused on individual stocks or individual asset classes and are not looking across the portfolio at asset allocation, at asset classes beyond traditional equity and fixed income, at risk management tools, and options and derivatives. I think it would be a really unusual advisor and a really valuable one to bring all of those services to a moderately sized individual portfolio.

Anjum: Advisors are sometimes focused on asset gathering; in those cases the less time they spend on the portfolio, the better. So they aren't going to give it that kind of attention.

Sally: We guard against this in the managers that we use as well. If we get a sense that our funds or managers are focused on generating assets rather than performing investment services, we look for an exit whenever possible.

What long-term return on capital should an individual investor expect, assuming they can mimic the investment strategies of endowments?

Anjum: About a 9.5 percent nominal return.

One of the things that has been slightly surprising is how much soft criteria goes into selection of advisors, funds of funds, and alternatives. How do you see this in manager selection?

Sally: There is a lot of soft stuff in the decision process. The analytics, of course, have to go on in the background and, increasingly, an understanding of the business organization of the fund, the manager, the service providers that they surround themselves with, including their support for legal, administrative functions, audit and accounting. But what we've always asked ourselves is, "How does a fund manager, whatever they're doing, whatever asset class they're working with, whatever structure they use, how do they achieve their returns? What's their value proposition and is that repeatable going forward?" A lot of that we can do analytically, but a lot of it comes down to our judgment about what kind of people are running the organization, what their devotion to it is, and how they will make sure that they repeat the records they have achieved so far.

Have you changed the way you think about liquidity in the past year?

Sally: Last November, December, we went into hyperactive liquidity management in order to make certain that under the most dire predicted circumstances—returns plunging, capital calls continuing, and distributions drying up—we could ensure we would be able to meet the endowment's liquidity needs for both its liability to the university and to the commitments it has to private partnerships.

We convinced ourselves inside and out that unless we had two or three years of negative double-digit returns that we would be able to handle our liquidity needs. But being sure of this requires us to turn a microscope on liquidity and to reevaluate everything new in terms of what it does to our liquidity profile.

I don't view liquidity as just cash and fixed income allocations that end up on the conservative side of the portfolio. So we substituted some structured and derivative transactions for what we otherwise would have put toward funding a manager. So if we could come up with a structure that had upside equal to or better than a partnership with a 10- or

12-year period without access to the money, then the structured transaction won out.

So there was a big need for liquidity, and you saw it a lot in the news because clearly all endowments and foundations are supporting their institutions' operating budgets. Have you seen the purveyors of investment vehicles ask for more aggressive lock-ups or has it been the other way around?

Sally: We've not seen that. In fact, we've been hammering away whenever we get a chance to loosen this provision.

The tables have turned in the LP's direction to say "those are kind of returns of yesteryear," whether fees or lock-up or key man agreement. We've learned to use our leverage and our persuasion with managers in this environment.

How comfortable do you feel with the current state of the public markets?

Anjum: Fairly comfortable that the depression scenario is off the table, but we still see some volatility over the next several years. We are more comfortable with the growth prospects in emerging markets and the growth in the demand for commodities (which are supply constrained).

What is your approach to a thematic versus strict asset allocation investment approach?

Sally: We come at it from both directions. Traditionally we've had an asset allocation exercise. Anjum tunes it up periodically. We certainly have that as the structure of the portfolio. But again, this is something that changed and evolved in the last year and a half. We have a much larger bucket for cash, but it's not cash to put under the mattress. It's cash to consider as the funding source for our opportunistic transactions that don't sit in any one asset allocation category or take advantage of volatility, which is not a traditional asset class—maybe should be, but it hasn't been. Or it cuts across the classic portfolio slices and links emerging markets, dollar weakness, inflation, commodity strains, and so on. So sometimes, if there is an obvious asset allocation slice, we will locate a transaction into that slice and sometimes we'll just let it sit in cash that we think of as opportunistic cash.

One thing we were very lucky to have already in place a year ago within our investment policy statement and on our list of authorized vehicles and securities was the ability to do futures, options and swaps. We did not have to go through a big discussion to get that approved and into our documentation. It's been there since we began vanilla rebalancing activity some years ago and that really allowed us to step up very quickly when we were ready to go. So, if you're going to spend a great deal of time agonizing over whether derivatives are appropriate vehicles, then you're going to spend a lot of time before you can get to what matters.

Tell us about the unique tools you've built at Case to manage the endowment.

Anjum: We thought this would be an important area of management. I had a lot of background in investment management technology from my work at Victory Capital Management. This helped in being familiar with system design and development. I recognize the need to have very accurate information if you want to make good decisions.

So the first thing I did when I came to Case was study how they did business, and look for opportunities to use technology for reporting and process.

We started with the in-house portfolio system. It has evolved over time, and we tweaked it and customized it to how we want to look at things. It allows us to look at our entire portfolio—not just the marketable side or the private side—in totality. It allows us to think about exposures from different angles, and also on a real-time basis we can almost see exposure on a daily basis and we can see what's gone on with the portfolio.

This lets us spend more time on strategy, deciding things like where do we need to increase our risk or decrease our risk? We meet weekly and we talk about these things and we make decisions as we go along. We've built tools or have the tools to monitor performance tracking, exposure tracking, risk management, controls, leverage, long exposures, short exposures, net exposures, tracking error, Sharpe ratio, past drawdowns, and more—at the manager level and at the portfolio level.

So it sounds like the tools at least in part are a response to wanting a lot of visibility and to be nimble. Do you think that's changed due to this very volatile past 18 months?

Anjum: When the markets are going up, nobody cares much about how you achieve your results. When I first started managing money it was back during the 2001–2002 recession. That was an environment where I learned that you have to have a good information system. And that was my first experience that when things aren't going your way, you need good information quickly. After that recession, everybody went to sleep again till 2008. And then, the industry woke up and said, "Wait a minute, we need all the tools." We had already invested the time to build them at Case so we were in a good position. We need people to manage business and any company that makes good decisions has to have a good information system. And if you don't have it, that means that you're missing out on opportunities.

Sally: We have the ability to cut the portfolio into more views than traditional institutional money management would use—more than just the asset allocation view. We include the volatility view, the geography view, the currency view, the industry view and the liquidity view. And the whole asset allocation exercise is more and more gray. There are so many more structures, vehicles that don't fit neatly into long-only public equity or corporate fixed income. Funds are harder to categorize. They may be market sector funds, they may be hedge funds with private side pockets, they may be private equity funds. There are public/private mixes. We could categorize some of our energy exposure as public equity or as a real asset. The traditional asset allocation plan is not so black and white.

So another major obstacle for individual investors is they don't have the views of their portfolios to be able to react to events that are happening or will happen quickly.

Anjum: Absolutely. We have to see what kind of macroeconomic risks we are exposed to and what opportunities we need to take advantage of.

And then you have to do this through the right asset allocation lens. It requires sophisticated systems.

What are the three or four new trends that you are thinking about over the coming two to three years that you're positioning yourself for now?

Sally: We are looking at number of things. But if you take one in particular—growth of emerging markets—we can execute that in so many different ways. It comes through traditional long-only emerging markets managers, long and short managers, private equity in emerging markets, energy, infrastructure, and commodities. It's a theme that can really fit into many different classes. We see this with a number of themes we are following.

So the challenge there may be combing through the opportunities to find the best ones and the best way to implement?

Sally: Yes. So, maybe we can find a terrific manager or maybe we can take advantage of option volatility that gives us 3x upside and only 1 for 1 downside, and then evaluate whether the likely payoff for that is beyond what any manager would be likely to produce in alpha versus an index.
Anjum: Another point with managers is that once you hire a manager, you're pretty much stuck with that idea until you fire the manager. So, you better identify whether something is of a secular nature or of a tactical nature. If it is tactical, then I think it's best executed internally.

So, for things that you think are tactics, you might just do something directly in the market versus going through a manager.

Sally: Right. But the other two members of our staff are focused on sourcing managers and funds and products in either public marketable products or private products. That is an active part of portfolio management as well, with two directors solely focused on that.
Anjum: Another thing in the decision to invest directly is that we also look at expense. When we can get direct exposure, we can do it much more cheaply than hiring a manager.

So, if you already know what you want, your tools are helping you decide how to implement, then you can execute it yourself and eliminate a layer of fees.

Anjum: Exactly. Also, we can cash manage better because we don't have to have fully funded positions.

Sally: We could have exposure without committing full cash. We reserve the cash and set it aside, but it's still there if we were to need it in an emergency.

What are your thoughts on future inflation, interest rates, and commodity values?

Sally: We expect deflation for the next couple of years. We do not believe that inflation will be a risk until unemployment falls drastically, which could be 5+ years out. The adjustment for monetary inflation will be reflected in a weakening dollar. We believe that interest rates will be higher 2–3 years out.

We expect commodity prices to be higher in response to a weaker dollar initially and then due to supply/demand imbalances as the economic recovery unfolds. Our strategy is to continue to incorporate better and broader risk management—both defensive and offensive; focus near-term on distressed, emerging markets, commodities, dollar weakness; focus longer-term on inflation; and real estate, which is the biggest current challenge but eventually will be an opportunity.

How concerned are you with currency risk and how are you managing it?

Anjum: From a benchmark perspective, we typically have unhedged benchmarks. Thus we do not directly engage in hedging this risk. Our managers occasionally hedge currency risk. However, from an alpha generation or risk reduction standpoint, we watch the trends in the currency markets and look for compelling opportunities where we can engage in cheap hedges. We do have trades which will benefit in a weakening dollar scenario.

Rebalancing—how often, how do you do it, what are the triggers?

Sally: We do not rebalance automatically. We watch our exposures on a daily basis and adjust as necessary to reflect our views. We have a proprietary system that we talked about earlier. It provides an almost-real-time view of our asset allocation, including the risk versus benchmarks and the daily cash position. We always make rebalancing decisions when we have significant cash inflows or outflows occurring. Being able to precisely manage exposures relative to benchmarks adds to our ability to be nimble. For marketable equities, the system also provides the ability to view exposures relative to the relevant benchmark as it relates to region, country, sector, and industry. This allows us to view the bets taken by our managers at the individual fund level, as well as at the aggregate level, and to hedge risks should they exceed tolerance levels.

What are your typical time horizons for investments (and variations by asset class)?

Anjum: One to two years for options that are near term hedges. Three to five years for equities, fixed income, and hedge funds. Five to eight years or longer for private investments. Five to 15 years for tail risk hedges.

Is the performance of the past decade in endowments unusually good? Will this be repeated?

Sally: Since 2001 and 2002, we had four, five years of returns in the double-digit upper teens to even low 20 percent range. And that just looked like it was all due to this wonderful endowment model and it certainly was, but then it reversed course on us. So, it was essentially borrowing from what usual long-term returns should be, but everyone somehow decided it was the new norm.

Was there perhaps a one-time return from adopting sophisticated techniques?

Sally: We weren't part of getting that trend started, but some other larger endowments were. But we caught onto it 10 years ago, when we started to say that the traditional equity/fixed income breakdown wasn't working so well, and there were probably better ways to look at things.

So, that began our evolution into a more sophisticated and diversified endowment model.

What information sources do you like to use? What do you read?

Anjum: The list of materials we typically read are manager commentaries, broker macroeconomic research, third-party macroeconomic research, consultant research, institutional investment magazines, research and white papers, newspapers (*Wall Street Journal*), *Barron's*, books, and research on nonprofit institutional governance. We also read a lot of the commentary from fund managers whom we regard highly.

What do you think about "liability-driven" investing used by pension funds? Is it applicable to endowments or individuals?

Sally: We're talking about that more ourselves and I'm thinking about it more in terms of endowments in general. One thing that really struck me in the last year of listening to my peers at other endowments large and small and my own work on a small school investment committee is that I think in many cases we've had a breakdown between what the endowment model can deliver, has delivered, and might deliver in the future and the reliance of a school on the revenue source coming from its endowment distributions.

And so, we've been talking a lot about how able we are to meet our liability to the university and whether that should be our very first investment goal rather than maximizing long-term returns, which has been our focus up until now. We are now thinking about our annual distribution to the university as our liability. It's at 10 percent of operating revenues. Of course, in other schools, it can be much larger than that—up to 50 percent in some cases. I've even heard 70, 80 percent in a couple of other places and that puts a whole different spin on what the portfolio should look like and its ability to withstand severe downturns.

So, we think that the liability view is much more important. We haven't put it first, but we are asking ourselves what can we do better, such as tail risk management, to avoid a future year like the one we just had.

Anjum: We believe that the future of asset management will be outcome-driven investments, which will give people a specific outcome at a future point in time for a certain amount of risk. The approach relies on defining exactly what you need your investments to deliver at certain points in time and then using derivatives and other products to ensure that those marks are met. For endowments to switch to this type of approach would require much less attention to peer group rankings.

Sally: It will be difficult for certain universities to adapt to the liability-driven view. We have become very peer conscious, especially among the larger endowments. Keeping up with the peer group and placing well in the rankings of peer performance is actually baked into investment documents in many places and even into some compensation plans. That has become a big trend in the last five or seven years. As investment committees and trustees search for meaningful ways to measure performance, peer group ranking is an easy-to-use yardstick. But we should be much more concerned about meeting our obligations to the university than we are about where we place in the peer rankings.

The performance review period is annual. You're being evaluated yearly on plans that can take five or more years to unfold.

Sally: Yes. The three-year return is the usual magic number everybody looks at. But there's a big mismatch between measuring results over short, three-year time periods when you are setting strategy for a perpetual pool of assets.

Universities have varying situations, which also makes it hard to compare.

Sally: There are a lot of things that go into a university's financial model, net tuition revenue and philanthropy, endowment distributions, and in some cases big research grants.

At Case, we're half academic and half research. But other places, of course, may have no research grants in their budget. The financial planning for an academic entity large or small has so many moving parts. In the turmoil, we wondered what would happen to enrollment and tuition? What financial needs would a starting class have? How would that drop to our bottom line in terms of net tuition revenue? Would benefactors and donors be able to continue giving or do we assume a drastic downturn in philanthropy, including giving to the endowment? All those things are critical. And they all were happening at the same time. This last year they were all subject to the same economic forces.

So, that is another example, that if your endowment provides 10 percent of your operating revenues or 50 percent, it should be a whole different conversation in terms of how you build the portfolio.

Chapter 9

Mary Cahill

Vice President of Investments and Chief Investment Officer

Emory University

"We look for the best opportunities to express the themes that we think will matter."

Emory University and the Emory University Endowment

Emory University is a private institution located in Atlanta. It has an enrollment of over 12,000 undergraduate and graduate students. The school was established in 1836 by the Methodist Episcopal church in honor of a bishop who dreamed of an education that molded character as well as the mind. The school was helped in the early 1900s by Asa Candler, founder of the Coca-Cola Company, with a $1 million donation and later, a land donation. The philanthropy of families associated with Coca-Cola, the Candlers, Woodruffs, and Goizuetas, formed the bedrock for the Emory endowment.

In 2001, Emory University created an investment management group to bring discipline and structure to the endowment's asset management program. The group is responsible for enhancing return opportunities and managing risk for Emory University's financial assets.

The mission of Emory Investment Management is to "enhance the investments and current purchasing power of Emory University while preserving its resources for future generations." The office is responsible for research, investment manager selection, portfolio management, risk management, and analysis.

The endowment has over $4.3 billion under management and is ranked 16th in terms of size in the 2009 NACUBO-Commonfund endowment survey.

Mary Cahill is the vice president of investments and chief investment officer at Emory University. She is responsible for overseeing investments of all endowment, trust, operating, and employee benefit funds for Emory University.

Mary joined Emory Investment Management in her current role in January 2001. She has an extensive background in pension and endowment management. Prior to joining Emory, she was deputy chief investment officer of Xerox Corporation where she was responsible for developing, recommending, and implementing investment alternatives for pension and savings plan assets in excess of $12 billion.

Mary has 25 years of investment experience with prior positions including deputy director of the Virginia Retirement System, director of the SmithKline pension fund, and pension management positions with BellSouth and Merck. She also has served as president of Pension Group East, president of Pension 21, and as an executive member of the Financial Executive Institute's Committee on Investment of Employee Benefit Assets.

Mary is a member of the NYSE Pension Managers Advisory Committee, a trustee of the Greenwich Roundtable, and has served on several advisory boards including Commonfund Capital Advisory Board, Pine Grove Advisory Board, and Yorktown Advisory Board. Mary has a bachelor of science in management science from Kean College, a master of business administration in finance from St. John's University, and holds the Chartered Financial Analyst designation.

Q: You joined Emory in 2001, which was just after a serious downturn in the markets. How did that influence how you reacted to the events of 2008–2009, and what if anything was different this time?

I have been in the investment management business a long time and have invested through a number of cycles, none of which were precisely the same. Clearly 2008–2009 felt very different than previous downturns that I experienced. Global financial markets experienced unprecedented volatility and price depreciation from the massive deleveraging precipitated by the bursting of the liquidity, leverage, and asset bubbles formed in the previous years. The economy contracted rapidly and the role of government increased dramatically. The state of the real economy, market liquidity, financial institution solvency, and the government's willingness—some might say requirement—to intervene in the markets were far more acute in this downturn than they were when the tech bubble burst at the beginning of the decade. When I joined in 2001, we began to migrate the endowment to higher allocations of private equity and hedge funds. Our objective was to implement a new blueprint for a durable, diversified portfolio that would endure over time, rather than simply react to the then current downturn.

When the next big downturn came in 2008, we were already further reducing our U.S. equities and continuing to add hedge funds. Our goal was to reduce volatility in the portfolio by reducing our exposure to equity risk. However, when you have a crisis like we experienced in 2008-2009, correlations tend to move towards 1.0, and so while our changes helped mitigate losses and reduce systematic risk, the broad decline across all asset classes overwhelmed these decisions leading to double digit losses.

When we got to early 2008 and could see clouds ahead, we made sure we were communicating with the investment committee appropriately. It was a good time to reevaluate everything we were doing and put each investment under the microscope. We made a few decisions, such as turning off securities lending, (which we did in May 2008), diversifying the counterparty exposure of our cash positions, and closely inspecting all of our collateral accounts (we found a global bond manager who was getting exposure in futures and had some collateral in subprime) all of which were very constructive in hindsight.

We went back and reviewed all of the hedge fund contracts so we understood precisely what our liquidity position might look like—what our redemption options were, where the gates were—so we could make contingency plans in a worst case scenario. We were in a good position to do all this because we had built a team that could handle the workload, both in terms of volume and content. Perhaps most importantly, we maintained regular and open communication with the investment committee so that they were closely engaged with the risks in the portfolio as the events began to unfold.

What is your approach to liquidity? Are there any parallels between endowment liquidity management and the "liability-driven investing" approaches used by pension funds?

I don't necessarily see parallels to pension funds. Endowments need to provide cash to their institutions based on an annual spending formula, and grow their portfolios to ensure intergenerational equity. Our approach to liquidity concentrates on annual cash needs and adequate flexibility. The latter is to avoid the need to sell assets after prices have declined. We stress test the liquidity profile of the portfolio and monitor liquidity continuously. We also have the ability as a university to determine how fast we want to grow and what things we decide to do in a given year. This is different than a pension fund where you can't really influence the liabilities with the same degree of freedom.

If, as a pension fund, you have promised someone a steady stream of income for the remainder of their life, then you need to have the cash to make good on that commitment. A university, on the other hand, can decide to accelerate or defer a building plan or other capital intensive commitments providing more levers to manage their spending commitments.

This provides endowments with an advantage; because the institution has some discretion in any given year or string of years on what the spending commitment will be, the endowment can have a bit more of a long-term view and can invest in assets that others can't necessarily buy. Universities would lose that advantage if we start looking at things from an LDI (liability-driven investing) perspective like the pensions use.

Some institutional investors have been adding liquidity by exiting their commitments to the private investments to hedge funds and private equity groups in a secondary market. Do you see any bargains to be had in this area?

We are satisfied with our investment allocations, and aren't looking to add to our private equity or hedge fund portions of the endowment at this point. I don't think that many of the sellers are as distressed as people think. And the pricing for many of the funds has not been all that attractive in our view.

What is your position on thematic investing versus asset allocation—focused approaches?

We do both, with a top-down and bottom-up approach to decision making. We conduct an asset allocation study every three to five years. It is an in-house exercise and we discuss it with the investment committee to determine the optimal allocation. The policy allocation is the best expression of our long-term expectations and our execution of the policy is particularly oriented to a value approach to investing. We have ranges around the asset classes that allow us enough latitude to gain exposure to opportunities we identify or move towards defensive strategies when uncompensated risks increase. Our intermediate term shifts within these ranges tend to be held 18 months to three years.

In addition to looking at our current allocation by asset class, we look at it in a matrix view, which also shows near-term opportunistic and/or defensive investments by asset class. For instance, during the recent crisis we added to corporate credit, which we saw as an opportunity to outperform equities. We also hedged a portion of the equity exposure using options as a defensive play. Our larger, long term themes are related to the acceleration of globalization, demographics, and innovation.

What are the top themes that you are thinking about currently?

Primarily globalization. We think there are opportunities in emerging markets and natural resources due to the rapid pace of globalization. We are also evaluating technology, and specifically, who is benefiting from large-scale changes in technology. The impact of government stimulus on the deficit as well as the impact of regulation that may fall out of this recent crisis will have a longer term impact on our markets and understanding this overall trend is going to be important.

As we look at these themes and trends, we allow ourselves to think about expressing our views in any asset class—U.S. public equities, venture capital, real assets—and seek to find the best asset class to express the themes that we think will matter.

Is it sometimes hard to find an investable asset for certain themes you identify?

Occasionally. At times it may take significant effort and time to find the best vehicle or most skilled investment manager to invest in line with these macro views, but our macro themes are not short term opportunities.

Going back to macroeconomic themes, what is your stance on inflation and the U.S. dollar in the mid- to near term?

There is a wall of inflation coming. What is uncertain is when it will get here or where it is right now, but it is on its way. So we are talking about this and concerned with it. Our natural resources portfolio has a good inflation component to it, so we feel that we are hedging our inflation risk. While the timing is not clear, we think it is probably better to be a little early on this rather than late.

As far as the dollar goes, there has been a lot of "gloom and doom" on it recently. I don't necessarily share this sentiment—the dollar isn't going away as the reserve currency of choice until an alternative becomes viable—but there are some concerning variables due to how much new money is being created right now and what stance the Chinese and other buyers of our debt will take. We have increased our exposure to international equities as a counter to this.

Endowments seem to be given considerable latitude from investment committees, which allows them to be flexible and to do some of the things you talked about in your opportunistic and defensive portions. Is this a trend?

We have certainly done that here at Emory. Our ranges in a given asset class allow us to make appropriate investment changes between committee meetings.

Further, we have the latitude to trade derivatives and ETFs if we see fit. If we are trying to increase our exposure to beta, we can simply go purchase it. Similarly, if we are trying to reduce our exposure to beta we can also accomplish that just as efficiently and inexpensively.

Endowments seemed to be aggressive in using their discretion to react quickly to the changes in the market over the past year. Is it fair to think of them as relatively nimble compared to other institutional pools?

In my experience, I see a great deal of flexibility in the endowment model of investing. The governance structure of an endowment, which is typically an investment committee or board made up of investment professionals and/or very successful business people, is the source and foundation for this flexibility.

What things are you doing to reduce risk in the portfolio, particularly for catastrophic or tail events, such as the fourth quarter of 2008?

That was a real liquidity event, and something that we are looking at in a number of ways. For example, we are making sure that we have a good lock on exactly what our realizable liquidity is and what our side pockets are. We understand that we can be paid a handsome premium for providing liquidity, but with every investment, we want to understand what the cost/benefit of its relative liquidity is and try to make sure that the premium is properly priced.

As far as hedging tail risk, there are a variety of tactics we are analyzing and implementing. Some involve the use of options, others employ exposures negatively correlated to extreme events; in each instance, however, we are seeking to purchase inexpensive but effective insurance against certain downside risks.

What do you do for portfolio management tools?

We have invested in a number of tools and have a number of people on the team dedicated to this area. There is no perfect solution for it, unfortunately, but one of the things we have worked on is automating the reporting as much as possible. What we have learned from our efforts is that it is a real challenge to do the detailed reporting you would like to have, and that certainly no individual investor or even a small endowment is going to easily be able to replicate this capability. The basic tools are inexpensive but require a fair amount of customization and vigilant data management to be effective.

What is your approach to manager selection?

We have certain things we look for. We like managers to be employee owned, have some kind of competitive advantage, display a value-investing orientation, and to have much of their personal net worth tied up alongside our investment. In particular, when managers have their own funds invested it helps with ensuring an alignment of interests.

We look at the management team's individual investing experience and confirm that it is appropriate for the strategy that they are undertaking. There are also things that we try to avoid, for example, if we believe a firm is merely trying to gather assets—for example, if they are growing assets before going to an IPO, or displaying other elements in their business that create a short-term focus.

The qualitative view, sitting down across the table from the managers and evaluating them, is part of it as well. We don't want to lead with it, because we have a lot of other sources of information and insight on the personnel such as background checks, references, going through the SEC filings that happen up front before we get to the soft-side issues. We want to rely on as many facts and quantifiable pieces of information as we can gather during the process.

How long should the fund be in existence?

We don't really have a hard criterion for fund duration, because this type of thing gets caught with the other checks that are part of our process. Clearly if someone who is not qualified decides one day they are going to be a hedge fund manager, we won't be looking to invest with them. Most often our general investment criteria will prevent us from doing business with a new firm, but not always.

There are periodically new firms or funds that are spin-outs from previously successful groups and these may be something we will evaluate. In that case we would want to be sure that the partners have the capacity to both execute the strategy that they were previously successful with, as well as manage the business at the same time.

How do you evaluate manager transparency and their use of leverage?

If you look at how hedge funds want to operate typically, they like it to be pretty wide open—they would like to be able to do nearly anything. Philosophically I don't believe in investing in something that creates a marginal positive return but has to be excessively leveraged to give you a reasonable return. I think those things can blow up when the leverage disappears and I don't know why I would give away 20 percent of the profits to someone when I am taking all the downside leverage risk.

In the end, if I want returns due to using a great deal of leverage, we believe there are other more direct and less fee-intensive ways to accomplish it.

How about the management of working capital in the endowment office?

We manage working capital guidelines at Emory and we think that makes sense, both for institutional efficiency as well as total portfolio management discipline.

This adds considerable complexity because of the different rules and time frames for these other types of funds?

Definitely. To help manage this complexity we have broken the over-all funds down into three groups: short-term, mid-term and long-term pools. The endowment is the long-term portion and the other investments fall into short or medium term.

The main reason you commonly see this is the consolidated management of all these pools of money usually achieves the best risk adjusted returns and the best management scale economies. Universities realized that they were leaving money on the table by not actively managing the short-term and mid-term pools of money, and the endowment management office was the natural place to put the responsibility.

What sorts of things do you read to stay current and to help in your work?

I read a considerable volume of material, and so do most people in the industry. A significant part of the job of investment management is reading. Our investment managers send a constant stream of information on what they are thinking, and of course the large investment houses also provide a wide variety of analyst reports. Journals such as the *Journal of Alternative Investments* and *Journal of Financial Analysts* are also common in this business. I will also use the Web for quick lookups of current market news.

Can an individual try to replicate some of the things endowments are doing? Endowments became sophisticated in the 1980s and 1990s. Can individuals follow in their footsteps?

They may be able to partially, but individual investors can't get access to the same investments that an endowment can and certainly not with the same fee structures. We travel the world looking for, mining for, really, investment managers that can help us execute our strategy. The individual would have a lot of trouble with even the amount of time and travel it takes to find and interview all the potential managers. I have over 18 professionals working on our portfolio full-time. An individual would have trouble replicating this, even at a simple level.

Furthermore, they likely would not have the expertise it takes to evaluate an investment manager. Relatively large family offices can do this, but that is probably where it ends. Smaller endowments can't do this either. They have to rely on advisors and consultants to help them figure it out.

Can individuals compensate for manager selection and access by using other vehicles such as ETFs?

You can't use an ETF for a long period of time because it won't necessarily follow its underlying asset. And they are expensive. They are good for some instant beta, so you can go in and out of them, or you can transition to an active manager for the strategy you want. They are a decent short-term solution.

Any other advice for the individual investor?

Keep it simple. Only put into a self-directed portfolio as much as you can devote the time to actively manage. If this is what you are going to do full time, you may be able to invest in individual stocks, but if you do not have much time to devote, then you may wind up using mutual funds. It is very difficult to mimic what an entire firm or endowment organization is doing, and individual should know their limits.

As far as asset allocation, I would make sure that you know what the major boxes are. For instance, your portfolio may have allocations to all the major asset classes: international exposure, bonds, U.S. equities, and so on. Within each box you should get the major subareas, so you might want your bonds to have high-quality corporate, a government component, and some high-yield.

It starts getting difficult if you try to break it down to the industry level unless you have a lot of time on your hands or if you happen to know the industry well. In the latter case, it can also add risk if your income is also in that industry, and so you need to be careful about unintended concentrations. For example, if you work for a pharmaceutical company and have a lot of stock options in your company, then you may not want to buy a health sector fund. Just because you know the industry is not necessarily a good reason to take on too much concentrated risk.

Chapter 10

Don Lindsey

Chief Investment Officer

George Washington University

"The process that we have developed here has always attempted to be asset class agnostic."

George Washington University

George Washington University (GWU), located in Washington, D.C., was founded in 1821. The university has an enrollment of nearly 25,000 undergraduate and graduate students.

The endowment at GWU has a notable history, originating with President George Washington. In his will, the president bequeathed shares in the Potomac Company to endow and establish a university in the District of Columbia.

Over a five-year period, the endowment has outperformed its benchmarks and the market. The GW endowment produced an annualized return of 5.57 percent compared to the S&P 500 Index return of –2.24 percent. The GW endowment grew by nearly 40 percent over the five years ending in July 2009.

SOURCE: GWU CIO 2009 report (http://investment.gwu.edu/merlin-cgi/p/downloadFile/d/23974/n/1/other/1/name/CIO-Report-09-FORWEBpdf/).

I n the 2008 NACUBO and Commonfund survey of endowments (year ending June 2008), GW ranked 58th in size for U.S. academic endowments. Figure 10.1 shows the GW endowment assets from 1989 through 2009, which reached $1.2 billion at its peak in 2008. Figure 10.2 shows the endowment's asset allocation target and actual as of June 30, 2009. Figure 10.3 shows the GW Pooled Endowment returns compared to benchmarks. The GW Pooled Endowment returned almost

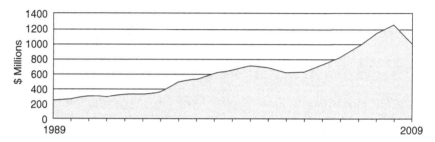

Figure 10.1   GW Endowment Assets, 1989–2009
SOURCE: George Washington University

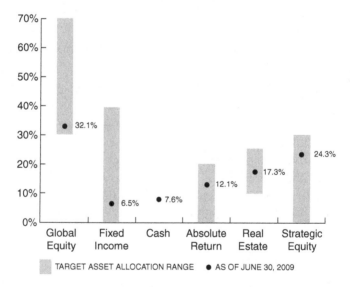

Figure 10.2   Pooled Endowment Asset Structure, as of 6/30/09
SOURCE: George Washington University

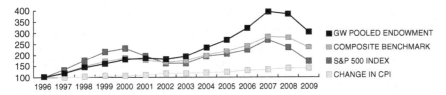

Figure 10.3 Pooled Endowment Returns Compared to Benchmarks since Portfolio Inception
SOURCE: George Washington University

7 percent net annualized excess return compared to the S&P 500 with less risk (Figure 10.4).

Donald W. Lindsey joined George Washington University in April 2003 as chief investment officer responsible for management of the university's $1.0 billion endowment. He is also a professorial lecturer of finance at GWU and teaches applied portfolio management in the MBA program.

Prior to joining GWU, Don established the University of Toronto Asset Management Corporation (UTAM) in May 2000 and served as its first president and chief executive officer. UTAM was established to

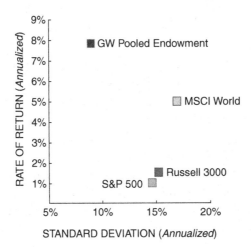

Figure 10.4 Risk vs. Return: July 1, 2004–June 30, 2009
SOURCE: George Washington University

manage the University of Toronto's CAD $4.0 billion in endowment and pension assets. He began his career with the University of Virginia Investment Management Company in 1987, where he served initially as investment analyst and proceeded to become assistant director of investments, senior investment officer, and director.

He has taught in the McIntire School of Commerce at the University of Virginia and the Rotman School of Management at the University of Toronto. In addition, he holds the CFA designation and has also taught CFA exam preparation and other courses in Croatia, Romania, Japan, South Africa, Italy, the United Kingdom, and Switzerland, and he has served on the CFA Institute Council of Examiners. He is a member of the Investment Advisory Committee of the Virginia Retirement System. Don holds a BA in political science from Virginia Tech and an MBA from James Madison University.

Q: How do you approach investment management at GWU?

The process that we have developed here has always attempted to be asset class agnostic. We are not starting with a belief that there are optimal fixed allocations to each asset class. Furthermore, even if there were, it is very difficult to define the universe of potential investments within each asset class designation. For instance, there are numerous investment strategies that incorporate both public and private equity into their structure. There are funds that incorporate both credit attributes as well as equity attributes. There has been a blend of asset classes over the past several years and that has come about as hedge fund managers, private equity managers, and other asset managers have tried to focus on absolute return as opposed to benchmark returns.

We look to drive our investment strategy based on what we believe are the macroeconomic trends. We try to determine what, from a macro perspective, are the best opportunities in the world. We then look for investment vehicles that make those opportunities implementable. This can be things that are industry specific, such as the energy industry in 2003. In that case it was clear that the sector had been undercapitalized for many decades, and that as energy demand went up there was going to be a commensurate need for capital. That became a dominant theme as part of our endowment investing.

Another theme that we are still in the midst of, and have made a significant commitment to, is agricultural land and agribusiness. We believe that there is a shortage of arable land in the world, and that irrigation of that land is going to be a problem, and that as income per capita in the emerging markets increases, there will be more demand for protein, and that changes in diets will drive commodity prices higher as a result. We see this as a great opportunity for long-term investment.

Another dominant theme is that we have reached a 45-year low in interest rates. The next cycle that we are likely to go into is going to be far more inflationary than deflationary. We have seen that playing out recently with weakness in the dollar and increases in precious metals prices, especially gold.

After we understand what the themes are, we look for assets that will let us make the appropriate play. We evaluate investment vehicles—hedge funds, public and private equity, debt, and real assets—across all types of markets—developed and emerging—and determine how best to implement.

In the end, while we are aware of what our allocation to asset classes is, and we look for some balance between them, our allocation is the result of a forward-looking analysis of the macroeconomic trends and the best investments across asset classes that will outperform based on the trends.

So, the real driver for GWU behind the implementation is your evaluation of important, broad economic trends that will drive growth over a period of years.

Yes. That is why our process never led us to invest in leveraged buyout funds. Many LBO funds, as a strategy, didn't have any basis to invest in from a macroeconomic standpoint. What we saw was that there was a lot of money flowing into LBO funds. The funds were taking a lot of companies at premiums and leveraging up their balance sheet, but we couldn't see what was the underlying investment thesis, other than that there was a huge amount of inexpensive liquidity available. Instead, everything we did in the private markets was very sector-specific, mostly in natural resources, where we felt that the risk-adjusted premium for the lack of liquidity was justified.

What have you learned from using this thematic investing approach?

First, it helps us determine which asset classes will be important, but just as importantly, it also helps us avoid investments that we think will be damaging to returns. There are a number of reasons we use this approach. First, it is difficult to determine what the target return is for an asset class over a long period of time. Different cycles will create different opportunities for different asset classes. The allocation you have to an asset class therefore should be based on your assessment of the current environment and not some projection for the long term.

For instance, right now you would be hard pressed to be entering U.S. Treasuries, because interest rates are at historic lows and the current projected rate on a forward-looking basis looks low to negative. So if you use a long-term projection on U.S. Treasuries and set your expectations, at this point you will not be able to achieve your goal over the next 5–10 years for that asset.

Likewise, correlations are difficult to manage. The correlation coefficients themselves can be volatile, meaning that assets that exhibit low correlation in one environment may have high correlation in another. In turn, this means that it is hard to determine the inputs for asset correlation coefficients that go into your models.

In principle, diversification is of course important. The risk factors to which your portfolio is exposed must be understood and diversified. We believe it is hard to simply put the data into an objective model and come out with an optimal allocation. The current and projected near- to mid-term environment is an important input to the moves you will make in a given year. This has been even more important for the past two years where things are changing more quickly than they have traditionally.

The biggest risks are the types of things that cause an unexpected drawdown in capital, such as the events of 2008–2009. Those risks are hard to plan for—you could look at the correlation of bank debt to equities and never have expected to get the result that you saw over that time period. This moving target of correlation coefficients, volatility, and returns makes it difficult to effectively implement a static model that only accounts for those inputs.

This technique means that you cannot build an asset allocation and then "set it and forget it" with periodic rebalancing. What does that mean for the team, managers, advisors, what does it mean for operations, investment policy, and other factors in managing the endowment?

From an investment policy standpoint it means that we have very wide ranges within each asset class. We have guidelines for what sorts of investments the endowment will make, but they are broad. This means that we very seldom, if ever, rebalance back to a target allocation. Target allocations are not the key driver for making changes in the portfolio.

From a staffing standpoint, it also means that you will have an emphasis on generalists on your team versus specialists within asset classes. Each member of the team needs to be able to think across the entire capital structure of a company and across a variety of asset classes in order to determine where to invest and with whom to invest. We don't have a person who just evaluates private equity or public equity or credit markets. The entire staff should be able to evaluate opportunities across the entire spectrum of investment vehicles to execute our approach.

The side effect of this approach is that it provides a great career path for the investment professionals, and it also prevents us from having a large hole to fill in a specific area in the event that someone leaves. It also lets us put multiple people on a specific deal, and so I can manage capacity better. We also believe that it helps develop broader analytical skills.

In the past few years, was inexpensive leverage driving the ever-increasing valuations of some companies, as opposed to some other market dynamic that was improving their intrinsic value? Did this mean that you avoided some investment opportunities in private equity and hedge funds?

Definitely. It was driven by the high availability of credit and the ability of the LBO industry to raise larger and larger funds each year. It seemed to be a financial phenomenon versus something being driven by fundamentals. In turn, we avoided LBO investments that didn't have a fundamentals component. As we evaluated funds we had trouble understanding what the nonfinancial rationale was in some cases.

We don't have a particular distaste for buyouts or private investment opportunities. In fact, we did make investments in funds that took advantage of opportunities we had identified as themes and liked—for instance, in energy. But in each case we shied away from investments that relied on a lot of leverage to generate or increase their returns and biased our investments in favor of equity-driven deals.

We were careful to understand the balance sheet of the individual investments within the fund so we could understand how leverage was being used. For specific natural resources and energy deals we wanted to understand how the valuation was based on discounted future cash flows from their proven reserves and from operations as opposed to use of debt.

For alternative or private investments, the question you really have to ask is, if I am giving up liquidity, am I getting the proper premium for that. In many cases there is not only an attractive premium, but you also get good diversification. For instance, even when energy prices were plummeting last year, firms that had ongoing oil and gas operations were still producing and selling product and still maintained cash flows from operations. They had hedged their production and so they were unharmed. The underlying investment was uncorrelated to what was happening in the public markets.

If you can get good diversification and a good risk premium, then private investments are certainly justified. Investors and managers are going to start asking this more and more. There is a dawning recognition that lack of liquidity on its own does not indicate a superior investment that pays the appropriate illiquidity premium.

What is your approach to keeping appropriate liquidity within the portfolio while maximizing overall return?

We have always managed liquidity very carefully. The importance of this has really been evident in the current environment. From a cash-flow standpoint, during my tenure GWU has always paid out more than we have received in a given year. This means that we have had to be precise and aggressive in ensuring the right levels of liquidity and that we couldn't necessarily count on new money to provide it.

Because we have always focused on liquidity management, last year didn't have as much of an impact. We have always managed based on what our liquidity needs would be and weren't relying on inflows to the fund to make our commitments.

In theory, endowments have infinite investment timelines and shouldn't mind long term lock-ups. Is it possible that endowments got overcommitted to illiquid investments due to the actual, or at least perceived, illiquidity premium and their unique ability to take advantage of it?

I think it is inaccurate to paint endowments with such a broad brush. This ability to access the illiquidity premium with a large part of the portfolio was viewed as being a characteristic of all endowments, and it was never the case. Endowments should operate very differently depending on their specific situation. Institutions should have been (and should be) looking at the things that affect their liquidity and payout requirements. These are factors such as forecast of new money coming in, what percentage of the operating budget they are asked to produce, what enrollment changes are predicted in the coming years, and how much external support the university will expect in the form of grants and other monies. Their risk profile should be set accordingly so that they can meet their commitments.

When you go into a particular private investment, characterized by a lock-up period or an uncertain return on the capital, you don't know whether you will receive cash back at the end of three years or six years or ten years. What happened recently is the return of capital started coming back faster and faster, which was really a unique phenomenon. This may have skewed the models, which showed the rate of cash flow coming back from private equity and hedge funds and made institutions too comfortable with the pace and frequency that illiquid investments returned cash. When the deal pace suddenly slowed down, everything changed. Today I think the expectation on the rate of return from capital is more in line.

Bottom line, the endowment time horizon is infinite with regard to the life of the fund, but not at all in terms of liquidity planning, and that is what people really missed. The idea that there is a single "endowment model" for investing is not accurate. How endowments allocate, organize, and invest will, and should, vary significantly based on specific attributes of the organization

Endowments managing over $1 billion have generally outperformed the market. Was this due to a one-time improvement in sophistication during the 1990s?

I don't think it is a one-time deal relative to other institutional money. For instance, public pension funds receive tremendous scrutiny, at least relative to endowments. I still expect that from a governance standpoint, endowment management will retain considerable flexibility. Pension funds have specific and uncertain liabilities in a given year relative to endowments. An endowment knows what their payout will be in a given year. Municipal, state, and local pensions are all public vehicles that are subject to a great deal of public scrutiny and public input, which can also have the effect of constraining their investment strategy and lowering their returns.

As endowments got more sophisticated, their staffs certainly had an impact, but I attribute a lot of the gains to the flexibility in governance, which provides a decisive advantage over other similar investment pools like pension funds and foundations.

Do you think that some of the governance differences you are observing also apply to differences between private and public university endowments?

Yes, and this gives the private universities an advantage. The university budget is subject to being changed by the state, which in turn affects the endowment. If you are managing an endowment, you clearly have more flexibility in the context of a private institution.

Do private school endowments have more flexibility than public universities?

Yes, although I believe the general trend for both public and private universities is going to be more scrutiny. First, there has been a lot of congressional interest in the past few years on endowment payouts. And second, the overall state of the economy will promote more interest in how endowments are being managed and what the risks are.

There is also going to be additional scrutiny with regard to investment staff compensation, which has been, in the last decade, outside the norm for the typical university faculty or staff member. For endowments to keep salaries competitive with the market of hedge funds, private equity groups, they will have to engage in the appropriate framing and public relations so that investment committees and other university constituencies can understand what the appropriate comparable occupations are and what impact having great talent can have over a large fund. However, as you would expect, compensation decisions also incorporate other considerations as well. This will be another challenge that endowments will face and should be factored into their management and governance process.

Can the individual learn from endowments?

First, individuals need to think more about diversification and less about how much money can they make in a particular asset class or a particular stock. Individuals tend to be more comfortable when everything is going up at the same time. However, this can also mean that things may be all going down at the same time as well.

Second, individual investors have traditionally had a huge "home bias." This is beginning to change now, but up until recently investors have had all or nearly all their investments in the United States. What you are seeing now in endowments over the past decade is a shift to global investing, and this probably makes sense for individual investors to think about as well.

What lessons can be learned from the 2008–2009 downturn?

It is almost impossible to structure a portfolio that performs well in a catastrophe. If you do, then you will have very low returns over the long haul. This means that you will look great during the one or two bad years, but your 5- or 10-year record will be subpar. The opportunity cost of being cautious is very, very high.

That said, the key lesson is that catastrophic events do happen, they can't be predicted, and they come far more frequently than most models tell us that they should. What you have to do is think constantly about what are the best strategies to protect the downside. For instance, something like using deep out-of-the-money puts on broad market indexes may make sense for insurance. I am comfortable giving up one or two points per year in order to pay for insurance against the catastrophic market failure.

The protection needs to be cheap—you don't want to buy it when volatility is high and the VIX is high. Instead, look to purchase it when the VIX is really low and the cost of the insurance is low. Similarly, when interest rates are high and 10-year Treasury yields are high, you can hedge against deflation and a downtown in the economy inexpensively. Right now you wouldn't want to do that because the cost of that protection is too high, with 10-year yields below 4 percent. While you can't plan for the disaster scenario, you have to at least attempt to have things that will help you when it does come.

Another barrier to entry for individuals seems to be access to managers and certain asset classes. Is this something that can be overcome? Do ETFs and other vehicles that have emerged in the past few years allow individuals to approximate the access that institutional investors have?

I think that access to a variety of asset classes for the individuals is less of a hurdle than it was. The explosion in ETFs has been huge and I think it will continue, because it does provide individual investors a great deal of flexibility. The caveat is that the individual also has an additional burden to understand exactly how it works, what risks they are taking, and exactly what they are getting. For example, if they get an ETF that does a 2X-leveraged return on the inverse of the S&P 500 Index, those can get fairly complicated and you can get a return stream that falls outside of what you would have expected in a particular market environment. ETFs are a great solution, but they are not a magic bullet and they can be hard to understand. ETFs also don't have as much historical track record, and so we haven't seen how they operate under a diversity of market conditions.

Beyond individuals, I think ETFs will help endowments and other institutional investors as well. We can use them to gain a certain exposure that we want to a specific strategy or asset class that we want and we can do it quickly and inexpensively. You can take temporary exposure without necessarily going to the work of entering a specific fund or engaging an external manager.

Endowments seem to be reacting quickly to themes they see developing. Is this going to be the "new normal" for academic institution money management?

Yes, although I should point out that when we go into an investment we are generally looking at it to be a three- to five-year investment and not something that comes and goes in a six-month period. You do not want to be trading-oriented and take your eye off the long-term objectives.

An example of this is gold. One of the first ETFs that we put on when I came to GWU was in gold. It was a good way to get exposure to gold because at the time the only other way to get exposure was to use futures contracts. Even for institutions commodity futures can be messy. You either have to put money with a commodity trader or do it directly, which involves daily margin calls and mark-to-market, which adds an operational burden for holding it. We bought the gold ETF in 2003 and held it through today, and clearly in 2009 this was a good holding. When we put it on, we didn't know what the time horizon would be and have now been in it for six-plus years.

Another example of this type of tactical shift was when we went into investment-grade credit at the end of 2008 because the spreads were quite wide. At the outset we believed this to have a three-year time horizon. Now the spreads have collapsed quite quickly, and so looking at that we may make changes sooner than expected. So, while you always go in with reasonably long time horizons for two to four years, as the investment progresses you may extend or trim your involvement.

The break point for big changes in how endowments work seems to be around the $1 billion mark. What things change as the asset base grows?

The biggest difference as you scale up the amount of assets under management is the number and type of investment professionals that you can bring to bear. It is very difficult to have a complex asset allocation under a billion and certainly under $500 million. You get forced into very simple 70–30 type allocations to public equities and fixed income or you have to outsource the management.

The complexity that emerges as the strategy becomes more sophisticated, the due diligence involved goes up exponentially. Additionally, larger portfolios become diverse geographically, and the staff spends a great deal of time outside the United States, which incurs the additional time and expense associated with that sort of travel.

Over the next five to 10 years you will see more and more outsourcing with the sub-$1 billion endowments and the multiple-billion-dollar endowments may become outsourcers for smaller institutions in a co-op type arrangement. The demand will be there, and the question and risk is will universities want to do this and can you carry it off operationally. Bottom line, to have a complex and internationally diversified portfolio is going to be much too complicated to do internally with a small asset base.

Are funds of funds and other types of advisors a good option for smaller endowments?

Using funds of funds is a suboptimal solution due to the tremendous layer of fees, which makes the hurdle quite large. Nonetheless, there are some funds of funds out there that can help subscale institutions close the gap. We do not use funds of funds and instead invest directly.

A challenge for smaller institutions is that they are not going to want to invest their entire portfolio in a single fund of funds, or even a material portion of their portfolio in a handful of funds of funds. It makes sense to have cheap beta and to have broad exposure to the market that you pay a small fee for, even for such things as Treasury bonds or investment-grade corporate bonds, where you want that operated by a long-only manager where the fee structure is low. Those types of decisions still have to be made whether you use a fund of funds or not. Since you have to manage and make decisions like this anyway, it reduces the value of what you are getting for the fees.

What macro trends are you thinking about for the near to mid-term?

The main thing we are looking for right now is subsectors within the real asset classes, as opposed to financial assets. One of these in particular within the energy sector has been alternatives such as wind and solar.

As you know, there have been a good number of funds raised around that particular theme. One of the things we have focused on is that the U.S. electricity distribution grid is aging and will need considerable technology upgrades to efficiently move nonbaseload electricity from the point of generation to the point of usage. Improving the electric grid infrastructure will be a focus for the industry in the coming years and so funds or companies in this area are interesting to us.

A second, and similar, subsector is water distribution. The aging infrastructure for this is showing up in increasingly frequent water-main breaks, which are very disruptive. Again, we would look for investment opportunities that will benefit from the necessary upgrades and infrastructure renewal that will be taking place in the coming five to 10 years. An analog to this is the natural gas mid-stream business over the past few years—distribution companies have done as well or better than companies focused on production or reserves.

What happened between 1980 and the late 2000s was tremendous financial innovation. An important part of this was democratization of credit—credit became available to a much wider base of both consumers and institutions. Much of this was good, although of course we found out recently that at least some of it was excessive. However, it was done to the detriment of investing in U.S. infrastructure and real assets. Instead of having capital flowing in to airports, roads, electric and water distribution, it went into less productive assets like credit default swaps and derivatives.

My view is that we are at the beginning of a new cycle over the coming decade where the investment capital will be flowing into real assets and not financial ones. I view real assets as those where the underlying cash flows are related to the physical properties of the investment and what those physical properties can provide. You see this real asset investment disparity in the United States when you go from the Hong Kong airport to downtown on their rail system and then you compare it to your options for getting from JFK airport to Manhattan.

How do you generate your themes and ideas?

We are doing this internally with the investment staff. This is done through reading and research. We don't typically engage outside firms to help generate our themes. One investment theme may even begin a thread that leads us to other ideas. For instance, when we began looking at infrastructure and water distribution, our research quite naturally led to agricultural demands for irrigation and to agriculture in general. These tangents can sometimes lead to the next idea.

Of course, not everything we identify as a big trend turns into something that is investable or implementable as a strategy. We spent time looking at nanotechnology, but couldn't find the large-scale commercial applications that led to an investment opportunity. We still think it is an interesting theme, but it needs time to develop before the right opportunity emerges.

Outside of the typical business reading, what sorts of things do you read that help you advance your thinking and identify opportunities?

I like reading trade journals, which allow me to delve down into an industry that we are evaluating. I want to spend time with the individuals who are doing the work—for example, the people managing the electrical infrastructure upgrades versus people from Wall Street. This detailed data allows us to be smarter about investing in our themes.

Because we believe strongly in international investments, we also need to keep track of geopolitics. This doesn't necessarily translate directly into a specific investment we make or asset class we are in, but it can clearly have a big impact on risk and opportunity across many themes. Things like global trade policy and what blocs may develop, what are the hot spots that will impact the overall geopolitical situation bear watching and will influence the investment themes you are either already in or considering entering. An important theme circulating right now is will there be an alternative to the U.S. dollar as a reserve currency. Central banks are trying to find a way to diversify their reserves much more than they have in the past, which, of course, will have a big impact on the U.S. dollar.

Chapter 11

Scott W. Wise

President

Rice Management Company

"We construct portfolios that don't require us to be right about current events every time in order to accomplish the mission."

Rice University and the Rice Management Company

Rice University, opened in 1912, is located in Houston, Texas. It has an enrollment of over 5,500 undergraduate and graduate students as of Fall, 2009. Rice's small size allows personal interaction between students and professors. The undergraduate students participate in research with distinguished faculty in the humanities, social sciences, engineering and natural sciences.

Rice was established with a founding endowment from William Marsh Rice, a successful Houston businessman. At his death in 1900, Rice left a $4.6 million estate dedicated to the founding of the Rice Institute, which became Rice University in 1960.

Today, at almost $4 billion, the endowment is one of the largest U.S. university investment pools. It was ranked number 19 in the 2009 NACUBO study. The endowment/student ratio is over $700,000 per student, one of the highest in the nation. During the period of 1989 to 2009, the Rice endowment grew from $990 million to almost $4 billion, reflecting an 11 percent average annual return vs. a 7 percent annual

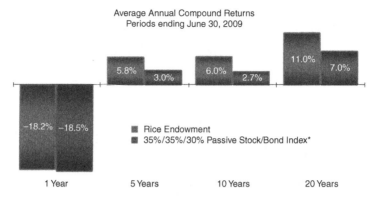

Figure 11.1 Rice University Endowment Performance

SOURCE: Rice University

NOTE: 35% Russell 3000/35% ACWI ex US/30% Barclays Capital Aggregate Bond
Index

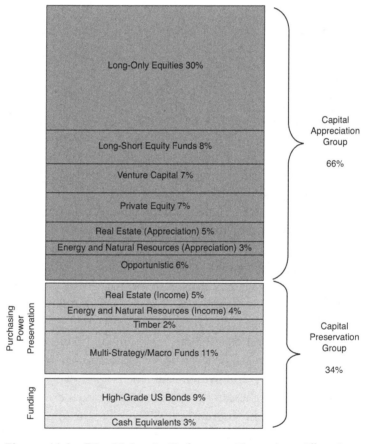

Figure 11.2 Rice University Endowment Target Asset Allocation

SOURCE: Rice University

return for a passive stock/bond portfolio shown in Figure 11.1. Figure 11.2 shows the asset allocation of the Rice endowment at the period ended June 30, 2009.

I n 2009, Rice University established the Rice Management Company to oversee the endowment. The group has existing staff of 16, including 13 investment professionals. The company is responsible for asset allocation, manager and consultant selection, performance monitoring, and portfolio management.

Scott Wise is president of the Rice Management Company. Wise joined Rice University in 1979 as its Comptroller, and has served at the University's Chief Investment Officer since 1989. He was among the four finalists for *Institutional Investor's* Award for Excellence in Endowment Investment Management in 2006. Wise has a BA in economics from Rice and a Master of Professional Accounting from the University of Texas at Austin.

Q: How do you approach investment strategy at Rice?

Most importantly, we seek to take advantage of the edge we have over other types of investors: the perpetual nature of our capital, and the access to managers that our size and mission provide.

Our process begins with establishing the role each investment is to play in our portfolio—at the highest level, we differentiate between investments with a capital preservation focus and those with a capital appreciation focus. From there, we establish asset classes with more defined goals. For instance, we break hedge funds into three buckets—the long/short managers are geared toward capital appreciation and are evaluated against active pure-play equity long-only managers. The second bucket is for the macro and multi-strategy managers. Their role is more capital preservation-oriented and the expectation is for them to produce monthly returns from 1 to 1.5 percent with relatively low volatility. Our third bucket, which has a capital appreciation focus, is for those hedge funds whose talent lies in deploying capital opportunistically. Some of our asset classes (real estate and natural resources in particular) actually have two allocations—one for capital appreciation oriented strategies and another for capital preservation and cash yield oriented strategies.

Once you have set strategy and asset class roles, how do you identify and select managers?

We have a variety of manager candidate sources including recommendations from our consultants. We have a consultant for hedge funds, and a consultant for private investments. We don't really think about manager selection on a project basis, but more as an ongoing process. When we have an opportunity to add a manager it doesn't create a big event, since we have been looking at different managers all along. A continuous process is what works best here.

Our board of directors also has a role. We have moved from an investment committee structure to an investment management company with its own board for governance. This allowed us to add investment expertise from individuals who are on the management company board, but are perhaps not on the Rice board. Input from the board members is important in both manager sourcing and manager screening.

Finally, we will talk to other investment offices, at both the CIO and investment staff level. We think an information exchange between endowment and foundation offices can be mutually helpful and we work to have relationships with comparable institutions to promote this.

When we identify a manager, we will look at their historical performance relative to the goal of the fund strategy. We look at fees, where alignment of interests is critical. Simply put, we want the general partner to make money when we make money. The manager should have incentives that reward performance in executing the fund goals so that the strategy plays the role we have selected for it in our overall portfolio.

Will things be changing in the manager-institution relationship?

The selection process and ongoing relationship have a good foundation when if you ask thoughtful questions. The investment staff must do a good job understanding and processing the manager's responses. Manager performance has to be evaluated net of all fees. When managers are generating high return numbers it is easy not to discount the importance of manager fees. Going forward I think there will be more focus to make sure that the fees are appropriate in a potentially lower-return environment. This will take on increased importance as institutions negotiate fees with manager candidates.

I don't think there will be much effort coming from institutional CIOs to retrade deals that already exist. However, there has been some movement coming from the fund manager side. Some of the managers have been good about initiating fee structure changes preemptively, in the cases where they have not been able to return or deploy capital in the way that was anticipated when they were marketing the funds.

This has been a positive differentiating element that we will take into account going forward as we look at managers. One of the side-effects of the market dislocation has been to expose what behavior we can expect of managers in a down market. We get to observe them under stress and see how they respond, and see what decisions they make. This is the kind of information we can and will incorporate into our manager selection process.

What are institutions looking for in manager transparency?

If you ask the right questions up front, you will most likely get what you want. This goes back to the process that I outlined for identifying, evaluating, and selecting managers. If you are executing those things well, the transparency should follow. The screening process results in only institutional-quality managers being on the short list.

Managers you would seriously consider are open about what positions they are taking, how they are using leverage, how their risk management regime operates—all the things that matter. The willingness to be open is critical. Our job is to ask the right questions. For instance, something we care about might not appear on a standard report that a manager is producing. In those cases, we need to ask for a different view or incremental information. There is a burden on the institution to do the homework—to visit the manager's office in person, to review the material they have sent in advance, determine what questions to ask ahead of time. These are just the basics that the institutional investment staff must do.

Would you characterize Rice as a thematic investor or asset allocation focused?

Our basic approach is a long-term asset allocation model. This has been true for a long time and will continue to be the way we work. When we did our asset allocation review a year or two ago, we did add an asset category for opportunistic investing.

This was something new, and allows us to do two things. First, we can take advantage of tactical investment opportunities, and second, we can add managers that we think are skillful at deploying capital across a variety of opportunities. With this structure, we have latitude to directly invest when we see something compelling but also have managers involved who are thinking about it every day.

One of the biggest issues in institutional money management, including endowments, over the past year or two has been liquidity management. How do you approach it?

We believe that the characteristics of the institution are key to determining the level of illiquidity that is comfortable and appropriate for each institution. Our university is going to be around forever—that is the underlying assumption. Therefore the capital should be managed with a long-term view, because it exists to support the institution. The other important aspect is the consistency of the distribution from the capital to support the institution. Every institution will have its own spending policy and formula, and there are several models commonly used to determine what an institution's endowment spending and liquidity needs are going to be.

A reasonable proxy for average endowment spending over time is about 5 percent. The important thing about managing cash outflows is looking for consistency from one year to the next. Then you have a well-defined call on capital from the pool. So those two things together, the long-term nature of the institution and the predictability of the distribution requirement, allow universities to accept a greater level of illiquidity than most pools of capital and certainly than most individuals. The way individuals in particular think about illiquidity is different because they don't share these two characteristics—individuals have more uncertainty and a much more limited time horizon.

We may have had a different approach and thinking about liquidity than other universities because of our unique situation. About half of the Rice operating budget is funded by the endowment. This has historically been 45–47 percent. I believe this would make us in the upper end of the spectrum in this area. Naturally this leads to some conservatism in the endowment and also in the working capital area. Any unexpected year-to-year variance in our liquidity can have a large impact on our ability to support the institution.

We see a number of changes to how institutions are approaching liquidity now. Like others, we have managed our unfunded commitments to private investments (including private equity, venture capital, real estate and natural resources). We looked at this carefully in the past couple of years, as the dynamic with private investments was changing considerably. In response, we have updated and improved our forecasting models for unfunded commitments and potential capital calls. We had traditionally had models that focused on the coming 12-month period. We would also look beyond 12 months, but the most important factors were within the next year. We analyzed and reevaluated all the assumptions that went into our near-term model and enhanced them.

We slowed the pace of commitments to new private investments. Our long-term goal is to make our private investment programs self-funding within each asset class. We look for the returns from each type—real estate, natural resources, private equity, and so on—to fund new commitments within that area. To do this, we need to have more capital coming back, more realizations, from each area. This has always been a soft goal for Rice, and something we tracked. Now we are making it a firmer goal. The challenge now is that there is not a lot of capital coming back.

If you are building a new program in a private asset area, the idea is that you are adding to your allocation in the area every couple of years. This means you are increasing your commitment to private funds every cycle. During those times you are focused on the pace of commitments and diversification across vintage years. When you get to your target allocation, then you change gears to the approach we are using now.

Further, we are looking at the capital withdrawal terms for private investments and side-pockets that exist with some hedge funds. This is something to pay increased attention to. In the past, hedge fund managers were providing quarterly liquidity, or in some cases annual withdrawal rights. We had not seen gates being put up or other withdrawal impediments in the past. After the dislocations in 2008 we wanted to evaluate this more closely.

There have also been external changes due to the emphasis on liquidity. Endowments are getting more questions from rating agencies in relation to their debt issuance programs. So, for instance, we are seeing Moody's asking for endowments to report liquidity levels as part of their data gathering. They are asking more in-depth questions in this area. Before, they might ask about capital calls from private investments, but now they will also want to know additional things. For instance, they would want to know about interest rate swaps. When a swap goes against you, you may be required to post collateral, which requires cash and therefore affects liquidity. The agencies ask these sorts of questions so they have a better understanding of an institution's liquidity, so they can more accurately gauge credit risk for the institution. Academic institutions will have debt programs of various types—for instance, tax exempt debt, or a liquidity line of credit—that are affected by the institution's rating. These may or may not be managed by the investment office, but the credit rating matters to an institution.

Finally, liquidity needs within managers' funds were another important trend from last year. Hedge funds and real estate funds were prominent examples in 2008–2009. Investors began asking for redemptions from the hedge fund managers in Q3 and Q4 of 2008. Many managers put up gates or suspended redemptions. In most cases this had an impact on the fund—it affected what sorts of investments they could make and also consumed a lot of fund management attention. This, in turn, affected all the investors in a fund, even if they were not withdrawing their money.

We saw an impact in real estate, which is by its nature a leveraged strategy. As the values of commercial property began dropping, the ratio of debt to equity moved considerably, which in turn meant liquidity (additional capital) needs in order to stay within the debt covenants. Some investment structures have recallable capital. This means that if the fund needs liquidity, they can ask investors to repay money that had been distributed to the limited partners previously. Current distributions also went down as the fund tried to conserve cash. In all, private investments were having a profound effect on the liquidity position of endowments.

Does the investment office manage the university's working capital as well as the endowment?

Yes, but it is not invested alongside the endowment, and it is not invested like the endowment. It is managed as a separate pool with different objectives and requirements. Managing working capital aggressively to generate extra return may have caused problems for some institutions over the past couple of years, but in fairness, it worked pretty well for the previous 20-plus years. However, we do not look for returns this way, because of the high liquidity requirements here at Rice.

We refined our approach on liquidity within the endowment port-folio in the past couple of years in reaction to the market dislocation. The main source of liquidity was the working capital account. Our tar-get for cash in the endowment could be as low as zero, or as high as 1 percent. We updated our target allocation for cash in the endowment to about 3 percent. This is over and above the liquidity we maintain in the working capital account. We also established an allocation to a short-duration fixed income strategy within our allocation to bonds. This was primarily a liquidity move.

Do you think endowments overall started trending toward overemphasis on peer group comparison (the "performance derby")?

Yes, some of that happened. One element that led to this over the years has been the various incentive compensation plans which were partly keyed to peer endowment performance comparisons.

Beyond this, however, is more public interest in what endowments are doing, how they are doing it, and what is the investment performance. Twenty years ago we would report returns to the board, but there wasn't much interest beyond that. Now people keep their eye on endowment returns. The numbers are published, there is interest from the press, student newspapers follow it, and there is much more visibility overall. This naturally leads to comparisons between institutions.

As a result, is investment committee approach to endowment staff compensation changing?

I think it is changing in the institutional money management indus-try. The comparison element as a part of investment staff compensation is being deemphasized now, with more focus on meeting the institutions endowment payout needs, asset class benchmarks, and board discretion.

It seems that investment committees are granting wider latitude to CIOs in response to market volatility. Have you seen this?

We haven't felt constrained by the committee in the past. Four years ago we added the ability to select managers and move capital among managers in between board meetings and then report our actions at the next board meeting. Before we would have needed board approval to hire or terminate managers within an asset class. This authority has been delegated to the investment staff.

Does the market dislocation we saw in 2008–2009 represent fundamental change in how markets will operate?

One fundamental that is different now is the speed with which markets move. Compare today to 1981, or even the early 1990s. That speed means more volatility and rapid dislocation when there is a downturn.

There has been a lot of conversation about previously unlinked, or at least lightly linked, markets being more tightly related, which made correlations go to one. I think that this linkage may have been present in other downturns as well. It tends to last for some number of months, but not necessarily years. We definitely saw it have an impact during 2008–2009. There will be a hangover for some time as we move through deleveraging.

How will endowments approach tail risk? Will the approach be different now?

For the long time horizon, I still believe that asset allocation and diversification is the best approach. This is how we plan and construct our portfolios.

For the shorter view, there is increased volatility that is influencing how people think about tail risk. Our goal is to have sufficient, truly liquid assets to support our institution and thereby mitigate the possibility of selling long-term investments at low prices. There are derivative instruments that try to address this issue also. We have looked at these options but haven't employed them, either for an opportunistic move or for hedging a risk that we see. The instruments are complex, and they can be expensive relative to the risk reduction or opportunity you are getting. There can be unforeseen consequences and the addition of risks that can be difficult to understand. In some cases you may not even be getting the protection you think you are getting.

Short-term tail risks are difficult to manage. We try to focus on the basics for an endowment—asset allocation, diversification, liquidity maintenance, manager selection, and transparency. This will serve us well for the long run.

What trends are you thinking about in the coming near to mid-term?

We are in the consensus camp with regard to relative growth rates being higher in underdeveloped markets. The evidence suggests that these will be areas of good opportunity in the coming few years.

When we think about inflation and deflation, we are more worried about unexpected changes than direction. This goes back to the basics of asset allocation and diversification. We want to always have some hedges that guard against unexpected inflation moves. For inflation we have hard assets that we own directly. For deflation we have a continual commitment to long-term U.S. Treasuries, which was great a year ago and not so great now. But we have it there for a reason, and so while we did reduce our investments in Treasuries, we have kept some exposure in the portfolio to give us a deflationary hedge.

Predicting what will happen and when is impossible. Our philosophy is to focus on what works over very long periods of time instead of trying to guess what will happen in the very near term. This allows us to do what the institution needs, which is to provide predictable cash flows. That is not to say we aren't interested in trends—we are. However, we construct portfolios that don't require us to be right about current events every time in order to accomplish the mission.

This also relates to endowment performance evaluation. We are primarily concerned with the interests of the institution and reflect that in our portfolio decisions. When we want to see how the endowment performs it means we don't necessarily engage in a lot of peer comparison. The metric is "did we provide what the institution needed?"

What advice would you pass on to individual investors?

Some of the points I made on manager selection demonstrate how difficult it is for individuals to replicate what endowments do. The complexity and level of effort in the manager selection process demonstrates some of the impediments an individual faces.

There are a few things individuals can take away. First, fees matter. Looking at what the investor receives net of all fees—not just the management fee, but the performance fees as well is important. Often the providers of investment performance information are not taking pains to highlight this data. Individual investors are not always equipped to ask the hard questions that get to this.

Another point is rebalancing. Averaging in and averaging out of asset classes is a relatively straightforward thing to do and within the capability of an individual investor. However, I think this gets overlooked. Rebalancing appropriately and periodically is a useful tool to help an individual investor deal with volatility in the markets.

Understanding your investment objectives is also important. This is going to be different for every individual, just like it is different among institutions. For instance, liquidity needs will vary—in some cases last year individuals became forced sellers of liquid assets in order to de-lever. Individuals can have wide variances in risk tolerance. They have different investment time horizons. Knowing what you are trying to accomplish is personal. It is something only an individual can do for himself or herself.

Chapter 12

James (Jim) Hille

Chief Investment Officer

Texas Christian University

Texas Christian University and the Texas Christian University Endowment

TCU is a private college located in Fort Worth, Texas, with a history that dates back to 1873. It was the first coeducational college in Texas. The school was founded as Add-Ran Male and Female College and became Texas Christian University in 1902. It was formed through an affiliation with the Christian Church (Disciples of Christ) but is not owned or managed by the church. The enrollment at TCU is approximately 8,900 undergraduate and graduate students.

The school was founded during the financial panic of 1873, which made it difficult for the founders, Randolph Clark and his brother Addison. Randolph decided in 1889 to transfer the college to the Christian Church. His decision was primarily driven by the desire to have an endowed college, writing: "If the college [is] to continue beyond the lives of the present workers it must have an endowment." The Clarks' gift of the now-sufficiently-financed college to the Christian Church was TCU's first endowment gift—appraised at $43,000. In 1908 an

153

endowment company was formed that focused on development. The first direct gift to the endowment came in 1911 in the amount of $25,000. The city of Fort Worth gave the school land at its current location and $200,000. In 1923, the school received a remarkable gift of $3 million plus several thousand acres of mineral- and oil-rich ranch land. Today, the endowment stands at nearly $1 billion, and reached $1.22 billion in 2008. The endowment is ranked number 58 in the 2009 NACUBO study. The endowment has a ratio of more than $112,000 per student.

J im Hille, the chief investment officer, is responsible for managing TCU's endowment. Jim works with the investment committee of TCU's board of trustees to set investment policy and execute the investment program.

Prior to TCU, Jim worked for the Teacher Retirement System of Texas in Austin, where he was chief investment officer. Formerly, he was the portfolio manager and analyst for the Employees Retirement System of Texas where he was responsible for managing multiple portfolios including international and domestic mid-cap equities. Before that, he served as the assistant international portfolio manager for Taylor & Company in Fort Worth, where he analyzed and pursued long and short investment strategies involving international securities.

Jim is a graduate of the United States Naval Academy and holds an MBA from the Neeley School of Business at TCU. He also is a former United States Marine Corps officer.

Q: What is evolving in the business of endowment investing?

The primary trend in the past decade is the thematic approach, as opposed to set allocations that you try to periodically rebalance against. The neoclassical approach now is to invest for themes for the long term. Develop your ideas for three- to five-year duration themes and stay true to that rather than some sort of slavish rebalancing to a 60/40 asset mix.

You have obvious themes that you can point to, like whether it's a bullish to dollar, negative to dollar, or bullish in commodities, or vice versa, or exploiting liquidity crunches, or having a pool of cash for opportunistic investing. Part of this new approach is making sure that you can do some things opportunistically, call it tactical if you want. This has liquidity implications.

Devoting a material portion of the portfolio to thematic and opportunistic investing is the biggest change I have observed in the business. Within my portfolio, it's not necessarily termed thematic. In what we are doing, the themes are largely exploited in the opportunistic portion of the portfolio.

Thematic investing seems to require more frequent decisions by the CIO and more latitude from the investment committee.

That is absolutely the case. At TCU it is something I began working on when I arrived in 2006. The investment committee wants to hear about it, but they don't want to be in the business of managing tactical moves or the opportunistic shifting of assets. Those decisions need to be consistent with the short-, medium-, or long-term approach that we're using. We will make sure the committee knows what we did and we have broad latitude to make moves between meetings.

This trend is something that differentiates endowments from pension funds. Pension funds generally have governance constraints that prevent or hinder them from operating with the kind of flexibility endowments enjoy. This reduces their return, and the phenomenon is reflected in long-term performance comparisons between endowments and pension funds.

Endowments seem to be organizing their long-term funds to generate a consistent low-risk return, and then using other portions to pursue themes, to go on offense, or to defensively hedge risk.

Yes. There are elements of all that in our endowment. I have a fairly balanced objectives-based allocation but roughly four segments of the portfolio are each focused on those sorts of things. Call it offense or defense, but we call it opportunistic and absolute return.

In other words, we need to absolutely get a certain level of return in a portion of our fund in order to meet annual payout for the TCU operating budget. We will do that through very low-risk strategies. Absolute return type of strategies, fixed income, cash, and all overlays of cash are the sort of instruments we use for that piece.

Depending upon the risk environment as we see it, we are going to dial-up risk or dial it down within the opportunistic portion. And we have the latitude to do that within our shop. Those two portions comprise about 40 percent of the fund.

There is another 35 percent of the fund that is fairly hard wired into equity, but it's not just the domestic stock market, it is also private equity and international stocks. We have a band of around 10 percent up or down in that portion. It is just focused on return seeking and is somewhat volatility agnostic.

The final portion is inflation hedging, which is another one of our core objectives. We have to keep pace with or out-earn inflation. This is where we have our real assets.

Is the latest crisis different from past downturns in some way?
Has the 2008–2009 crisis changed the way endowments will
think about investing?

Liquidity is the obvious thing that will get more attention, but the crisis will get managers to think differently about how they approach asset allocation. Coming through the 2000–2001 tech bubble, I was in the pension business. Even though we were deeply underweight stocks, we were severely impacted by the equity markets blowing up like they did.

Meanwhile, I studied what endowments did and the endowments came through that particular crisis pretty well. It was because of this focus on absolute return, making sure you get a minimum rate of return first and use the risk environment with your opportunistic money to go for some extra return.

When you study what successful endowment CIOs have done and what they have written, it shows you need a balanced approach that is not overly biased to equities. Also, you cannot allow your total fund to be dominated by any one asset class, no matter how attractive it is. I can see signs of the next bubble coming, and I believe it will be the emerging markets, and it's because there is so much love for them. There are some good reasons for investing in emerging markets because they are going to be the determiner of investment returns and risks going forward. The story is based largely on the contrast between the huge fiscal imbalances that the developed markets have versus the large savings balances that many emerging markets have. I think they have become too popular right now, however.

They have many things going for them, but the things that they don't have going for them is valuations, which will ebb and flow, and they're flowing right now. Emerging markets and developed market fiscal imbalances are going to be the determining factor in the coming decade. That is a function of what we just came through.

But with that said, emerging markets have been a primary determinant of the returns for the last 20 years. They're going to be that for the next 20 years. You've got to have an idea of what the themes are going to be that are driven by emerging markets and fiscal imbalances in the next 3–5-year horizon because our careers depend on that.

I detailed our four segments of the fund that we're focused on. And I feel really good about how balanced we are across those. No one segment or fund or asset class is going to unduly influence the returns on the fund. They are all going to add something, whether it's a stabilizing effect or return to the fund.

The struggle in this last year that we went through is making sure that the people I report to are comfortable with that. We lagged the stock market this last year (2009). We lagged our benchmarks this year because of the undue influence of the stock market in the rebound year.

If they get dissatisfied with not keeping up with the stock market, that takes some communication. The market giveth and the market taketh away. And you know what, we had to step back and say, "Okay, what are our objectives? Did we meet our objectives?"

We exceeded our objectives by a factor of three this last year. We should be very happy with that. And yeah, we had a setback last year and the prior year (2007–2008), but we came through that better than about 97 percent of all funds.

So, we're set up for managing those tails, not the big rebound tails or the positive tail, but certainly the down tail, and that's when you're going to make your money: by not losing it.

What is the right benchmark and time frame for evaluating endowment performance?

First and foremost, that's why our investment policy utilizes this objective-based approach: Number 1, did we meet our objective for the university? And if the answer is "no," then there is no variable compensation for the investment staff. You also have to take a look at what was the landscape and the opportunity set, and did you participate satisfactorily with that opportunity set. This must be viewed within a reasonable time period, and we're looking at more like, three- to five-year time frame for that.

We also evaluate relative ranking versus peers. We stack up really nicely with that, but that comparison is far down the list of metrics we care about. Relative performance is a fair question, but you don't want it to be the primary thing that is driving you and determining what you are doing.

There has been a lot of focus on liquidity in endowments. The CIO has to strike the right balance of maximizing return while meeting commitments. How do you do this?

The events of 2008–2009 were unprecedented, and we had to pay much more attention to liquidity than we ever had to here at TCU. However, we didn't have a lot of the issues that you read about. I've read about the large endowments that were really alternative focused-type of funds with 60 percent private equity and higher or 60 percent private equity and the rest in hedge funds. We didn't have that here. We have close to 50 percent in alternative asset illiquid-type strategies, but we didn't experience liquidity issues. The controversy in liquidity came about, with respect to endowments, this last year because of overconcentration in illiquid private investments. It could have been worse than it was, had we not had lots of bailouts and zero percent interest rates.

But the reason everyone really came through it is because very large endowments have triple A credit ratings or double A credit ratings. They were able to issue debt, although that is not the most desirable thing to have to do in order to make your capital calls.

Furthermore, many institutions got bailed out by the stock market rally. What we have at the end of the 2009 is a reverse denominator effect where in March of 2008, the denominator effect was crushing everyone and they were relatively overweight in private equity. They didn't have anything to fund their private equity capital calls, which can be done through fund redemptions, but when they are massively undervalued, you are really loath to do that. With the stock market rally, the assets they had in equities or in high-beta hedge funds provided a way to redeem some funds in order to make capital calls in other parts of the portfolio if need be.

We're not completely out of the woods, but we're really close. Had the public equities market rally not happened, it could have been considerably worse for illiquid institutional money.

I suspect that what people are going to do differently is view the idea of an illiquidity premium a bit more carefully, making sure they're managing their tail risk. It means they might want to go about their hedging or they might just have a pool of capital set aside that they take lower risk with.

The very large endowments that were affected will be fine in the long term, but in the short term, the institutions themselves have been knocked back a step or two. The affected universities had to implement pay freezes or program cutting. And any institution that is not dealing with those sorts of budget issues is going to be a net beneficiary in the short term.

Did your background in pension funds, where liability-driven investing is used, lead you to a philosophy that helped you maintain greater liquidity?

At an endowment, the liability is the annual payout to the University. We foresaw the crisis to some degree heading into it, and, we were ahead of it by investing in some funds that were short credit, and we had some fairly decent-sized equity hedges on our equity book. We were compelled to do this because of the hard cash liability we face year in and year out. Not many public pension fund managers think this way, though corporate plan managers do.

So we were managing our tail risk in that regard. We actually didn't have a set amount for the payout until fall 2008, actually right after the Lehman crisis. We already had a big redemption for hedge funds, and we got it in October and that was enough to set aside for our payout for the coming fiscal year. We were not totally ahead, but we did make advance moves that allowed us to satisfy current operating budget needs.

Where I differed from the industry, I think, was in willingness for lock-ups in private equity or long-term lock-ups, and hedge funds. I wasn't willing to go beyond where we were at 45 percent in private or semiprivate type of assets just because I saw that it would impose challenges in managing liquidity needs. It is possible our size helped here as well. With a small investment group and relatively small endowment, I am less willing to manage excess complexity. Larger endowments had the staff and size to take on much higher levels of complexity. It is possible they will rethink it because it is part of what hurt them later. There is an illiquidity premium, but there is also an illiquidity cost that must be evaluated.

What is your approach to managing working capital?

We looked at it pretty hard largely because the TCU CFO, Brian Gutierrez, came from University of Texas System and he worked with Bob Boldt to establish such a program there. We wanted to see if it was appropriate for our environment.

One interesting thing we considered for getting returns from working capital was a barbell approach. We could put a portion, maybe one-third of the really long-term working capital and manage it as quasi-endowment. Then if you lose some money, then you have time to make it back. We were also looking at perhaps doing an absolute return type of strategy that is very similar to our absolute return strategy within the endowment. This has been stable for us and was well above its high-water mark just nine months into the recovery.

After we evaluated our options, we determined that we simply did not want to do it. The risk-return was not right for TCU's culture. Following that, in fall 2007, we decided to go to 100 percent Treasuries with our working capital. This has produced very low returns, clearly, but it has also been stable and in fact, certain.

The investment committee is aware that we are probably leaving money on the table; however, as an institution we decided to focus on the endowment as the place where we will be taking risks and generating returns. I think the decision will vary from university to university—some have implemented aggressive working capital investment management and done well with it.

Endowments have clearly gotten more complex. Is it possible to overcomplicate things?

Yes. It is tempting because the investment offices are staffed with very smart people, who are capable of doing very sophisticated things. You can be the victim of overconfidence here, or just simply the victim of unintended consequences or the black swan event that no one sees coming.

This idea probably goes back to the question of, "What's the right size of an institution endowment?" To optimize management and return, I would say it is larger than TCU, but much smaller than Harvard or Stanford. In this business we talk a lot about economies of scale. However, I think there are also diseconomies of scale. I experienced it to some degree at the pension fund, which was over a $100 billion. We had an abundance of resources—staff, research, access to managers, whatever you would need. All the information you have at your fingertips, if you are not careful, can become noise, however. I had a chance to talk with Jack Myer [former CIO for the Harvard endowment]. About eight years ago, I was thinking about making a switch to the endowment world. At the time, the Harvard endowment was around $25 billion. I asked him what he thought his challenges were, and I was surprised with what he said. I thought $25 billion was very manageable because I was managing $100 billion. But he said, "I'm worried about how large we've become and not being able to allocate optimally."

I took heed of his advice, and I came to the determination that I should focus on an endowment fund of at least a billion. Now that I have been in the endowment business for some time, I have concluded that the sweet spot is probably $2 billion, maybe $2 to $3 billion. At that level you absolutely will have appropriate scale to be well resourced, but not cross the line into the overly complex and succumb to overconfidence. When you get that large, you can do virtually anything, and so you do. This can lead to unexpected problems from the over-complexity.

It appears that the very largest endowments have a lot of advantages that come from size.

It is true. A number of folks who have stepped into the endowment management role have thought, "Well, I'm running an endowment. I can do all the sophisticated things that endowments do." They find, though, over time that they don't have the same kinds of advantages that some of the best endowments have.

Let's talk about the other end of it. When you start looking at smaller endowments they look to outsourced advisors for a lot of help. How do CIOs strike the balance between doing some things themselves versus using consultants versus outsourcing and funds of funds?

Besides scale, it is philosophical. At the $1 billion level and above, your need for funds of funds starts to diminish, although there are a few unique ones we have considered. Any place we don't have the bandwidth, the expertise, or the ability to do manager selection and due diligence ourselves we might outsource to a fund of funds (FoF). We see this in certain specific circumstances.

For instance, we used a fund of funds in the credit opportunity space in 2009 because we were being inundated by proposals. We knew we wanted to top off in credit opportunities. We didn't have much capital to deploy and we wanted to be smart about it, and we wanted to be timely. We went to a fund of funds, which solved those issues. If we had significant resources and a staff that could quickly execute the diligence, we would have done it ourselves. A fund of funds made sense in this case.

There are other cases as well. For some international private equity or international opportunistic themes, we've gone to fund of funds. It also works for smaller funds. It takes the same time to do due diligence on a large fund as it does on a small fund, and so an FoF arrangement distributes the diligence cost and effort, but still lets you get the exposure you want.

There are also certain compelling reasons to do things in a small way, or in small cap, or small private equity or small mid-market. We may establish a core position via fund of funds and then we do some satellite or niche investing on our own.

There are some smart CIOs managing smaller pools. They have to accomplish a lot with very limited resources and bandwidth. It all comes down to the math on 20 basis points or so on assets. That's roughly the level of resources you can devote to endowment portfolio management. That is why the $800 million to a billion dollar range is the threshold for staffing up. Every now and then, you get that smart guy who is willing to do it for a lot less, and they are able to execute, but this is the exception.

What are some of the themes you are evaluating for the coming six to 36 months?

I pay attention to themes that create the herd mentality and then try to be in front of it. We have this opportunistic approach for when it all goes bad or goes in the direction that people don't expect. We are patient and a little contrarian, so the typical themes that I hear about, the conventional wisdom, is inflation and emerging markets, commodities and commercial real estate. These themes today are the worst kept secrets in the entire investment world.

To get a good return in a thematic investment, you either have to be participating in size ahead of time or you have to wait for the inevitable downturn in order to get your position in, if you've missed it in some cases. Everybody's got an opinion, and they should. I have some contrarian views on the whole inflation story. I don't believe it will come about for quite some time. There is a lot of excess capacity in the market. Everyone is worried about the monetary situation and you've got to watch that, but I'm more in a Keynes camp where excess capacity is going to keep inflation in check for quite some time. I'd like to be clear though that I am not in the Keynes camp in regards to all the government stimulus. This is likely to create its own debacle.

A good example of how this can play out is what we have seen in the gold market. A lot of people were very early in it. When it doesn't meet expectations for three, four years, people will get impatient with those investments. Look at TIPS, as another example. I predict the breakevens will be wretched. The investors won't make any money, and may actually lose money in TIPS, and they will get impatient and blow them out at some point. At that point we will step in and buy some TIPS.

There will be other commodities that see a temporary dip due to anemic growth or supply and demand imbalances, so there will be opportunities there. The monetary situation is manifesting itself today in financial assets, as it always does, but it won't manifest itself in the real economy for a while. We will be patient and keep looking for ways to play those sorts of things with the opportunistic part of our fund.

For emerging markets, they are more expensive than developed markets but they're not grossly overvalued relative to their growth. Therefore we have a fair allocation to emerging markets at the moment, and we're not going to reduce it for a while. If you add some on pullbacks at the bottom of the cycle, I think you can be rewarded. You just have to pay attention to it because it will get overdone. It's probably six months from being overdone, which isn't long enough to make a good solid investment in them. There are a few places we think are becoming overvalued—certain markets like China and the Hong Kong real estate markets and certain commodity markets like Brazil and Russia.

As far as contrarian viewpoints, one way we determine where the consensus is going is by attending various conferences. If I sense too much consensus, that tells me what things to watch out for. It often reaffirms what not to do.

Can you talk about your philosophy and/or process for manager selection?

We take our time with the manager selection and we're deliberate and patient. Once we make an allocation to a manager, we stick with them for at least one cycle. Due diligence can take six to nine months between passive due diligence (just observing) and active due diligence where we step it up to onsite due diligence, reference checks, and background checks.

As far as what data to gather, there's a standard detailed checklist that everybody uses. Of course you absolutely have to have that. Going beyond that, we want to spend time observing and talking with others about a particular fund just to make sure that they're staying consistent and their actions and what they are saying line up over time.

We are also not big fans of very large funds or very small funds. The very large funds we worry are prone to the scale diseconomies we discussed. The small funds have a higher risk of failure. The market demonstrated that risk last year. For the small fund, it is a function of having to get over the business risk hump, and there is a new normal there now. The new minimum fund size is at least half a billion. Previously it was probably $100–$200 million.

Do you feel the LPs are ascendant now in fee and term negotiations?

That is hard to say because it is something that happens on a case-by-case basis. You need to do your homework on every deal so that you can be sure you are armed with the right information to make a deal that works for both parties. I think the markets rebounded too quickly in 2009 to have much of a lasting impact on how managers are thinking about fees.

The other thing that came out of last year is probably a diminished appetite for lock-ups and restrictions in private investments. This will be something that gets more scrutiny from institutional money managers going forward.

How do you feel about leverage? Has your viewpoint on it changed?

We haven't changed our view on it. We are not going to be scared of leverage but during certain periods, we certainly need to pay attention to it. We are never going to be in a two times leverage fund and we are not going to be in a real estate fund that uses 90 percent leverage. We're not going to be using leverage to any appreciable degree at the fund level either. So, we never were big advocates of leverage. I think leverage has its role, but we're not seeking it.

In places where a manager is using leverage, how do you differentiate the return they generate from leverage versus the underlying investment?

One way we have done that is investing in one-and-a-half-time levered funds, where there is also an unlevered or one-time levered fund with the same strategy. You can discern the value add because you are also watching their one-time levered funds or the nonlevered funds.

Do you have any books or reading material that you recommend?

Everybody reads the obvious things like *The Economist* and *Barron's* and *The Wall Street Journal*. *Grant's Interest Rate Observer* is popular in the endowment world. Geopolitical-oriented newsletters and web sites like Stratfor are also helpful. People in this business read voluminously. Most useful market intelligence, though, comes from our investment managers.

As far as books go, *Pioneering Portfolio Management* was everybody's guide from the start and then, what's on my big bookshelf, *Winning the Loser's Game*. Other interesting books on risk are *Fooled by Randomness* and *Against the Gods*.

Chapter 13

Jeremy Crigler

Chief Investment Officer

Tulane University

"At Tulane ... we keep a particular eye on hurricane season. When it comes along we may ramp up liquidity to provide a hedge against natural disasters."

Tulane University and the Tulane Educational Fund

Tulane University, founded in 1834, is located in New Orleans. The university was originally chartered as a public medical school. In the late 1800s, a donation from Paul Tulane provided the initial capital for the Tulane Educational Fund. The Louisiana State Legislature transferred control of the university to the fund in 1884, privatizing the university. Tulane is unique as the only university in the United States to have transitioned from a public to a private institution.

The school has an enrollment of over 11,000 graduate and undergraduate students.

Tulane University's endowment reached $1 billion in 2007. The investment office employs eight full-time professionals. Tulane's goal for the endowment is to "achieve the highest long-term total investment return on investment assets that is compatible with the university's risk tolerance and time horizons and consistent with prudent investment practices." As shown in Figure 13.1, Tulane allocates about 35 percent to

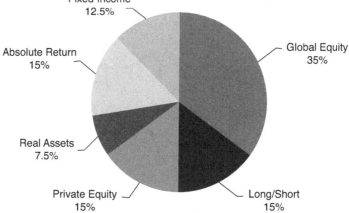

Figure 13.1   Tulane Endowment Allocation, as of March 31, 2009
SOURCE: Tulane University

global equities, 15 percent to absolute return strategies, and 12.5 percent to fixed income.

Tulane University was named the 2008 Mid-Size Nonprofit of the Year by *Foundation & Endowment Money* magazine.

The endowment is ranked number 75 in the 2009 NACUBO study, with estimated assets of over $800 million.

J eremy Crigler is the chief investment officer for Tulane University. Crigler previously served as senior investment officer for Cornell University in Ithaca, New York, where he was part of a team responsible for developing and implementing investment policies and performance measures for the university's $6 billion endowment. He also managed a team responsible for investing $2.5 billion in public equity, hedge funds, and other assets for Cornell.

Prior to working for Cornell, Jeremy founded the investment consulting firm Trusten Capital Management in Durham, North Carolina, where he worked for seven years as a consultant and portfolio manager. Before Trusten, he served as investment director of public equity for

Duke Management Company, which is responsible for investing Duke University's endowment and other assets. Crigler was part of a team responsible for managing $1.4 billion in assets.

Crigler earned his MBA at the Fuqua School of Business at Duke University. He is also a graduate of Tulane University's A.B. Freeman School of Business, where he earned an undergraduate degree in finance.

Q: *An interesting issue in the industry seems to be a move away from the "performance derby" of measuring institution endowment performance relative to a peer group, and a return to evaluating performance relative to what the institution needs from a budget standpoint. What are you seeing?*

Institutions are recognizing that they have different needs and that they operate under different circumstances. At Tulane we don't do peer group relative comparisons. We are aware of what other endowments are doing, which we think is appropriate, but we keep an eye on what our needs are first and foremost.

We will look at the list of universities that are in our size range— universities with between $500 million and $1.5 billion in assets. We also look at benchmarking from an admissions standpoint, competing schools that attract the same students that Tulane does—we know what other schools that our admitted students are also considering or opting for and use this as another data point.

The performance of our size peer group or academic peer group, then, is something in the background that we are keeping track of, but we don't base investment staff compensation on it.

How are you managing liquidity? Is this changing in the industry?

Like most institutions, we have to evaluate our unique situation to understand what our liquidity needs are. At Tulane, because of our geography, we keep a particular eye on hurricane season. When it comes along we may ramp up liquidity to provide a hedge against natural disasters.

Our liquidity needs also influence the way we may implement a given strategy. We hold the same asset allocation that we would regardless of our geography. However, our implementation within an asset class may make greater use of indexes and ETFs when possible.

These instruments have better liquidity—I can move in and out of them easily—and I don't have to disrupt relationships with our fund managers to free up capital. The disadvantage is that the return may be impaired slightly, but the liquidity benefits in some instances take precedence. This goes back to the benchmarking issue where our unique, seasonal liquidity needs may make it more difficult to compare us to a peer institution.

As I talk to other CIOs I get the impression that they are adding more liquidity to their approach right now as well. This lets them rebalance with greater frequency or add specific exposures or hedges that they feel they need in the short- to mid-term.

There was a "perfect storm" in 2008–2009 facing endowments—credit markets drying up, operating budgets more reliant on endowment income, private investments that once returned cash now making capital calls, and so on. How did you approach this?

We did just fine. Some of this was historical happenstance for the institution. The sophistication and complexity of the Tulane endowment picked up only in the last decade and so our commitment to illiquid private investments lagged the market to some extent. This was helpful in 2008 and 2009 because we didn't have the liquidity problems that some in the industry faced. We had fewer investments in illiquid private funds, and we had adequate liquidity on hand that we didn't need to go back to managers for redemptions.

At the moment we have an advantage. One of the results of the past 18 months is that private partnerships that were previously closed to us are opening up. Endowments with adequate liquidity are in a good position to enter selected private investments that may have been difficult to access in the past. We are evaluating these opportunities and are using this chance to selectively build and balance our portfolio. It is a nice opportunity to evaluate some high-quality private investments, even though it is the result of the unfortunate events of the past two years.

Another event that inadvertently helped was Hurricane Katrina. Buyout groups and private investments were rapidly increasing in popularity during the time that Tulane and the city of New Orleans were recovering from the devastation. This meant Tulane was focused on recovery and we were limiting our evaluation of new private investment opportunities. Although we didn't draw on the endowment for the recovery, the institution's risk profile was different during this time. The appetite for private investments was low. This meant, in turn, that we didn't have a lot of exposure to 2005, 2006, and 2007 vintage year hedge funds, private equity, and buyout groups.

Now, in a changed environment, we are gradually moving to a higher allocation for alternatives.

What makes for effective governance and interaction with investment committees? What is the impact on investment staff compensation and retention?

The dynamic between the investment committee and the investment staff is critical to the success of the institution overall. Each group has its appropriate role which is specific to that institution. The board must have a commitment to let the investment committee and staff make their respective decisions and hold each accountable for the results. This balance between the two will be the important issue in endowment governance going forward. Further complicating this balance is that in the past decade, some of the largest donors to academic institutions are hedge fund and private equity managers. As a result, they often become part of the investment committee that often oversees asset allocation as well as the investment staff.

Also, the tenure of the CIO and the success of the team's track record influences the interaction with the investment committee. CIOs with lengthy and successful track records have much more latitude to do innovative things in rapidly changing markets. If you have a successful 10-year track record with an institution, then you will not be as worried about your one- or two-year numbers because you have a successful history with the institution. This probably means that more tenured CIOs have the latitude in the current environment to take advantage of unique opportunities. The occasional one-year hiccups won't be looked at askance if you have a successful tenured investment team, which in turn changes the decision-making dynamic with the investment committee.

The current environment is particularly difficult for a CIO to position the portfolio. The tails of the distribution of outcomes appear to have gotten fatter. You don't know whether you will have inflation or deflation, or even stagflation. Positioning the portfolio for any specific outcome and being wrong can have dire consequences, which goes back to good communication and clear lines of authority between the CIO and the investment committee.

There seems to be an industry trend toward thematic investing over fixed asset allocations. Are endowments becoming more nimble and making investment decisions more frequently?

We try to be cognizant of macro factors in our decision making but not overly so. The increasing economic and market volatility means that you are reevaluating these factors more frequently, which means that we are probably more dynamic in the way that we rebalance the portfolio today than in past years.

Generally speaking, I think investment committees are granting wider latitude to endowments to move more quickly to play both defense and offense in this environment. It wouldn't be unheard of for us to have a material amount of the endowment, say 10 percent, in cash at any given time as we respond to an economic shift and are working to identify opportunities to put the money to work. I think we are now less wed to a tight adherence to our asset allocation targets. Of course, this varies by institution—some will still set precise asset allocation targets and then rebalance when things vary by as little as a few basis points.

The events of the past few years have resulted in more scrutiny of the endowment model. One of the things we have been able to do at Tulane is have some latitude around our targets for asset allocation. Our targets still drive our long-term thinking. We won't stray significantly from our asset allocation targets we have set as a long-term goal, but we believe it is important to be nimble over short periods.

Is this dynamic approach the new normal for endowment management?

I believe you have to be more flexible when the markets are moving this much. When volatility is high, as it was in 2008 and 2009, you have to react. But if the market volatility goes back down and stays consistently low, then I think the need dissipates. The more dynamic approach recently is a reaction to the rapid changes in the markets.

Over the longer term, there may be a more permanent move to an active approach. Part of it is the presence of new instruments for implementation. It has become easier to get exposure to a specific theme quickly using an ETF or some other instrument. This means that you can play both offense and defense without disrupting the long-term work you are doing with fund managers.

Also, we use ETFs as a placeholder for a given investment theme until we can find a manager we like. This lets us move on an idea sooner and takes some of the time pressure off the manager selection and diligence process. In other cases the amount we would want to allocate to a theme or idea may not reach the threshold that a manager requires, or the threshold for covering the effort of our own internal evaluation and selection process. Manager selection is a time-consuming and detailed process and you are generally entering a fund intending it to be a long-term relationship. The presence of these newer tools makes us more efficient on all these fronts.

How do you approach manager selection?

Clearly it is an important aspect of being a CIO. As I mentioned, after you select a manager you intend to stay with them for some time. The events of the past couple of years have been clarifying in some ways. You saw which managers did a good job managing their business and their team under stress. It was surprising to see how some alternative investment funds reacted to the downturn, and how they interacted and communicated with their investors and how they operated the business end. Managers in the alternative asset business can be brilliant investors but frequently not as effective at some of the other aspects that can be important to long-term success—staffing, operations, investor relations, communications, and so on.

In general, I believe fewer managers are better so long as you have the correct mix of assets overall. Now that we have low-cost, liquid alternatives to get exposure, it raises the bar on more permanent manager relationships that we select for the portfolio. We look closely at the stability of the team and the culture in the office because when things go bad we want to know how the manager will react, regardless of what the terms and conditions say.

In all, there is a lot more to hiring a manager than just evaluating returns. Endowments will likely be more selective going forward, look to fewer managers, and more closely evaluate qualitative factors. The downturn, combined with the emergence of reasonable marketable proxies for most asset classes, will put pressure on the manager selection process, raising the standard overall.

An example of how this plays out happened in early 2009. We wanted to start adding risk back to the portfolio in March and April. We focused on emerging markets as a theme. We implemented it by buying emerging market indexes and BRIC market ETFs. If we had waited to find a manager for each one of those countries, then it would have extended the process by weeks or months. Instead, we were able to add to our exposure at the rate we wanted.

Fast forward to late 2009 and most of our holdings were up considerably, and we decided to start reducing our exposure. The rate of change in the market was driving this. The traditional manager selection process is still appropriate for the long-haul asset allocation, but a more rapidly moving theme needs a different approach. Also remember that there is a fair amount of work that goes on after you have selected a manager—monitoring and meetings, so there is some overhead that goes with every one you add.

Another thing we look for in managers is a productive dialogue about what they are seeing in the market. Talking to them provides helpful input into our decision-making process. One thing we especially listen for is a manager with a contrarian view relative to market consensus. We like to understand why they are taking that view and what we can learn from it. Managers may have a varying approach to this, but reasonable ongoing access to them and their staff and good transparency are things we look for. A good manager relationship works in both directions. Managers are looking for clients that will be reasonable to work with. One thing that happened during the market downturn was that managers saw some panicked investors seeking redemptions. After things turned around again, some of those same investors wanted back in. We want to be sure we are invested with managers that are both open to dialogue and where our interests are aligned as much as possible.

Finally, Tulane, as a relatively smaller pool of money—compared to a large pension fund—is able to look at managers who have a unique strategy or view of the world. We don't have to put quite so much money to work in each transaction. Of course, looking at less well-known managers also means more careful due diligence and making sure the investment committee is comfortable with the trade-off.

What are you seeing as some of the trends in the coming near to mid-term?

Like everyone else, we are keeping our eye on is what is happening with inflation. There is a consensus right now that this first half of the year will be strong and the second half weak, eventually leading to inflation. We are looking at this, mainly because we are always wary when we see a consensus forming. One old saying about the market is that it will tend to do whatever it takes to hurt the most number of people at any given time. There is some truth to that and so we are cautious not to overcorrect even when conventional wisdom has coalesced. Nevertheless, it seems like we should be concerned about inflation and the dollar.

We believe that while the world economy is working its way out of the current situation, there will probably be a few panics and scares along the way. There seems to be a disconnect regarding the second half of the year while the VIX (market volatility index) continues to trend downward.

Overall, the probabilities at the tails of the distribution appear fatter and so there is a wider range of outcomes you have to anticipate and for which you need to have a portfolio strategy. This means that we are modeling potential portfolios under a wide variety of conditions—rampant inflation, mild inflation, a near-term recovery and a long-term recovery, and so on. Then we do a sensitivity analysis on how those portfolios perform when you are wrong and when you are right. The challenge is that the optimal portfolio is materially different under the different scenarios that we can picture. We have tough decisions to make about how much risk in either direction we want, and we will we be more biased toward defense or offense.

Another option in times of uncertainty is to try to hedge tail risk, and this has been tried in various ways over the years. In the 1990s Wall

Street was selling "portfolio protection" with mixed results. Hedging tail risk is a complex process and can be expensive. In the worst cases it can also be unpredictable or fail to produce the result you intended. Our evaluation includes comparing the cost and effort of insurance to simple things like keeping more liquidity. Cash can be a good asset class in highly uncertain environments.

Universities sometimes invest operating working capital along with the long-term endowment portfolio. What does Tulane do in this area?

I know other institutions do it, but we have not. The events of Hurricane Katrina underscore the importance of maintaining liquidity. Investing operating funds in the endowment is something we would only do if we were certain that we would not need the liquidity for an extended period. Tulane is a conservative institution and it is not something we are moving toward at the moment.

What is your position on using leverage in the portfolio?

We don't use leverage at the portfolio level and aren't planning to at the moment. We are exposed to leverage at the manager level, and it is dependent on the strategy. We aren't looking at heavily levered funds right now. I don't think leverage is good or bad on its own but think that it is dependent on what you are trying to accomplish and the portfolio needs.

We are aware of environmental leverage that reflects the balance sheets of companies in which you are invested. This isn't something that we attempt to compensate for at the portfolio level. We tend to look more at the aggregate level of net and gross exposure of our long-short equity managers, for example. If they all start raising their net exposure, then I start paying attention. This goes back to good manager transparency and dialog.

Are there some important break points in how endowments will be managed across various total asset sizes?

This is something I have seen, going from a relatively large endowment to Tulane, which is mid-sized. One difference is how complex your strategy can be and what tools you can use to implement that strategy. Larger funds can use more esoteric investments. They have the time and resources to perform the diligence and ongoing monitoring, and they can meet the minimums more easily without committing as much of the portfolio.

What lessons can individuals take away from what CIOs and endowments do?

There are a few lessons that individuals can learn from the endowment model. It is not necessarily specific implementation—what to invest in—but philosophical.

First, develop a good perspective on the relationship between risk and return. If an endowment has a year that is up 20 percent, and the historical return is 10 percent, then they know it was an exceptional year but not something they should expect to repeat. Individual investors can become overconfident and after an unusually good year will pour more money in instead of taking some gains. In 2009 someone might say "I did great—I bought gold when it was below $600," but my question would be when did you start trimming your position back. There is a tendency to add more to a position that has done well.

The reverse happens as well, where individuals have a bad year and either don't put additional cash to work or take money out. I think there was a lot of that in early 2009, in fact, and many people missed a significant rally in the second half of the year.

Endowments tend to sell their recent winners, looking for inexpensive assets with a lot of room to grow. When the market was down dramatically in 2008 and early 2009 we saw it as an opportunity and were looking for things to buy. When the market goes up materially over a short period we get concerned and start looking for vulnerabilities. In addition to being able to recognize what is happening, individuals have to manage their emotions—euphoria on the upside and depression when things are down.

On that front, I would recommend deciding what your basic asset allocation strategy is going to be and then try to stick with it. You shouldn't be reviewing your allocations overfrequently. Understanding what you want your portfolio to accomplish for you, knowing how much risk you are willing to take, and consistently putting money to work are all things an individual investor may want to consider.

What things are helpful to read?

I think it helps investors to be well read and to be well read outside of normal financial news. Everyone will, and should, read the top financial publications and keep track of the industry. Additionally, it is helpful and context-setting to read related history. So, if you are investing in China, then studying the history of China will be helpful in building a perspective.

I am also interested in what contrarians are saying. Managers who are currently out of favor or who are short-only may have interesting views. Look for disconfirming evidence so you can avoid the herd instinct.

In general I think being an avid consumer of a wide variety of inputs is an important part of being successful as an investor. I also think it is important to get a broad cross-section of input to ensure a good perspective. Furthermore, a diversity of opinion will help prevent falling prey to conventional wisdom.

Part IV

ADVISORS
AND MANAGERS

Chapter 14

Sandy Urie

President and Chief Executive Officer

Celia Dallas

Co-Director of Research and Managing Director

Cambridge Associates

"Cambridge has been in the investment consulting business with endowments since 1973."

Cambridge Associates

Cambridge Associates is a privately held independent firm that provides consulting and investment oversight services to more than 800 clients worldwide. Cambridge works with global institutional investors and private clients to achieve their investment objectives by offering advice grounded in intensive and independent research.

Cambridge Associates was formed in 1973 to provide investment research and consulting services to a group of major university endowments in the United States. The firm grew out of a project undertaken for Harvard University. Soon 11 other major university endowments asked Cambridge to provide research and recommendations. More than

35 years later, these 12 original clients still use the firm's extensive research and peer data.

Cambridge also serves foundations and other nonprofit clients. In the early 1980s, the firm expanded into the private client business. In the 1990s, the firm began developing an international presence, working with global institutional investors as well as large institutional investors beyond the nonprofit world. Over time, clients also included pensions, sovereign wealth funds, and other government funds. With more than 100 research reports published each year and a wealth of unmatched comparative peer data, the firm's global research provides the foundation for all client relationships at Cambridge Associates.

Some clients seek a sounding board to provide advice and insights into their decision-making processes. Others request an intensive partnership where the firm's investment staff provides day-to-day oversight of portfolio assets. Cambridge Associates' consulting approach provides any combination of services needed to properly execute an investment strategy. For clients seeking a complete investment solution, outsourcing provides the opportunity to delegate day-to-day oversight responsibility directly to Cambridge Associates, either on a discretionary or nondiscretionary basis.

For clients who wish to build direct alternative assets programs, focus on mission-related investing, improve their governance structure, or require other financial planning services, the firm's specialized expertise allows it to provide assistance for these important components of overall endowment oversight.

U.S. foundations and endowments have long been considered the most successful global institutional investors. Their early adoption of a diversified portfolio approach has led to enviable long-term risk-adjusted returns. Cambridge Associates is the leading investment consultant to these sophisticated investors. Today, the firm's clients' assets represent more than 70 percent of total U.S. higher education endowment assets and 40 percent of U.S. foundation assets.

Some clients have a full-time staff or an investment committee that is available to spend significant time on endowment oversight. In these cases, Cambridge Associates serves as a sounding board to the staff and committee, providing insights and advice to help them properly oversee the endowment's portfolio, tailoring the level of involvement based on client input, allowing them to benefit from its extensive resources in the way that best works for them.

Other clients have a strong CIO in place, but limited staff available to help the CIO implement and execute portfolio decisions. For these types of clients, the firm works closely with the CIO to serve as an extension of the investment office staff or as a fully integrated partner in endowment oversight. In these cases, the firm provides a more proactive "advisory" consulting approach that includes day-to-day oversight of the entire portfolio, including direct alternative asset programs, if needed. Cambridge operates from its principal locations in Boston and Arlington with other offices in Dallas, London, Menlo Park, Singapore, and Sydney.

S andy Urie is Cambridge Associates' president and chief executive officer and has been with the firm since 1985. Prior to assuming the CEO position, she was the chief operating officer with responsibility for directing the firm's consulting practice.

Prior to joining Cambridge Associates, she worked as a member of the faculty at Phillips Academy (Andover), where she taught Russian language and served on the Admissions Office staff. She also served on the school's development office staff where she had responsibility for capital fund raising and eventually assumed the position of associate secretary of the academy with responsibility for the school's annual giving and alumni programs.

Sandy is a member and vice-chair of the Investors' Committee of the Presidents' Working Group on Financial Markets, focusing on defining best practices in alternative assets, including due diligence and ongoing oversight. She currently serves on the board of advisors for the Yale School of Management, the board of overseers of the DeCordova Museum, the board of visitors of the New England Baptist Hospital, and the board of 100 Women in Hedge Funds. Sandy also currently serves on the boards of The Plymouth Rock Company and Homesite Group Incorporated. She formerly served on the boards of Phillips Academy, Belmont Day School, and Buckingham, Browne & Nichols School. Sandy was an honoree at the 2005 "Women Who Make a Difference" award ceremony, hosted annually by the National Council for Research on Women.

Sandy graduated from Stanford University and received an MPPM degree from the Yale School of Organization and Management. She has earned the Chartered Financial Analyst designation

Celia Dallas is the co-director of research and a managing director at Cambridge Associates. Celia oversees the firm's published research, and she is responsible for establishing the firm's view on asset allocation in the current environment and for editing and providing guidance to the various authors of the research reports produced by the firm. Celia specializes in topics involving capital markets and investment planning and has authored a variety of research reports throughout her tenure with the firm. In addition to her research responsibilities, she frequently leads discussions at the firm's client roundtables.

Before Celia joined Cambridge Associates, she was a consultant for Harlan Brown & Co., a competitive intelligence consulting firm. In this position, she researched, wrote, and presented market analysis commissioned by Fortune 500 clients on a variety of consumer and industrial products. She also worked for the Employee Benefit Research Institute (EBRI), where she conducted research and wrote reports on retirement income security issues.

Celia graduated from the University of Pennsylvania and received an MBA from the Darden Graduate School of Business Administration at the University of Virginia.

Q: Cambridge has come up repeatedly in our research as a leading advisor and provider of research and services to endowments and foundations. Can you tell us a little about the firm and your approach?

Cambridge has been in the investment consulting business with endowments since 1973. We started as the external research arm for a consortium of major university endowments in the United States. Our first clients were many of the leading academic institutions such as Harvard and Yale. The idea was that by combining efforts they could achieve economies of scale in research and evaluation. They all needed to cover the markets and the managers, which created a lot of redundant activity and expense in each endowment. Cambridge was launched to provide the shared research platform off which each investment staff could then develop a customized approach to investment planning, implementation, and oversight of their assets. During the firm's formation period we had 12 institutions join as clients and they are all still clients to this day.

While we have a wider range of services today, the original core activities of the firm remain an important part of what we do for clients. We have significant and expansive research capability at the firm that truly covers the world. When we started in 1973 we were only looking at U.S. public equities and bonds but quickly expanded our research coverage to include just about anything one could invest in across the globe. We have over 200 college and university endowments as clients worldwide, making our client base international. On average, our academic endowment clients have been with us for 14 years. This means that we have considerable experience in what works for endowments and what the best practices are in this space, in addition to a historical understanding of how they have evolved over time. Our clients were among the first to invest in alternatives such as venture capital and hedge funds and to engage in global investing, and we helped take them into those investments working side by side with their investment committees and their professional staffs.

After our successful launch as a research organization, we began to consult from the platform we had developed. The way that we deliver and customize our research to clients is an important part of our consulting services that is instrumental in helping them implement tailored policies based on their specific situation. Increasingly we have moved into the outsourced space where clients have asked us to serve as their investment office or as a very engaged partner to their investment office.

Today we have a continuum of services ranging from primarily research, to an array of traditional investment consulting services, to a complete outsourced investment office function. This flexibility allows us to work with each client according to their need. We have over 800 clients that include academic endowments, foundations, sovereign wealth funds, pension funds, and other investment pools. We also have a private client base. Our clients are in 26 different countries. For about one-quarter of our clients we provide full portfolio investment outsourcing services.

Our client base is diverse across investment type—endowments, foundations, private funds—and across geographies.

You have a diverse client base that includes not only endowments, but foundations, pensions, and private wealth as well. What are some of the key differences that you see between these entities?

Different types of entities operate under very different constraints given the liabilities that they need to support, the nature of these liabilities (e.g., the degree to which they are fixed or variable), the availability of income sources and financial resources outside of the endowment (or main asset pool) to meet cash needs, and investment time horizons. For instance, U.S. foundations have a required payout rate of 5 percent of endowment value each year, and so their liquidity requirements may be different, since they have limited flexibility to lower the payout in a given year when compared to most colleges or universities. Many foundations like other perpetual endowments typically want to preserve their purchasing power into perpetuity. This is quite difficult to do when keeping up a relatively high payout on a consistent basis. Just as there are differences in investment considerations across investor types, there are also significant differentiating characteristics among investors within an investor group such that any given investment pool will be laboring under very specific constraints.

Will endowments start operating more like foundations or pensions with defined payout, given some of the liquidity issues of the past year?

Perhaps, but the liquidity issues have not been as significant as you might think. We completed an extensive look at this topic late in 2008 with our own nonprofit and academic endowment clients and interviewed a material percentage of them. Roughly 90 percent of them were not dealing with any of the liquidity issues of the type that were so widely reported in the press. A few large, high-profile, and well-publicized cases may have created the impression that this was a more widespread issue than it is. The publicity certainly gets everyone talking and thinking more about issues regarding liquidity. This was already on the radar for most before the credit crisis, but concerns and discussions accelerated as the magnitude and duration of liquidity constraints were more severe than most imagined. Thoughtful investors have been developing means to evaluate risk from multiple dimensions, including illiquidity risk, and looking at asset allocation with an eye to risk diversification, rather than focusing on maximizing return for a certain level of volatility risk. It is not just the college and university endowments that are looking at this, but all types of sophisticated investors.

Peer comparison has been a common theme in our conversations with investment professionals. Can you elaborate your views on benchmarking and what time period one should consider when looking at total performance?

This is a good question, but cannot be answered without considering another question: What are you trying to understand by looking at the comparison? If you are trying to understand the performance of one institution relative to another, you really need a long time horizon, the longer the better to allow at least a full investment cycle, if not multiple investment cycles. Further, the main reason we are given for adopting peer comparison is to understand the degree to which institutions that compete against one another for students, faculty, research grants, and the like have a competitive advantage because their endowment can provide more support to the operating budget. This question requires a long time horizon (e.g., at least 10 years) to evaluate. Naturally, this is not practical as other things intrude—for instance, the tenure of investment professionals and individuals on an investment committee can be much shorter than that. From a practical perspective, three to five years is a reasonable time horizon for peer comparisons. Such a time horizon is consistent with typical endowment value averages used in spending rules and is also somewhat comparable to typical market cycles. While it is useful for institutions, particularly those in direct competition with one another, to know how their endowment's performance compares, this question is less relevant to foundations and other endowed institutions. We are hopeful that the current environment will provide an opportunity to reduce such comparisons because we do not think it is generally as productive to focus on peer comparisons as it is to evaluate the specific objectives for the institution—answering questions such as how do I meet the financial goals of my institution. Such specifics include understanding how much risk the institution should be taking, what are the institution's liquidity requirements, staffing levels, and return goals, which in turn affects their volatility and performance in a given short period of time.

Endowments may seem similar on the outside, but because they are subject to a wide variety of factors such as the amount of the institution's operating budget they are expected to support, the amount of new giving coming into the endowment, maturity of their alternative asset allocation, culture of the institution, composition of the investment committee, investment goals of the institution, it turns out that the "right" strategy for a given endowment can be very different to that of a superficially similar peer.

Incentive compensation that is tied to peer performance can be quite dangerous, as it provides investment professionals with incentives to focus on the short term and to leverage the portfolio, even if this is detrimental over the long term. Investment fiduciaries should do some careful and strategic thinking about whether compensation should be based on peer comparisons, and if so, who are the appropriate peers and what are reasonable time frames? If the investment opportunities available to "peers" are different from those available to the specific institution, and if the risk tolerance of "peers" is not comparable, then the benchmark is not particularly relevant and may encourage more risk-taking than is appropriate. Benchmarks should reflect an investible opportunity set. As such, these benchmarks suffer at the outset, as investors do not know peers' asset allocations in any detail on a real-time basis and cannot replicate such investments *ex ante*.

What dictates your investment actions most—your asset class allocations or macroeconomic trends?

Recently, investors have been very focused on macroeconomics trends. Historically, endowments have focused on maintaining strategic policy allocations to a range of asset classes. Within this context, many have been nimble in shifting across asset classes or making bets within asset classes in order to enhance returns, typically driven by relative valuations. The idea of having mid- to long-term macroeconomic trends play a more prominent role in investing is new to most investors. In the last couple of years, for obvious reasons, the macro environment has been playing a much more significant role than it previously has. However, we have long advocated that investors maintain relatively stable policy allocation targets to exposures designed to protect equity-dominated portfolios against macroeconomic risks, particularly unexpected inflation and malign deflation, as such risks historically have been devastating to equities. In other words, we consider the need to hedge against macroeconomic risks when establishing a strategic asset allocation plan. We are not willing to structure portfolios too biased to any one macroeconomic view, as it is essential to consider the consequences if you should be wrong.

Another element that is influencing this is that the lines across traditional asset classes have blurred somewhat. For example, hedge funds have side pockets and they have private investments. If you are thinking that distressed is a good place to be, then you can implement that in your long-only portfolio, you can implement that in your hedge fund portfolio, you can implement it in your nonmarketable portfolio. So then the question is where is the best place to implement this strategy and it may be across all three. So, we think there are changes that have occurred across the asset classes that have influenced how people think about implementation. A much higher premium has been placed on implementation in the past 5–10 years as opposed to just strictly thinking that it is all about asset allocation.

How do you conduct manager selection? Is it important to establish and maintain manager relationships in order to preserve access to successive funds over time?

On this notion of wanting to preserve relationships with managers to get into the next great fund—we think investors should be exceptionally selective in doing this and have spent a good bit of time working on how we can help our clients build relationships with managers that balance the needs of general partners and limited partners.

Over the last couple of decades, as hedge fund, venture capital, and private equity asset managers have experienced periods of strong performance, terms and fees have moved significantly in favor of general partners (managers). When the market crashed in 2008, in our view, it provided an opportunity to take a step back and think about what the right balance is on terms and fees. We believe that striking the right balance really benefits both the general and limited partners (manager and clients). However, in order to make this change, limited partners need to communicate more with each other and with general partners to determine what changes are feasible and most desirable and must also be prepared to walk away from an investment opportunity if they don't believe that the terms and fees are fair. We have written a research paper on various terms and conditions that should be considered when evaluating investments in limited partnerships of all sorts. It takes a tremendous amount of work to build up good relationships with managers. Institutions just need to be selective in this process—some managers absolutely have a track record that justifies their fees and we believe in their ability to continue to be a valuable partner. Our view is that when market conditions for a particular strategy in alternatives becomes less attractive, then the institution has to be extremely selective in which managers they will re-sign, and they should pay close attention to the terms. This is particularly true for managers with long lock-up periods—you should be compensated by higher returns for the illiquidity net of fees on a risk-adjusted basis.

On manager selection more broadly, we always start with the basic question: Is there a way to passively invest in this market and if there is, that should be the default position. If one can invest easily and cheaply, then there is no reason to invest with an active manager unless a compelling case can be made that the manager can add value, net of fees, on a risk-adjusted basis. Just as important is the qualitative manager analysis—understanding their process, staff, back office, controls, and how their strategies are expected to perform under a variety of conditions and time horizons.

Qualitative concepts like "trustworthiness" come up a lot when investment professionals talk about manager selection, especially in this environment.

That has been a fundamental part of our manager evaluation. It is important, and especially so for some strategies like hedge funds where it is more difficult to monitor what they are doing on a real-time basis. They move positions frequently and the result is delayed transparency.

This really goes back to our fundamental belief that you need to know what the investment really is and how the manager will be generating returns. Simply put, if we can't understand what someone is doing, then we don't want to be invested. This sort of screening has served us well over time and has helped avoid situations with managers where they drift from their intent and do something different than proposed and you don't necessarily know due to transparency issues.

How do you feel about returns from leverage in investments? Investment professionals are often leery of managers who generate returns from leverage because they feel that if a material part of the return is from leverage, then they could use leverage directly to get the same returns, with higher liquidity or no lock-up and no layer of fees.

We agree with this. We don't want to invest with managers who rely mostly on leverage to generate returns. It is simple to replicate, and you don't want to pay the fees for this type of investment, and the current environment isn't really a good one for it anyway.

How do you understand where managers are using leverage so you can monitor it?

It takes work to understand it, and you also have to put it in context of what is happening in the market and in business overall. There are periods, for example 2002–2007, where leverage was pervasive—it rose across all industries and capital markets in general—corporations increased their balance sheet leverage, we saw it in real estate, we saw it in buyout activity, and we certainly saw it in managers that already used leverage. In cases where it is generally rising, you may not be able to do anything about the investments you have already made because you are locked up. However, if you are concerned about it, you can make other moves in your overall portfolio that will hedge the risk you see due to changes in leverage.

Much of this gets dealt with as part of the manager selection process. When you understand how a manager is going to use leverage, it would be unusual for them to suddenly take a dramatically different approach after you have made the investment. Hedge funds in particular have to be evaluated periodically, usually using quarterly information, because of all asset classes they may change their approach to leverage the most. When they are going to be applying large amounts of leverage as part of their style you will usually know it. The management of leverage is done through manager selection and ongoing oversight.

What are the global economic trends that you are following at macro level?

Many of the same influences you indicated that other investment professionals are concerned with: deflation in the near term, inflation longer term, a weaker dollar, the search for investments that will benefit from the development of a domestic demand, particularly in emerging markets, changes in commodity costs. We are also closely watching the potential for asset bubbles, as stimulus may continue to push financial markets higher, as well as the potential for economic growth to stagnate as governments and central banks begin their "exit strategy." Finally, like others, we are closely watching supply and demand dynamics regarding sovereign bonds, particularly across major developed markets, as supply increases, while the source of demand growth is far from certain.

These are converging themes in the endowment CIO community. Is there a risk if everyone is concerned with the same trends?

It is not concerning that people are worried about the same thing—the question is what are they doing about it? Are they moving their portfolios in the same way based on their conclusions? For instance, there seems to be high consensus that inflation is inevitable. The timing is uncertain, although, if you look at what is priced into the bond market and the swaps markets today, it is pretty clear they are pricing in relatively low inflation in the coming few years, and roughly average historical inflation rates for the five years after that. We continue to watch what the markets are pricing in, as inflation expectations do not match the heightened inflationary concerns we see in much of the commentary we read.

We happen to agree with the view that deflation is more of a concern today; inflation the larger risk for tomorrow. While we regard inflation as likely to increase down the road, we recognize that it is possible this won't happen. For example, the experience of Japan over the last couple

of decades provides a clear example of an economy that continued to experience economic stagnation even after significant monetary expansion
and stimulus. Investors that position portfolios for a specific scenario,
such as a bout of unexpected inflation, without considering the potential for continued deflationary pressure may find they are unprepared
should their view prove incorrect.

Further, as investors respond to the same macroeconomic views,
they can drive up the prices of securities beyond their fundamental
values. In such cases, regardless of the attractiveness of an investment,
valuations matter. For example, while we continue to believe in the
long-term secular case for many emerging markets, we believe investors
should move slowly into this area today given their significant and rapid
appreciation.

Two of the most important principles of endowment management
are not overcommitting to a trend and having too many "eggs" in one
basket, and to think through "what if we are wrong?" You don't want
to position a portfolio too dramatically based on your forecast if the
outcome would be unacceptable if you are wrong.

What is the break point in assets under management where the economies of scale start influencing ability to afford staff, gain access to managers, and achieve higher returns?

These are big-picture governance issues and there is not necessarily a
single rule of thumb for this. The marketplace often cites that when
assets exceed $750 million to $1 billion that a fully staffed investment
office is feasible. That said, we have seen some smaller sized endowments
build very credible internal organizations as well as multibillion-dollar
pools decide to outsource their investment oversight. Institutions need
to be self-reflective on what they can accomplish with the three potential
parties at the table: the investment committee, the internal professional
investment staff, and the outside advisor. They must realistically assess
what is the talent pool they can access and retain, what is the con-
tribution of the investment committee, and what components do they
need an outside advisor to bring. In cases where the investment professionals and the committee believe that scale economies are missing,
they can bring in consulting firms like Cambridge to cover that gap and

complement their in-house skills. The outside advisory relationship can take a number of forms, depending on what the institution needs. A more well-staffed endowment may choose a research-oriented advisory relationship, whereas an endowment with limited staff may elect to outsource the investment decision making. In our opinion, the appropriate solution cannot simply be boiled down to a break point in assets under management.

There is considerable expertise, bandwidth, and tools required to be effective as an individual or institution in this space.

There are definitely important economies of scale in portfolio management and that is why outsourced investment houses have seen good growth in recent years. A number of institutions have looked at their own situation and decided that there is a good middle ground that exists between full outsourcing of the endowment management and no assistance at all. This lets them still maintain considerable control and maintain relationships with the fund managers directly, while also having a tightly engaged and capable external partner helping.

There is no question that in order to do this well, human and financial resources are required in order to emulate the endowment strategies that have been successful. We also want to reemphasize that it is not always appropriate to do this. It really comes back to the unique situation of the institution, and each one may make materially different decisions based on their needs and culture. The same thing is true for the individual investor.

Cambridge has been in business for a long time and, as an institution, has seen the markets and global economy under a wide variety of conditions, including numerous downturns. What is your take on the events of 2008–2009? Do you believe that it was just another downturn or that something fundamental has changed? What lessons should we have learned from 2008–2009?

This is an important question and something our clients are asking as well. First, were the events of 2008–2009 unprecedented? If you look at the wide scope of history, no. If you look at the last couple of decades, then yes. The period from 1982 through 2000, or even 2007 (both years that we see as inflection points for different reasons), was largely a period of stable economic growth, low inflation, falling interest rates, and expanding credit. All of these conditions are positive for financial assets broadly, creating a disinflationary "economic boom" environment. It's just part of a broader cycle of boom and bust, but this boom lasted longer than is typical without a real bust.

What happened starting in 2007, from our perspective, was we reached the point where the low-cost, easy-to-access leverage that investors, households, and corporations had come to take for granted simply became more constrained and expensive. Credit could no longer be used as a replacement for savings. We can't expect that corporations and consumers will continue to want to lever up, either. The effects of deleveraging should be felt for an extended period of time. Just as it took decades for consumers to expand their debt, we believe it will take a long time to delever. In 2008–2009 public sector spending has primarily offset private sector saving, but has left the U.S. government (and many other governments, particularly the United Kingdom and parts of Europe) with a significant debt burden.

Normally, economic recovery takes root when interest rates come down and encourage the corporate sector to borrow and households to spend down savings. This has not occurred in developed economies today. Easy-to-access, inexpensive debt has been harder to find. At the same time, consumers, corporations, and banks have been more focused on stabilizing their balance sheets. Not only is there less credit available, there is less demand for credit. This has obvious implications for economic growth prospects, as U.S. consumers have accounted for about two-thirds of U.S. GDP growth and nearly 20 percent of global GDP growth. Of course, this can change as emerging market economies seek to build a domestic consumer base, but this adjustment cannot occur easily or quickly. While everyone would like for this global rebalancing to be something that changes overnight, it seems likely that it will take years.

So, it is important to consider that the economic backdrop will not be as favorable as it has been in the past and that investors can't just always expect this huge tailwind at their backs where it is easy to make money. It will be harder to preserve wealth and still spend at the levels that institutions have previously enjoyed.

We can't, however, just throw out everything we have known. While it is sensible to consider if various models or theories are "dead," and we have been examining these issues closely over the last couple of years in particular, it is not constructive to throw everything we know about modern portfolio theory out the window. The important thing to remember here is that models and frameworks serve their purpose of informing decisions and, if used with a critical eye to aid evaluation, rather than to find the answer, they are going to continue to be relevant. Model results are only as good as the assumptions that go into them and we have always known that the assumptions are flawed. A clear lesson learned by some in the recent environment is not to rely exclusively on models and not to assume that the future will look like history, particularly when based on short periods of data. Asking "what could be different this time" and "what has happened under different conditions historically" will help in using the models properly. Age-old best practices like stress testing portfolios are practices that will help institutions.

Other key lessons learned—there is a lot more attention being paid to liquidity. Some clients with higher allocations to nonmarketable alternative investments have been making sure that they have adequate liquidity, at times creating a reserve of cash. A lot more double checking is going on here to make sure that clients understand their liquidity position.

Further, diversification, or rather, true diversification is very important. There are very few investments that have a fundamentally different basis of return. Having such investments in a portfolio is important in protecting against fat-tail risks. Having some allocation to sovereign bonds, for example, was particularly helpful in 2008. While diversification across different types of equities and risk assets provided limited benefit during 2008–early 2009, investors should not take away that such diversification is not important. Rather, the lesson learned here is that when a common factor causes all assets to rise together, as was the case in 2003–2007 when cheap financing bid up the price of all risk assets to very overvalued levels, diversification should not be expected to work when the tide turns. This factor also reinforces the benefits of valuation analysis. Valuations do matter.

Finally, investors have learned that there are many sorts of risk, other than volatility, which are important to understand and measure, and seek to manage. An increasing number of institutions are taking a multidimensional approach to evaluating portfolio risk.

Is cash something that endowments are now considering an asset? In the past there was low interest in holding very much cash.

Investors should continue to consider the opportunity cost of holding cash and the degree to which they really need additional liquidity, as investments other than cash can be very liquid even during periods of stress. Still, in the current environment we have recommended that clients hold more cash than normal as "dry powder" to facilitate investing in good values as they materialize, particularly in distressed investments.

What can individuals look to learn from endowment investing principles?

As much as there are differences between colleges and universities, it geometrically expands once you get to individuals and their families. All the things that make each endowment unique are even more so with private wealth, and furthermore the individual is not only the fiduciary of the investment, they are the owner of it. They have come into possession of the assets in different ways—some created it, some inherited it. This diversity of interests means that they do not all necessarily aim to emulate what endowments do. They are interested in what endowments are doing, they would like to learn from it, but their viewpoint is more focused on implementation than asset allocation. For instance, many private clients that are taxable have a large allocation to municipal bonds. When they look at their bond portfolio they are not thinking of deflation hedging but instead what that allocation should be and how to structure things relative to their taxes. Most high-net-worth individual investors we work with are not necessarily driven by their tax strategy, but they are aware of it and they should be. There are some hedge strategies that are not tax-friendly and therefore may not be suitable for the private investor.

What is in common is that you start in the same place with the individual that you do with the institution: understanding the unique characteristics of their situation. For a private investor, it is things like what is their anticipated spending—do they want this to be a wealth-preservation pool or a wealth-creation pool? What are their philanthropic interests? How many beneficiaries do they have? The answers to these questions will lead to very different allocations. Because of these differences, directly taking a template from an endowment environment and placing it over any individual is not a sensible thing to do.

This has been controversial. Is it helpful at least philosophically?

There are process issues that they can at least be mindful of. Engaging in a disciplined process for the management of their assets can be good, and not reacting to the momentum of the moment but to instead create a roadmap for how they want to manage their assets, and to stick to it and not be swayed by the noise that is out there. The process pieces are the things that are transferable. The asset allocation or implementation issues will be quite different.

The individual can ask the same sorts of questions of a variety of advisors and the responses will be illuminating. You don't invest in different strategies that have a lot of dispersion across returns, like private equity, for example, just to get the average return or a bottom-quartile return, because you won't be compensated for the extra risk you are taking—operations risk, more leverage, more liquidity risk. Instead, think through what advisors and managers and funds you might have access to and what that means for your approach. Endowments that have identified their core competency as finding alpha, for example, have sought out active managers they believe are best positioned to succeed in this effort and have therefore tended to have high allocations to equity managers in illiquid and/or inefficient markets and hedge funds. This might be inappropriate for the small-net-worth individual who just can't get access to the funds and can't find the managers who can help them.

Chapter 15

Lyn Hutton

Chief Investment Officer

Commonfund

"What individuals . . . can learn from nonprofit and long-term investors is a philosophical approach."

Commonfund

Founded in 1971, Commonfund is devoted to enhancing the financial resources of educational and other nonprofit institutions, through fund management, investment advice, and treasury operations.

Commonfund manages approximately $26 billion in long-term and endowment investment assets for more than 1,500 educational institutions, foundations, health-care and other nonprofit institutions. This is one of the largest pools of educational endowment funds in the world. The firm employs a full-time staff of more than 240, including over 80 investment professionals.

Commonfund has a balance of large and small nonprofits—they serve 72 of the largest endowments in the United States, while one-third of their clients have assets under $100 million. Commonfund offers these clients more than 30 different investment programs.

The firm is located in Connecticut, with offices in Los Angeles and London.

L yn Hutton joined Commonfund in 2003 as chief investment officer. She has oversight responsibility for all aspects of invest- ment strategy, portfolio management, manager due diligence, and selection for all of the organization's investment funds, as well as non-investment programs and services.

Before joining the firm, Lyn served as the vice president and chief financial officer of the John D. and Catherine T. MacArthur Foundation since June 1998. She was responsible for the financial administration of the foundation and for management of the foundation's (then) $4.0 billion investment portfolio.

Prior to MacArthur, Lyn served at Dartmouth College as vice president and treasurer, handling its investments and treasury, budgeting and planning, the controller's office, internal audit, administrative services, facilities operations, and human resources. She was also senior vice president, administration and treasurer for the University of Southern California.

Lyn is a Chartered Financial Analyst and was a Certified Public Accountant (currently nonpracticing) and a member of the CFA Institute. She serves on several boards, including the MSCI/Barra Editorial Advisory Board, and has been a trustee for Commonfund, Commonfund Realty, and Commonfund Capital. She is an alumna of the University of Southern California and graduated with honors from USC School of Business Administration. In 2010 she was awarded Institutional Investor's investor lifetime achievement award.

Q: How did you become involved in institutional investing?

My involvement with Commonfund and nonprofit investment management goes back to the late 1970s and began when I was the Treasurer of the University of Southern California and, subsequently, its executive VP for administration and finance. I served in similar capacities at Dartmouth and the MacArthur Foundation prior to joining Commonfund. Both USC and Dartmouth were investors with Commonfund. I was chair of the board of Commonfund when I was still at USC and was asked to come on board as CIO at Commonfund while I was at MacArthur Foundation.

Tell us a little about the history of Commonfund.

Commonfund was founded in 1971 to serve educational nonprofits, and is itself a nonprofit corporation. Commonfund's beginning was the result of a project by the Ford Foundation initiated by George McBundy in the 1960s. There is a lengthy history here, but to sum up as simply as possible—at that time, gifts to most educational endowments were given as a separate trust with the income to be used to support the purpose of the gift, be it a scholarship or in support of a specific program, in perpetuity. The idea was that the institution would sustain itself from income from that trust. In the 1700s and through the 1900s endowments could only spend the income (yield) in support of the named purpose and the corpus was not to be touched. The recipient institution couldn't commingle these individual trusts for investment purposes, meaning that the institution couldn't manage the assets in the aggregate. These constraints generally meant that the trusts were invested to generate current income for spending and not for total return.

What came out of the Ford Foundation study was a number of important new ideas about nonprofit institutional money management. First, was the notion of separating spending policy from investment policy to allow for total return investing. The Ford Foundation studies showed that educational endowments should do this by having a "spending rule" so that they could reduce the volatility of income in their operating budgets due to changing interest rates and dividends, and allow for total return; in sum, educational institutions should be indifferent to spending from income or capital gains. Second was the idea that institutions really needed economies of scale to access the best managers and achieve the best investment results to support the mission of the institution to which the gift had been given, which meant commingling of investment assets. Third was the idea that these very long horizon investors—these perpetual pools—really should have an equity bias for the long term to preserve purchasing power. There were two direct outcomes of the Ford Foundation's work: the Uniform

Management of Institutional Funds Act, which allowed for the commingling of separate trusts and a total return objective, and a grant that
started Commonfund, which provided for the benefits of scale, allowed
for professional management, and gave smaller institutions access to funds
and fee structures they could not get on their own. Interestingly, many
of the early Commonfund participants were some of the larger endowments. Commonfund was established as a nonprofit, with the mission
of helping educational nonprofits manage their financial resources. We
also have an educational mission to identify and promote best practices
for endowment management in addition to offering investment management services. Commonfund established the original "outsourced
CIO" model, and today we help clients with everything from designing
their investment policy, asset allocation, governance, helping them think
through spending and distribution policy, liquidity management, working with donors, rebalancing their portfolio, manager due-diligence and
risk management.

How did things develop from educational nonprofits to other types of nonprofits that needed investment management services?

As we were having success with educational endowments, other institutions in the nonprofit community asked to be part of what we were
doing. Starting in the 1980s we began taking our investment strategies beyond traditional long-only marketable securities (publicly traded
global equities and fixed income). We moved into marketable alternative investments in 1982, real estate, private equity, venture capital and
natural resources in 1988, and distressed debt investing in 1989. We kept
expanding areas of the capital markets in which we worked. This led to
investment successes that were attractive to other nonprofits that were
looking for improved returns but did not have the budget or the resources
it takes to run their investment pools, especially in alternatives. We built
our suite of investment funds and services in response to demand.

What is the asset base at which an endowment can consider having their own investment management office?

We see it as different for different types of non-profits—educational
endowments versus private foundations, for example.

For a foundation, the number is higher—about $3 billion. For an educational institution, it is probably somewhere between $2.5 and $3 billion. Educational endowments are different because the investment office gets used in many different ways, and therefore can justify an allocation of more resources. In this environment the internal investment team often provides other finance-related services for an educational endowment—things like managing overall university finances.

For example, at Dartmouth the investment office also managed the debt portfolio—the liability side of the balance sheet—and banking relations. The office also did operational financial planning and execution for the university. Dartmouth has its own heating plant and water/utility infrastructure. For example, the investment office hedged commodity price changes to manage budget risk. These types of activities provide some staff cost absorption and incremental benefits that allow an institutional endowment to have resources to deploy in support of the mission.

In a foundation, there just aren't enough additional finance activities to provide the cost absorption and so the cost burden on the managed investment pool is higher. In addition to the cost of recruiting and retaining a sufficient number of qualified people, there are other fixed costs to an investment management office as well—for example, over head charges, risk management systems, and office space—so scale is important.

There are a few other important differences. Foundations are subject to excise taxes while endowments are not. Foundations do not get to count investment expenses toward their mandatory IRS distribution requirements. And, private foundations have no new contributions or frictional cash flow. At a private foundation, every payroll, every grant, every capital call and every portfolio rebalancing decision requires a "sell decision"—there are no "new money buys" to rebalance the portfolio or take advantage of new opportunities. An academic endowment, depending on restrictions, has a different set of circumstances—no excise taxes, no mandatory distributions, and additional sources of funds (new money coming in). Furthermore, an educational endowment can offset the office and management expenses against distributions. In all, this makes the liquidity requirements for foundations higher and it gives academic endowments more latitude.

What is your thinking on university finance offices using the endowment office to also manage working capital?

From an operational standpoint, many institutions separate the working capital accounts and outsource the management of the long-term investment pool or endowment separately. It is easier for the institution to outsource the endowment investment management, due to the nature of the activities. Within the institution, the working capital management may even fall to a different part of the finance organization than the investment office. There are also differences between public or state-run universities and private universities. In particular, public universities may have policies that affect how they can manage working capital that are implemented by the state legislature or state treasurer.

I think that the financial events of 2008–2009 have changed how this approach to working capital management will work in the future. Before the crisis, many universities took their excess working capital, what was really their liquidity buffer, and invested those funds alongside the endowment funds. When the 2008 financial crisis struck, their long-term and working capital accounts simultaneously took a 20, 25, or even 30 percent hit. This had a tremendous impact on their liquidity. Not only were they challenged to meet their operating budget commitments to the university from the long-term endowment funds, their operating cash had been materially diminished as well. Some institutions had been very aggressive in their working capital management—they had given what was thought to be an excess of liquidity to the investment office in pursuit of additional returns and got whipsawed.

The trend now is for the investment office to work very closely with the finance area in managing working capital to ensure a consistent liquidity strategy and implementation approach, but the pools of money aren't managed the same way. Colleges and universities don't want the endowment investment professionals worrying about how overnight working capital deposits are invested.

Endowments have been rethinking their approach to liquidity in the past year. What is driving this?

The events of 2007–2009 have pointed out the importance of clearly defining what the appropriate role of the endowment is in the institution's capital structure. Now we have a new stress test for long term investment pools as well as for the balance sheets of many nonprofits, especially educational institutions. Why was there a liquidity problem for endowments? It wasn't just the public markets and the declining value of their endowment assets. In 2007 many educational nonprofits experienced what is called "the auction rate problem." Many nonprofits on the liability side of their balance sheet, got hammered. They couldn't roll their debt. The swap rates were incredible. The amount of variable rate debt on their balance sheet really hurt them. At the same time, many banks were exiting the student loan market, and the schools were left providing the financing for their students. This also had an enormous impact on their working capital requirements.

Furthermore, there were institutions that had their working capital lines of credit eliminated or diminished without warning. The debt market, even beyond the auction rate market, shut down for them and they had no access to debt capital.

The events of the past two years have had a profound impact on educational institutions that goes beyond negative returns in their long-term endowment accounts. The intersection of troubled credit markets for the institution and students, the aggressive management of working capital, the allocation to illiquid alternative investments with long lock-ups, and the losses in the endowments themselves combined in way that made for a particularly difficult environment. I think there is a fundamental change in the way many endowments will be thinking about liquidity requirements going forward. The evaluation of liquidity will not just be for the endowment but for the institution as whole. They will be asking things like: What will the tiers of liquidity be? What will be core assets versus near-term liquid assets? How should we prearrange our credit lines for backup access to working capital?

For individuals there may be a few lessons learned from the liquidity crisis; for example, doing a clinical evaluation of what your net worth is and what your personal balance sheet looks like. For personal liquidity it is important to know what your risk tolerance is. Do you really want to chase yield with your liquidity bucket or are you better off taking the risk someplace else? Some individuals are beginning to "barbell" their liquidity and risk. They divide their assets into very high- and very low-risk pools. In the high-risk pool, they take as much illiquidity premium and risk as they can, because that's where the returns are. On the other end they have a large pool of very safe, low-risk, low-return assets. What this looks like in implementation could be a large pool of Treasuries and a smaller pool invested in illiquid investments such as real estate, venture capital and private equity, or other opportunistic or distressed investments. The risk pool may have some amount in cash at any given time to aggressively provide dry powder to go after high risk/high return opportunities as they appear.

Is the endowment investment model evolving? What has changed in response to the latest market downturn?

We seem to be in an environment where "what is old is new again." Remember that endowments are, in substance, perpetual pools of assets—the ultimate long-term investor. An endowment is a gift or bequest of money or property that carries the stipulation that the gift be invested and the principal remain intact in perpetuity. By definition, endowments are designed to be as enduring as the institution and the purposes they support. The endowment model trend we are seeing is a return to the ideas that were important early in my career. The important driver of modern endowment investment policy has been the notion of intergenerational equity, the idea that once you separated investment policy from spending policy, you invested as much as you could into ownership assets—own not loan—to achieve growth and preserve purchasing power. As an endowment, you wanted the benefits from owning assets—meaning owning the means of production if it is a company, owning the rents if a real estate asset. Then, as a result of the Great Depression, long term investors decided they needed to guard against deflation, and so had an allocation to deflation hedging assets, which were Treasury securities and other sovereign bonds. Then hyperinflation came along, so everyone added another allocation called inflation hedges. Then we all learned about modern portfolio theory and CAPM (capital asset pricing model), so we added another portion called "diversifiers."

This approach gives you four categories or columns across the horizontal axis: growth with risk assets and equities, deflation hedges from bonds, inflation hedges like real assets and commodities and diversifiers to reduce correlation.

On the vertical is a continuum of liquidity, from highly liquid to illiquid. From there you can take every type of asset class and strategy you might invest in and categorize them and plot them. For instance, opportunistic real estate strategies are typically in the growth category, and they are typically illiquid while short sellers might be a deflation hedge and/or a portfolio diversifier. See figure 2.5, "Evolving Asset Classes and Portfolio Dynamics" which shows this concept.

In some cases, an asset may have characteristics of multiple categories, like real estate, which might be both growth and a diversifier and an inflation hedge. Another example is gold. As a currency, it's a store of value. If I own the bullion, it is illiquid. If I own long-dated futures contracts, it is less illiquid. Emerging markets, for example, offer some liquidity, but their securities are not as liquid as Dow stocks, so it would fall further down the liquidity axis. This is what endowments are going back to, a bottoms-up analysis by asset class, strategy and investment type. That simple endowment model that worked so well for so long in real terms is really the concept that individuals can take away from what endowments do.

What did the events of 2008–2009 mean for endowments? How did this happen?

In my view, a lot has to do with governance structures of nonprofit institutions. Trustees needed to demonstrate that they were good stewards, which came to mean showing great relative peer-group performance. At the same time, competition for students, faculty research grants—the "arms race" in higher education, lead to increased demands on the operating budget. If you needed more money for the operating budget, then you had to add risk to the endowment portfolio in order to generate higher returns which, in turn allowed for increased spending or at least a faster rate of growth in spending, depending on the institution's spending policy. The inter-institution comparisons led to chasing returns, which naturally added more and more risk. When most assets were headed up quarter after quarter, the incremental risk didn't really manifest itself. When the credit bubble burst, correlations went to one and it was clear that institutions had added a lot more risk than perhaps they knew, or could afford.

Has endowment investing become a performance derby?

There is an agency problem that has been growing and centers around performance and investment staff compensation. Compensation based on performance is necessary and is typical in the financial services business. To get the best talent you have to compensate them appropriately. What has happened is that the investment committees have often established CIO and investment professional compensation based on endowment performance relative to a peer group.

This is tricky because it isn't necessarily appropriate to compare one endowment to an apparent peer in a given year or even over a long period of time. The number of things that affect the return in an endowment over a short period is large and highly variable. And, as I said earlier, the role that the long-term investment pool—the endowment—plays in the capital structure of the institution can be very different, even among schools that, on the surface, look to be "peers." The illiquidity premium they can take is directly influenced by how much cash they need on hand. This in turn is dependent on things such as how much cash is returned from previous investments in a given year (which can be lumpy), new money from donors, and other factors driving the institution's operating budget. Investment committees and the institutions have varying appetites for risk. These are just a few of the things that make it difficult to compare the performance of one seemingly peer endowment to another. Compensation based on peer group rankings can incent the staff to structure a portfolio and take risks so as to beat the peer group that might be inappropriate for the individual institution that they serve.

In the end, the board has to solve these issues. They hire the CIO. Their job is to make the CIO as successful as possible while measuring performance and holding the CIO accountable. Boards and investment committees initiated this relative peer group benchmarking. Previously, institutions would look to earn a real return, net of all investment management expenses, which covered their spending needs and inflation. There was a period of time where this goal was very easy to achieve. So boards started looking for more rigorous ways of evaluating performance and performance relative to other institutions instead of relative to the needs of their own institution became the norm.

In the coming years I believe that there will be a reevaluation of how boards want to measure and compensate CIOs and investment staff. I think there will be more emphasis on understanding what risks the institution can or should tolerate and look for returns that correspond to the risk appetite, and there will be less emphasis on looking at your neighbor's work. This will be better for the long-term health of the institutions.

Did a similar performance derby affect decision making and risk taking in the hedge fund business in the past few years? The compensation structure can potentially promote an "all-or-nothing" approach that entails a lot of risk to generate unusually high returns.

Hedge funds that operate this way don't survive long term. There are plenty of hedge funds that do things right. They are thoughtful about their business plan, how they add value for their investors, compensate their people, manage risk, and use leverage. These are the long-term players who have a good business. They keep their firm's own interests aligned with their clients and their fees and compensation programs reflect it. These managers have been around a long time and probably will continue to be. In today's environment they will also be the groups that can attract and retain the best talent.

Were there too many hedge funds two years ago?

We have probably always had too many. However, hedge funds serve an important role in the investing community and for long term investors as these funds are often the best diversifiers in a portfolio and a necessary source of downside protection. There is a tremendous concentration of assets in the top funds. I saw a recent study showing that a small fraction of the firms in the business, around 16 percent, are managing the majority of the money—over 87 percent of total assets. This means that there are numerous small firms hanging on the periphery. The largest firms can attract great talent and they can also be selective when it comes to investor access. For individuals, there are a number of hedge funds that have focused on private, high-net-worth investors and have not pursued institutional money. They have done a great job taking care of their clients and have served that segment very well.

How do you approach manager selection?

We have established a rigorous process for manager selection. It has a dozen steps from sourcing through funding. An important part that makes the process very efficient is our up-front screening checklist. The checklist has both quantifiable and qualitative criteria that a firm must meet. For instance, for a hedge fund it might be things such as asset custody, who is the fund administrator, who is the auditor, who are the prime brokers, can they provide position-level data for the strategy going back for a reasonable period of time and do the principals have their own money invested in the fund. We have specific red flags that we look for that will eliminate a fund from consideration; and, we have to have transparency with a manager or we can't work with them. The initial checklist screen eliminates managers that are unlikely to make it through the later in-depth due diligence.

We don't pay a lot of attention to performance numbers during the initial screen. If you can't pass our checklist, or our operational due diligence, or you can't satisfy our risk management team, then the performance of the fund, the terms of the investment, or the unique strategy, or the qualifications of the managers is not really relevant. Process rigor in manager due diligence is important because it protects our client's interests and helps us execute diligence in the most efficient sequence. Starting with performance numbers is not the most time-efficient way to do this. This happens sometimes, but it can lead to chasing past performance.

The stringency of the process may mean that every now and then we miss a difficult-to-spot gem. However, we believe that the trade-off is worth it. We save a lot of time in the process, which lets us look at more managers overall. Furthermore, and most importantly, it keeps us out of trouble by dramatically reducing the risk that we get entangled with a bad manager.

At the same time, we are not necessarily concerned about how long someone has been in business. There can be new managers that have been spun out of other firms that have a great approach and a solid, well-thought-out business. These can get through our screen because the process doesn't necessarily eliminate the firm from consideration based on time in business.

Is this a result of Commonfund's history in the institutional money management business?

Yes, but the process is not exclusive to Commonfund. I have seen other entities—for instance, high-net-worth family offices—that have established a similar up-front rigorous screening methodology. This is a step that saves time for all parties involved and should be a critical part of the manager selection process.

Did the events of the past year fundamentally change anything? Is it possible that the ongoing good times meant that some bad habits developed in the investment management world?

Some bad habits developed during the good times. After all, it was easy to do. We had really strong bull markets for a prolonged period. There was a huge amount of excess liquidity, low interest rates, and easy credit. Fundamentally this comes back to risk, which, in my view, was horribly mispriced in the capital markets. This has been seen at various times in history—the mispricing can happen, but sooner or later it is going to correct. You don't know when or how but when it does, it will be painful and unavoidable.

It was possible to see this coming. We wrote about it, as did others. We published an article in fall 2006 on excess liquidity, making the case that no good would come of it. We worried about a "regime" change: what would happen if the then environment of very low volatility, rising equity markets around the globe and the narrowest credit spreads in a generation suddenly reversed. And, what would be the trigger to such a change: what would cause volatility to increase, equity markets to fall and credit spreads to widen. We were worried about the possibility of an accident in the credit markets but thought any trigger to the re-pricing of risk—a regime change—would be in the CDS—credit default swaps—and not in sub-prime. But in a euphoric bull market everyone is too busy making money. Even those who see it can sometimes ignore it because they are counting on having a chair for themselves when the music stops. However, I don't think that anyone thought that the correction would be this profound or turn into a full blown financial crisis. No one was expecting an 11 standard deviation event.

This is what is taking endowments back to the basics. However, there is a danger of swinging too far in favor of caution. We've spent a lot of time talking about tail risk, but what we see institutions subject to now is worrying too much about managing to the left tail and not thinking at all about the right tail. There could be a huge opportunity cost to the institution.

What else did we learn from 2008–2009?

The interesting thing that emerged from the 2008–2009 period, for institutions and individuals alike, is how to think about portfolio insurance. You should know how much you are willing to pay to insure or hedge against risk. For the institutions that escaped some of the problems last year, they need to now take a hard look at how they escaped. Were they smart or were they lucky? It is important that they know.

In either case they will want to try to be smart for the next round. I think there is more willingness now for both individuals and institutions to think about the rainy-day portfolio and to decide an appropriate level of downside insurance and what premium to pay for it. They don't have to give up pursuit of the upside, they just need to give up a portion of the return to pay for the insurance.

What are some specific ways that institutions will implement an insurance purchase?

It depends on what your portfolio has in it and what you think the risks might be. Long-dated, deep out-of-the-money options are one thing you can use. For instance, at the moment I think there is something you could do with long-dated options on interest rates. Ask yourself, what would happen to your portfolio if Treasuries suddenly moved to a six-handle (6 percent interest), for whatever reason—which could be a change in inflation expectations, currency debasement, or other factors. If you were concerned about what happens with rising rates as a factor exposure, you would want to know what happens to your portfolio if interest rates rise? You would want something with a big convexity in its payoff. You would want to understand what happens to some of your risk assets and might want to have some insurance against a fall in your equity portfolio in this scenario. Clearly, your deflation hedges become less viable in rising rate environments. The insurance process really means thinking about things on a factor basis instead of an asset class basis. You want to understand how the factor will affect all your asset classes. Think about if we went to an eight-handle on the 10-year Treasury—what would happen?

Is thematic investing going to become more important going forward?

The investment decision process is becoming more bottom-up and driven by the themes that you can forecast. For instance, now it seems that emerging markets and Asia in particular will be the driver of global economic growth in the near to mid-term—it is no longer the American consumer. You could reach a reasonable level of consensus on that. Going further, you might marry this outlook with demographic trends in those geographies. This analysis will help you decide what you want to own and let you look for investment opportunities that provide exposure to that growth. You might decide that a the best way to exploit this opportunity is to own a group of mid-cap Japanese exporters and that this is a better way to have exposure to the growth in the emerging markets than owning, say, a "China fund." You will seek the best risk-return balanced mechanism of accessing the trend. The themes and trends that you believe are coming will drive asset allocation, versus a top-down approach which dictates specific targets for assets without consideration to the risk factor exposures you are taking.

This means, though, that CIOs and investment teams will need to develop a comprehensive macroeconomic world view and get to a relatively deep and detailed understanding of what investment vehicles will let them harness the trends that they identify.

The other thing that is happening is that risk management and modeling are becoming more sophisticated. Institutions are arming themselves with as many facts and analysis as they can and evaluating a wide variety of scenarios. You can concoct any number of high-potential scenarios and simulate how the portfolio might perform, and what new investments you might take on in a changed environment. The fundamental decisions on where you want to incur risk, what assets you want to own, and how long you want to own them will hinge on good modeling, an understanding of the macroeconomic factors, and detailed comprehension of the given industry and trends that you have identified.

Did the use of leverage go too far in the last few years?

I think so. Clearly there were some hedge funds where the "alpha" or excess returns were solely from leverage. And abundant, cheap debt fueled some private equity returns for a period. We avoided some of the bigger LBOs partially for this reason. The top quartile and the top-performing funds were not necessarily the big LBOs. The mid-market, the less efficient areas of the market, where investors provided what amounted to growth or expansion capital, have performed well. In private equity you can only make money by either improving earnings or changing the earnings multiple. You can't do this with leverage alone. Whenever you look at where the big returns come from in private equity, the leveraged players don't generate the top returns consistently over time, especially on a risk-adjusted basis.

What is the minimum size of investable assets where you can be helpful to a client?

Our mission is to help as many nonprofits as we can. Since all of our programs are structured as private investment vehicles, the SEC sets a couple of thresholds for what makes a qualified investor. If you don't qualify, there are many of managers who cannot accept your investment and a number of strategies you cannot touch. So, for institutions under $5 million it is challenging to add real value, but we try.

The notion that individuals can learn from endowments is not without controversy. What would you tell individuals they can use?

What individuals, ultra-high-net-worth or not, can learn from non-profit and long-term investors is a philosophical approach. Things like evaluating the risk-return trade off, optimizing the benefit of diversification, and hedging the risk of inflation and deflation. All investors should think about managing their assets in a total port-folio context—"wholistically"—and using this to evaluate their own

decision making and their own specific situation, goals and time horizon, instead of getting caught up in the "performance derby." I think
from that standpoint, individuals can learn important ways of thinking
about investing from endowments.

What is your advice for an individual?

Think about your investment objectives. Think about the long term and
what you want this pool of assets to do for you. Are you trying to retire
with this? Is it your grandchildren's education? Do you want to establish
a foundation that survives you? Deciding the objectives—the purpose of
the pool of assets to be invested—is the first principle. We do this with
our clients at the outset and again periodically and individuals should do
it for themselves.

Can individuals do a better job in selecting an investment advisor?

There are a lot of very good firms available to the individual investor. The
few "bad apples" often get a lot of attention and that can be discouraging.

The selection process for an individual goes back to the screening
that we discussed earlier. If you look at some of the fraudulent investment groups that have hurt individuals, they generally wouldn't pass
some of the easy screens: they had self-custody of the assets, including
marketable securities, they had relatively unknown audit firms, and there
was little to no transparency into their investment philosophy, strategy or
process. This last point is, especially as it relates to hedge funds—while
few hedge fund managers are able or willing to disclose their current
positions—what they are long or short on at the moment—they should
be willing to explain and verify past performance—how and why they
were able to generate returns for their investors and how they manage
risk. There are some basic checks that can be done with relative ease that
will quickly weed out firms that you may want to avoid. If a manager
can't provide some of these basics, you don't even need to hold the
meeting.

We will sometimes see a hesitance on the part of boards to do some
of the heavy lifting or slightly invasive parts of manager due diligence,
such as background or reference checks. They will say, "We should be
able to trust these people." We say, "trust but verify." We believe that

you must do all these things, every time, and do them continuously as part of the monitoring process. Investors need to "re-underwrite" their managers on a regular basis. Usually you don't find out anything new, but you have to confirm that the investment thesis that drove you to place your money with the manager still holds and, not just assume that nothing has changed or be blinded by exceptional performance. It might be the case that exceptional performance was generated by taking exceptional risks. Having a rigorous process to which you adhere in manager selection and monitoring can also eliminate the inherent vulnerabilities of the human emotional elements of the decision-making process. People are naturally flattered if they get invited to invest in a fund that is perceived as exclusive, or in something that their friends have used. Similarly, it is very hard to scrutinize or question very good performance. This is part of what we saw with Madoff.

Any additional thoughts for individual investors?

It is always hard to predict the future. We can worry about lots of things. The number of possible and reasonable specific scenarios you can develop is large. Investment management is really about managing risk—there is no return without risk but taking risk doesn't mean you will always be rewarded with return—and you can't "manage" returns. Sophisticated endowment investors know that, and so they think about what the significant drivers of future returns and risk are—things like economic growth, inflation and interest rates—and then try to understand how these factors will affect their portfolio. They think about diversification: do they have too many eggs in the same basket, not enough baskets, or not enough eggs in different baskets? They try to identify those economic and capital market factors that will have an impact across multiple asset classes and holdings they ask: where are the opportunities and what are the risks of exploiting those opportunities? Most important, they ask: what can go wrong, and manage accordingly.

Chapter 16

Thruston Morton

Chief Executive Officer
and Chief Investment Officer

Global Endowment Management

"You've got to watch out when endowment people tell you, 'we deliver returns with less risk' because half of their portfolio is not marked properly."

"Inevitably it is much harder to implement some of these grand secular themes even if you call them right."

Global Endowment Management (GEM)

GEM employs an endowment management approach to investing globally for a select group of investors. It pursues varied and nontraditional investment opportunities to provide a long-term, diversified investment strategy for its institutional, family office, and individual clients. Its structure provides for shared asset allocation, but allows for sensitivity to investor tax status.

The GEM team comprises a diverse, international group of professionals. Many of its senior members have years of principal investing as well as endowment and foundation management experience. The team includes three former endowment/foundation chief investment officers, each of whom generated top-ranked performance in their respective peer groups.

T hruston Morton is the chief executive officer and chief investment officer for GEM. He was formerly CEO and CIO of DUMAC, the endowment management company for Duke University.

Q: What you are doing for clients at Global Endowment Management?

We are replicating the endowment investing approach for institutional-sized clients. Our senior team successfully executed this approach at Duke, an industry leader, and we wanted to provide this same investment process and philosophy for these clients.

You were chief investment officer at Duke. When you started at Duke it was right after the tech bubble crash in 2000.

Yes, it was September 2000 to be exact—about five months after the NASDAQ had peaked, signaling the beginning of the end of the tech bubble. The portfolio at Duke at that time was heavy in private equity, particularly technology venture capital, which had served the university very well up to that point. As you would expect, with the ensuing correction, there was a lot of work to do to restructure the portfolio for different times. Historically, say 35 years ago, Duke was a very strong regional school and had aspirations to be a leading research university at the national level. But having been created only in the 1920s, it was relatively under endowed versus the bigger Ivies and Stanfords of the world. And so, the trustees in the '70s had the foresight to realize that there were only a couple of ways to make the endowment bigger. The first is to cultivate donors who will be generous to the institution. Duke has loyal alumni and friends, so this was something that was possible. The other was to realize high investment returns, and to do that you have to be willing to accept more risk. The trustees demonstrated a lot of foresight in that regard, and Duke became one of the very early institutional investors in venture capital. I think the first Duke venture capital investment was in 1976, actually, along with Yale, Harvard, and a couple of others. Then in 1990, DUMAC, the wholly-owned investment management subsidiary, was set up to be professionally staffed and separately managed.

By the time the mid-1990s came along, Duke was a familiar limited partner in the venture capital world. The combination of the endowment being fairly small relative to other schools and Duke's fairly aggressive allocation policy meant that we often had proportionately larger venture investments in our endowment. During the tech boom this worked very well for the university. In fact, for the fiscal year ending in June 2000 Duke had the number one performing endowment in the Cambridge University for 1-, 3-, 5-, and 10-year periods.

The downside is that the equity portfolio was small cap and tech-heavy when the tech bubble burst. When I came into the picture, we started in earnest to restructure the portfolio to diversify much of this embedded private equity exposure. It took a couple of years to really have an impact.

It seems that your first two years at DUMAC were really characterized by rebalancing and rearchitecting the endowment.

That is correct. When the equity markets started to rebound in early 2003, we climbed back out of the hole relatively quickly. We got back into the top decile of performance in our peer group in my last couple of years there.

At that point I had been at Duke $6\frac{1}{2}$ years. The endowment was doing well, we'd built a good team, and we had a very talented young guy in the group, Neal Triplett, all set to take over. I thought it was a good time to move on, and see if I could do the same sort of thing in the private sector.

Endowments seem to be more activist now. They are taking direct positions in some cases.

Yes, that's true. First, let's look at private investments. It's important to distinguish between 'direct' investments and 'co'-investments. Co-investing is taking a 'direct' position but alongside an existing GP investment—that is, the GP has sourced the deal, done all the work and is putting it in their fund. You the LP are essentially riding on their coat-tails, and investing a little extra outside of the fund in the specific deal. True 'direct' investing is basically what the GPs do, and frankly most endowment staffs don't have the appropriate experience set to be doing this, which of course doesn't necessarily stop anybody. But it's one thing to choose a fund as an LP; it's another thing altogether to be sourcing deals and investing in operating companies directly. Some endowment investors have the requisite skill set, but most do not. Even if you have the skills, it doesn't mean it's a smart use of capital and resources. The three senior members of our private team have been principal investors in their former lives and do have the required skills. But we still make relatively few direct investments, if for nothing else because the size is rarely going to be big enough to matter (due to single company concentration risk) yet the time intensity required to make a direct investment tends to be greater than a typical fund investment. The benefits of course are that as a direct investor, you keep much more of the economics. If you're seeing more of this activity at endowments, it could be for that very reason—in a low return world particularly, you want to keep as much of the return as you can and dis-intermediating can help reduce the often egregious fee burden imposed by the average private fund structure. Whether you go direct or through a fund, it's always 'caveat emptor'.

Beyond that kind of direct investing, many endowments, and other institutional investors, are putting on direct positions as portfolio hedges. Having lived through the recent Great Recession bear market (if it's in fact over), it has become quite popular for committees to discuss hedging tail risk. Of course the most straightforward way to hedge tail risk is just to take less risk in the first place. But that doesn't sound sophisticated enough, and besides, we all like to have our cake and eat it too, right? Let's all stay loaded to the gills with equity risk, and we'll just go out and buy some of that tail insurance. Well good luck with that. The hurricane hit already, and guess what—now everyone wants to buy insurance and the price has gone up. So you can certainly put tail risk hedges on, but they typically cost more than you'd like and it's hard to buy enough to really matter. You either have to sell some of your upside away or just be willing to spend a lot of basis points outright. And even if you can buy cheaply and your position goes in the money, you'll be lucky to get the exit right—in other words, to monetize your profits.

Another reason endowments are probably feeling pressure to be more 'activist' as you say, is that their return objectives have not changed, but the world has. I think when most investors reflect on where things are going over the coming years, they come out with answers like: "More subdued growth," "Higher savings rates," "Lower consumer spending," "Lower leverage," "Lower absolute level of return." In spite of this, the bogey for most endowments, and foundations for that matter, hasn't changed. It's still 5 percent real.

It is one thing to deliver 5 percent real when nearly every asset class is up in the teens. It is really something else when interest rates are rock bottom and equity markets have run a long way ahead of economic recovery—true, organic recovery anyway. You're probably looking at high-single-digits returns at best. I would imagine that this is going to cause endowments to rethink how they benchmark, how they set their payout targets, how they compensate their teams and, most importantly, what they actually invest in.

Lower prospective returns will also likely cause a rethink of manager/client economic relationships. It can be argued that the consumer and financial institution balance sheet deleveraging we're continuing to witness is in fact a secular change. Without the credit octane in the tank, economic growth and financial market returns are likely to be more subdued—. In a lower absolute return world, 2 and 20+ fees with no hard hurdle and long term lock-ups are really that much tougher to swallow. They just consume too much share of total return while constraining flexibility.

The other big issue being rethought is the level of illiquidity endowments can tolerate. Traditionally, the tolerance level has been high—the argument being that you earn a return premium if you can "pay" a liquidity premium, so if you can tolerate the illiquidity, you should do so. Endowments as perpetual annuities can tolerate more illiquidity than, say, the typical pension fund, so the leading endowments have had pretty hefty illiquid asset allocations. However, in order to maintain a target level of illiquid assets, say, private equity for example, investors typically make commitments that exceed their targets. This is to compensate for the fact that capital is returned over the course of a fund's life. In 2008, though, the perfect storm of declining portfolio values, zero private distributions and fixed future commitments threw asset allocations out of kilter, and caused private asset NAV's plus unfunded commitments to soar as a percentage of portfolio values. The inadvertent percentage increase in illiquid assets and future obligations constrained institutions' ability to rebalance their portfolios.

In our portfolio at GEM, we had no legacy private investments and we had been quite bearish anyway, committing very little to private investments in '07 and '08. Nonetheless, the market experience caused us to rethink our asset allocation approach to private assets. We eliminated specific target allocations for private investments of any type—venture, buyout, natural resources, real estate. Instead, we gauged the *maximum* level of private NAV plus unfunded commitments we could tolerate, and ran stress scenarios, e.g., with the whole portfolio down 20 percent, to determine if we would have enough liquidity to meet our unfunded obligations and retain flexibility?

The other important aspect about illiquid assets is that beyond their liquidity characteristics, they are fundamentally the same risk exposure as their more liquid brethren. That is, private equity and public equity both constitute 'equity risk.' The point is to decide how much equity risk you want to take, then determine the best vehicle to effect that exposure. You need to set an allocation for equities as an asset class and then assess the relative merits of any particular private or public investment within that context. Private and public opportunities should compete for the same risk or exposure capacity. The hurdle for privates is naturally higher given the higher fee structure and longer lock-ups, but that is as it should be—every private investment *should* compete with a public alternative if available.

What is your view on the thematic investing approach?

One of the things that has distinguished the more successful endowments over time is that they do think fairly creatively. Often this is having the courage to be truly contrarian, or sometimes it's correctly identifying secular themes and adding exposure aggressively. Both are hard to do, and even harder to do consistently. We do look for themes, whether secular shifts or just transient opportunities that seem to be interesting and priced right. I remember about 8 years ago at Duke trying to pursue the "water as a scarce resource" theme. We spent a lot of time looking at it and trying to find a vehicle. It turns out it's really hard to invest in the resource itself, and you're left with tangential plays like purification/filtering/utility stocks, etc. So that's an example of a theme you might want to develop in the portfolio but finding the right vehicle is harder. People love to talk about themes. You can play visionary or investment guru. But leaving aside whether your idea has merit, it's not worth much if you can't implement.

Some of the exceptional returns in private investments have been due to leverage. Is this approach going to fall out of favor now?

I think a lot of returns in the big buyout space were almost entirely defined by that dynamic. We never invested in the big mega buyouts at Duke. You could say that for the period of 2004 to 2006 that was a mistake, because these funds had great returns.

But the outsized returns were because of leverage. I remember one private equity king pin being asked "How much leverage is appropriate for your portfolio companies?" His answer was "As much as we can possibly get." And that's why we didn't invest with them. And of course, that particular fund did very well, but I wouldn't have wanted to be in their follow-on fund.

There have been several studies, including a recent one I think by the Kaufmann Foundation, who are private equity pioneers, that have demonstrated pretty decisively that most private equity fund returns after fees are pretty underwhelming. In fact, levering the S&P 500 index by the amount the typical private equity fund is levered would have historically produced superior returns. Personally, I find it tough to pay 2 and 20 plus for an arguably higher risk, locked-up fund when I can do it myself in the public markets at very little cost and unwind it tomorrow if need be. Thus, the hurdle is high for private equity investments—you've really got to identify groups with a true market niche or edge.

Why didn't endowments do this in the mid-2000s when leverage was a good approach?

You've got to watch out when endowment people tell you, "We deliver returns with less risk," because half of their portfolio is not marked properly. Similarly, with individual private equity investments, you need to adjust for leverage—buyout structures are riskier than they appear, they're just not marked regularly. But what this does is it allows you to put stealth leverage in the portfolio without having to suffer the volatility of public investments. This is what's rather ironic—endowments *should* be the perfect investment vehicles to employ sensible levels of leverage precisely because they have perpetual investment horizons. Why should they care about short term volatility? But they, or more accurately, their staffs and investment committees do. This is why, in my view, most endowment managers do not lever their public portfolios. It's too blatant. It's too uncomfortable to get the marks on a daily basis.

Now that there is less appetite for leverage in illiquid investments, what will happen in private equity?

Not all private equity is created equal. The kind of private equity funds that we look for tend to be smaller and do things the old-fashioned way. These are people who actually go in and improve the operations of a company, not just financial engineers who can use your LP equity capital to borrow money and goose their returns. Venture capital is a different story in that it is not levered. But the VC fund business is crowded. There's too much capital chasing not enough really good opportunities. Plus the basic math in venture is challenging. By definition, venture is the riskiest end of the equity spectrum and should command the highest expected return. As an LP you'd like to see a return of 4x your capital, but the funds typically market 3x and you'll be lucky to get 2x after fees. Given that most venture investments at the company level return little to nothing, every fund needs a few home runs to carry the whole portfolio to a decent return. There just aren't that many home runs out there. So while venture capital does not suffer from the "less available leverage" issue that the big buyout funds now face, it's still a very challenging proposition for an LP. And just as the average private equity or buyout fund does not outperform a levered S&P, the average venture fund is not a good place to be. If you're not in the top quartile of buyouts or venture capital, you shouldn't be doing it. Cambridge and others have done research on that. That's pretty well documented.

When you joined DUMAC you were in the midst of a downturn. The causes were different from the 2008–2009 downturn, and it was less broad. What did you learn from each downturn and how would you compare them?

I learned two important lessons in my time at Duke. First, relationships are really very important in this business and probably more important in the private investment space than in the public—due to typically smaller fund sizes, and therefore capacity, and longer hold periods. When I joined Duke, although the public markets had already started to tank, in the private equity and venture arena, the top funds were still in huge demand. Having access and good relationships was really paramount because there was so much money chasing those funds. I learned the value of cultivating those relationships, and it's one of the reasons you must have a very competent investment team that's going to be respected by GPs and represent you professionally. This has changed somewhat in the current environment, but I think it will probably always be true for the top managers—the superstars are always oversubscribed.

The second thing I learned is that speed is of the essence. That's not something you might think is important to a true long term investor like an endowment, but it really is when you've had such dislocations as we did in 2001, 2002, and in this past couple of years. When you think you've identified something really attractive, you now often need to move quickly and get onto it. The world has gotten more competitive with information and ideas moving more quickly.

I learned one of those lessons the hard way at Duke in 2002. In the late summer of 2002, with the world still cratering, junk bond spreads blew way out to where they had spiked back in 1992. It was a really attractive opportunity. In classic endowment style, we tried to be thoroughgoing and process-oriented. This meant finding a manager to implement the opportunity.

If you're starting from scratch, the process of finding a manager can take months. After getting the board to buy off on the idea and approach, establishing a new asset class and all the rest of the formalities, we set out to narrow down the universe to two or three really good managers. During the process, spreads started narrowing and by fall 2002, about half the spread had been compressed already.

We ended up hiring a strong manager in December, and while the party wasn't over we had missed about 40 percent of the move. The lesson learned is that things move fast. If you see the perfect wave coming, you just want to get on a surfboard to ride it. Waste too much time searching for the perfect board and you miss the wave. In this more recent downturn, one thing we've witnessed is that the speed of change is faster, and I think that has altered the investing dynamic. Everything has accelerated in these last 10 years—instant global communication and analysis, lightening fast quant traders, etc. Speed turns out to be so important in some strategies that you've seen firms physically moving their offices closer to the exchange, trying to shave microseconds off their order times. A fallout of the compressed time horizon phenomenon is higher price volatility. So one lesson for investors and endowments is that the new normal is fast-paced and volatile. You will need more tools in the bag, and a stronger stomach to stay the course. There are certainly more tools available now, like ETF's and other derivative instruments, but as always it becomes a question of how and when to use them.

Paying this much attention to the trends and investing is a full-time job. Can the individual reasonably do this?

I suppose some individuals can, but most certainly should not be trying to call trends and trade their way to wealth creation. For that matter, neither should most institutions. Most do-it-yourself people should hold a diversified portfolio, look at it maybe once a quarter or after major market moves, and rebalance only when their asset mix has changed noticeably. Institutions that take a more active approach generally have pretty big teams thinking things through full time. For every idea that gets into a portfolio, there's probably ten that have been researched and dropped. And they're not looking at one thing at a time—there's a lot of concurrent activity across different teams, each looking at a specific area. Pretty tough for an individual investor to be able to cover as many bases. Of course, individuals can identify trends and get it right, but that's not for most people, and fewer still can do it consistently.

Is there anything the individual can do?

Well a good old 60–40 split between equities and bonds is not the worst portfolio in the world. But an individual can get more clever than that without too much trouble. At a minimum the components of the 60–40 can be subdivided into subcategories to gain broader exposures; for example, international equities, REITs, resource stocks or ETFs, international bonds, etc.. But I think the average person should avoid making things too complicated or falling prey to the marketing pitches of mutual fund companies who constantly churn out sexy sounding funds—you can end up with all sorts of unnecessary and obscure noise in your portfolio. In addition, as an individual, or even a smaller institution without a large internal staff, I would not set as a goal trying to closely mimic the leading endowments. First, you will likely always be at the end of the line, getting into things too late. Second, the better endowment investors succeed over time through a combination of asset allocation *and* manager selection. Again, the average individual or smaller institution just doesn't have the resources and access to do this.

Managers like institutional money for a variety of reasons. Is there a difference in access when you are operating a private fund?

Well, it depends on what kind of private fund you're talking about. We manage funds in an endowment format, with those same long term characteristics that managers like. So we have had great access.

Having said that, I also think that endowments and foundations may be somewhat overrated in this area. When I was at Duke, we backed a hot new venture capital firm. Duke, Yale, Princeton, MIT were the key backers of their first institutional fund in 2001 I think it was. When they came around for their second fund a couple of years later, we sat down with the managing partner to talk through terms. They were raising $350 million. We had a $10 million allocation in the first fund and were interested in taking it to $15 million for the second. Even though we had been in a prior fund with them and knew them well, we would expect to give it a thorough due diligence review. We sat down to discuss this with the general partner and he said: "Here is my dilemma. On the one hand, Duke is going to put me and my partners through months of navel examination, spending time with every partner, requiring us to go through every deal we've done in excruciating detail, and all you're going to take is $15 million dollars. On the other hand, a large Dutch pension fund called me the other day to say they would take all $350 million of the fund, and due diligence I'm sure would be light. Gee, what would I rather do?"

We did re-up with the fund, and they did suffer through our due diligence, but endowments may be less influential with managers than they had been historically. The experience of 2008 probably exacerbated this shift as a number of endowments turned out not to be not such stalwart long-term investors, when they had to go back and ask for commitments to be canceled due to liquidity challenges.

You seem to be near-term bearish. Do you think the 2009 recovery is a prelude to a double dip?

The economy is one thing. The market is another. However, I think the odds are better than even that the economy will have some sort of relapse, and the market will either anticipate it or follow it.

Government support has begun to recede, and by mid-2010 should be pretty much behind us. And what we're likely to be left with is years of high unemployment, anemic wage growth, consumer de-leveraging, higher taxes, etc. And this is not just in the US. Most of the OECD is in similar, if not worse, shape and before we write off the importance of the western world and Japan, let's remember that this group still comprises about 2/3 of global GDP. I just don't see what the engine is that's going to generate sustainable revenue and earnings growth we need to support current stock prices.

What trends will you be evaluating in the near to mid-term?

Here it seems that consensus has formed that emerging markets will be strong, the US dollar will be weaker, and inflation will be higher. It is slightly unnerving that almost everybody has the same opinion about those three issues. Yes, Asia and Latin America are where the growth is. Yes, the dollar is probably a slow-motion disaster, versus hard assets anyway. And yes, obviously, there is the risk of inflation if the Fed and other central banks cannot drain fast enough all the as yet dormant liquidity they've created—bank excess reserves.

What makes me nervous is that it seems so obvious and everybody believes it, and usually when everyone is lined up like that something else happens. We are trying to think about what else might happen and why? Where do we find growth that's not overpriced? How can we best invest to (a) participate in a cyclical recovery but (b) protect against the deflationary forces from the huge secular challenges facing the entire western world?

Portfolio managers are often skeptical of conventional wisdom when they see it developing.

Yes but they are just as often aligned with conventional wisdom, or perhaps conventional ways of looking at things. In 2003, we came out of the '01–'02 recession, and conventional metrics told you that certain assets were cheap. For instance, commodities looked cheap. Emerging markets looked cheap just on standard metrics. So in that sense, sticking to conventional ways of assessing value was a good thing to do.

At the market trough in early March 09, however, stocks had by conventional metrics not reached real bear market lows. The market never got down to single digit P/E's, or the 10x Shiller P/E that was seen at classic lows like '32, '49, '82. So people who ignored that conventional wisdom that the market needed to correct further, and instead said "stocks are certainly cheaper than they've been in a couple decades" and bought obviously did well. Now, though, to say something looks cheap, you have to make rather heroic assumptions. For instance, emerging market stocks, and commodities, look cheap if China becomes the growth engine of the world, which ultimately requires a huge shift upward in domestic consumption. After the last downturn, you didn't have to say "well if such and such happens" then things are cheap then—many assets were just absolutely cheap. Today, for most asset classes, you need something more to happen to be able to make the case.

As for the dollar, it is hard to find reasons why it shouldn't go down, beyond its as yet still intact flight-to-safety characteristics. But go down against what? It's hard to find another major currency you'd rather own, and there's a limit to how much Norwegian krone or Singapore dollars investors can buy. I think it is likely that over time the dollar, and the other major currencies at least, do go down against hard assets, like commodities. It's just the math of the expanding supply of paper currency versus the much more slowly expanding supply, and in some cases depleting supply, of hard assets.

What do you read to help you identify trends and stay current?

For starters, I usually scan the *Financial Times* and the *Wall Street Journal* every day. I have a handful of my favorite 'regular reads'—certain economists, strategists, market observers. I also try to find a good iconoclast or two and some contrarians just so I don't get too comfortable, stacking the deck with opinions supportive of my own—which we all tend to do. Beyond that, it's just keeping up with and siphoning through current market, economic and geopolitical data and reports. In fact, the real challenge is that there is so much information, disseminated so broadly and so quickly, that you can easily get overwhelmed. Most of it is noise. At the end of the day, you have to form your own opinions and develop conviction. But there's a fine line in this business between conviction and dogmatism. So I try to have conviction but I'm constantly skeptical of my own and everyone else's opinion. In short, you'd better have some humility if you're going to invest in markets.

Chapter 17

Mark W. Yusko

Chief Executive Officer
and Chief Investment Officer

Morgan Creek Capital Management

"It isn't fair to the intellect and the capabilities of the individual investor to say that they can't understand what endowments do and can't replicate any of the strategies."

"Investment is the only business, when things go on sale, people run out of the store."

Morgan Creek Capital Management

Morgan Creek Capital Management, located in Chapel Hill, North Carolina, provides investment management and advisory services. The firm employs investment programs for clients based on the university endowment model and manages or assists with asset allocation, manager selection, and portfolio construction. The firm also provides an Outsourced Investment office solution.

Morgan Creek was founded in 2004 by Mark Yusko. Mark later brought the majority of his investment team, including Mike Hennessy. Prior to founding the firm, the Morgan Creek investment team worked together managing complex university endowments. Mark Yusko and

Mike Hennessy were responsible for building the Investment Office and subsequent Management Company operations for the University of North Carolina Endowment at Chapel Hill.

M ark W. Yusko is the chief executive officer and chief investment officer of Morgan Creek Capital Management. Prior to forming Morgan Creek, he was president, chief investment officer, and founder of UNC Management Company, the endowment investment office for the University of North Carolina at Chapel Hill. During his tenure at UNC, from 1998 to 2004, he oversaw strategic and tactical asset allocation recommendations to the investment fund board, investment manager selection, manager performance evaluation, spending policy management, and performance reporting. Endowment assets under management totaled $1.5 billion. Until 1998, Mark was a Senior Investment Director for the University of Notre Dame Investment Office, where he joined as the Assistant Investment Officer in 1993.

Mark received a bachelor's degree in biology and chemistry from the University of Notre Dame and an MBA in accounting and finance from the University of Chicago.

Q: You have been a CIO for a leading endowment, and have built a business advising endowments as well as high-net-worth private investors. What can an individual investor learn from endowment investment principles?

There are definitely parts of the endowment model that can apply to individual investors, given the right vehicle. Utilizing institutional money management techniques for individuals is part of why we founded Morgan Creek. We saw a gap in what was available for the "mass affluent"—individuals and families with $1.5 million to $25 million in investable assets. They can benefit from endowment investing approaches. What we set out to accomplish was to democratize investing and make available and accessible the process and the philosophy that had historically been only available to the elite universities.

Tell us a bit about how you founded Morgan Creek and what you learned as you added institutional and private money to the fund.

We strongly believed that individuals could benefit from what we had learned as the investment team for a major university. There had been some things written that made the case that individuals should not try to invest like endowments. The conventional wisdom was to steer investors to simple investments like index funds. It isn't fair to the intellect and the capabilities of the individual investor to say that they can't understand what endowments do and can't replicate any of the strategies.

The evolution in my thinking on this topic took place over my career in investment management and is worth a brief recap here.

I did undergraduate work at Notre Dame in biology and chemistry, and then graduated from the University of Chicago with an MBA in accounting and finance. I went to work in the investment business for an insurance company and an asset management firm. I realized that I enjoyed investment management and had the opportunity to return to Notre Dame in their investment office, working with Scott Malpass.

After I had been in the endowment world for a while, I reflected on my time working in private capital management. In the institutional money management field there was an idea that security selection was the most important part of the investment process. In working with an endowment I discovered how significant the impact and the power of asset allocation was to portfolios. I determined that while both parts of the process were important (of the four steps in investing: asset allocation, manager selection, portfolio construction, and then security selection), asset allocation was the most dominant.

Each of these components contributes to the overall return. Asset allocation is 60–70 percent of returns, manager selection is another 15–20, and another 10–15 comes from portfolio construction—how much you give to each manager—and you need another 10–15 for security selection. What this implies is that asset allocation is the most important factor and you have to get that right first. The proof was in the Endowment portfolio results—the large schools were crushing the average investor, outperforming them by 1,000 basis points a year over many decades.

The results are embarrassingly far apart. If you break it down a little further, about 600 of those 1,000 basis points come from just having a better asset allocation model. A more diversified model that includes hedge funds and private equity and real estate and commodities and that lowers the volatility of the overall fund and gives you a higher compound long-term rate of return because, ultimately, the way you make long-term wealth is to compound the low volatility rate.

So, the other 400 basis points came from manager selection and portfolio construction. The problem for the individual investor has always been manager access. There was this elite club of stock managers, bond managers, hedge fund managers, private equity managers that were not available to individual investors. An individual couldn't meet the minimums and might be frightened off by the fee structures. Incidentally, we always saw these fee structures as a positive because the investment business, above all, is a pay-for-performance industry. I think there is a bias against fees in the advice that individual investors typically get. Fees are not bad if they are accompanied by appropriate performance.

I could also see that Commonfund was helping small endowments overcome these obstacles and achieve scale economies and get good management. TIFF was doing the same for foundations, but there was nothing that served individuals.

So we were thinking about the idea for Morgan Creek at that point, but the timing was not right to start it. A few years later, I had the offer to be the Chief Investment Officer at North Carolina. It was a great opportunity. The fund was in need of moving to a more sophisticated model—it was basically 65 percent stocks, 30 percent bonds, a little tiny bit of hedge funds. We decided to diversify across a much broader list of asset classes and we began employing advanced techniques and adding the best managers. We thought this would improve performance, and it did. We went from an 84th percentile to today, where UNC is in the top 5 percent of all endowments.

After seven years at UNC I felt that we had accomplished what we set out to do, and I was still interested in applying endowment investing to the private market and to smaller institutions. We started raising money and built a fund with a few hundred million to start with. This was in the 2003–2004 time frame. Now we've got 40 people in Chapel Hill and we've got 8 people in New York and 8 people in China—23 people on the investment side, and the rest on operations and diligence. We also partner with a firm with close to 50 people that provide infrastructure services such as wholesaling and compliance and all the things that you have to do to run the business. In all we've got about 100 people dedicated to our largest fund for individual investors.

One of the keys to our success was finding leverage in fund-raising. Part of what is difficult to do in addressing the "mass affluent" market is keeping your per-client acquisition cost low and having enough clients that the asset base allows us to invest for them like an endowment does. We decided to look to distribution partners, and we started with a couple of regional banks, one in Texas and one in Oklahoma. We also worked with a brokerage firm, which was helpful. We knew we were on to something, because we were keeping up with large endowments in our returns, even on a fee-adjusted basis. We still felt that we needed to scale up significantly and looked to some larger firms to partner with. We decided to partner with Merrill Lynch, which gave us access to a large client base and was a mutually beneficial relationship.

Their clients were looking for good returns, with lower volatility. Everyone was still thinking about the big downturn from 2000 through 2002 and wanted to make sure they could take advantage of growth while hedging downside risk. That is something endowments can do well.

The only other hurdle was making sure that our fee structure was appropriate. Our philosophy is that outstanding performance warrants good fees. If you are doing well for your client, and doing better than the benchmarks net of fees, then everyone will be satisfied. Because we were still investing with managers we had their fees and ours, which meant that the burden was on us to show our clients that they were getting their money's worth, something that we were confident of.

You said manager selection is part of what matters. How do you approach it?

As we grew Morgan Creek, we got people believing in the construct and the concept of asset allocation and manager selection as big determinants of return. We had to be good at manager selection, and the process reminds me a little of the old Groucho Marx line, "Never join a club that would take you." Often you don't want your money with managers who want your money. You want your money with managers who really don't want or need your money. One of the things we could help private clients with is access to managers, based on our relationships, background and experience in the business.

On manager selection, the handicap to the individual goes beyond access and expertise and experience, though. It is also just simply hard work. We have 23 investment professionals. We look at thousands of managers per year. We only invest in about 3 percent of the people we see and we work really hard. In the last month, I've been to Seoul, South Korea, Shanghai, Beijing, Tokyo, London, New York, and Boston meeting with managers. We think China is going to be important and so we have eight people full-time there. The process and the travel is expensive and time consuming and that is why individuals have a hard time replicating it.

So, manager access and the experience required to evaluate managers is a big difference between endowments and individuals. What else do you see there?

I agree that access is one. Time horizon is another—endowments typically have a very long-term, even perpetual viewpoint. Taxes are different. There are also some more subtle things, like the process and tools you need for evaluating and monitoring investments. These help you to clearly understand what you have in your portfolio, how it correlates, and how much leverage there really is.

As I mentioned, one of the biggest ones turns out to be bandwidth. That is, you've got an endowment with two or three dozen investment professionals, and they are spending most of their time interviewing, selecting, and monitoring fund managers. It is hard for the individual to overcome just the sheer manpower advantage.

Also, many individuals who have a reasonable amount of investable net worth are focused on the job they already have and don't have time to spend with their investments. If you are a highly paid professional, a doctor or a lawyer, you will want to be working to keep your current income.

The other thing that you cannot overlook is experience and run-time in the investment business. If you survive mistakes in this business and you have been through numerous cycles, that is how you develop judgment.

Another issue we see with individuals is that they generated their wealth through a business or their own efforts. I think this leads to confusion between wealth creation and wealth preservation. Wealth creation always comes from concentration. Concentrated business ownership, concentrated stock positions, betting it all on black in Vegas. All great fortunes are made from concentration. Likewise, all small fortunes are made from concentration. It is reminiscent of the old joke: "How do you make a small fortune? Start with a large one and keep it concentrated." There is a tendency for private wealth to want to continue to keep concentration, which may or may not work out. We are interested in preservation and then growth.

What should individual investors be thinking about?

We all know about the lost decade. Superficial or unsophisticated asset allocation is going to hurt you. Endowments figured this out and that is why they have been able to grow during that same period. The individual investor needs to be educated, informed, and active. No, they can't necessarily replicate what endowments do, but they can at least try to understand it and incorporate it as much as possible into their strategy.

You might not be able to do it on your own as an individual investor because you don't have the bandwidth and you probably have different constraints than an endowment, but you should learn at least philosophically from them, and that will help you pick a good advisor that uses these principles, and then you can get these better returns.

The interesting thing is that people haven't really come to grips with this issue. In the end, as I mentioned, there are only four ways that you can make a return and all four of them require taking risks. If you take no risk, you get the risk-free rate of return, which basically equals inflation and you make no real returns. So, you destroy the purchasing power of your assets over time. So, you know, people who put their money in cash or buy many bonds think they are making a good investment. Well, municipal bonds after inflation and currency changes this year lost eight percent. People should be focused on the real rate of return, not the nominal return on their brokerage statement.

How do endowments approach balancing risk and return? What can an individual learn from their process?

As you know, risk and return should be balanced. You can buy a bond with a risk of default and you get paid 2 percent risk premium to do that, above the risk-free rate. You can take equity risks. You earn another 5 percent on top of that so that's 7 percent real. Then you can take illiquidity risk, and this is the other reason endowments have outperformed so dramatically, they can take the long view. Illiquidity gives you another 5 percent over long term on top of equity returns.

You go from 4 percent long-term T-bill rate to 6 percent for bonds, to 11 percent for stocks, to 16 percent for private investments. Then you can use leverage to amplify your returns, and leverage can add (or subtract) a few hundred basis points here and there depending on its availability and prudent usage. What all the improvements in return have in common is that every single one of them entails taking risk. Most investors should not employ leverage.

What I see in individuals is that they aren't explicitly gauging risk and return. Risk that you know about is okay—this is just active risk and if your portfolio is balanced and the return you are getting justifies the risk, then it is a good approach. What I see instead is that people take risks that they don't understand.

For instance, muni bonds carry currency risk and purchasing power risk. In general people are not thinking about this—they may only be focused on default risk when the real danger is from changes in value in the dollar, or changes in inflation. Another example is someone who buys a mutual fund that they think is a great fund, and they won't understand that it's concentrated in large-cap growth stocks in developed markets that are all highly levered. That's probably not going to be a very good place to be invested in a de-leveraging world. Understanding what you own, what real risks you are incurring, and making sure you are getting an adequate return is key.

Another point for the individual investor is discipline. Discipline in accomplishing anything is hard—discipline in a workout regimen, in a diet, in studying for an exam—all difficult. And discipline in investing, particularly when you're talking about multiple decade time horizons, which is what most individuals are really dealing with, is particularly difficult.

Part of discipline is being able to take the long view on things. Even when you are 65 you have potentially another 20 years ahead that you need to navigate financially. This is a time in your life when advisors are steering you toward bonds. I am not sure it is appropriate—even at 65 you need to be thinking about asset allocation and moving assets between and among the best asset classes.

Does having an advisor help impose some discipline for the individual, because it makes them less likely to whipsaw their portfolio with constant tinkering?

Definitely. However, a good advisor will also understand all the principles we have talked about. They can also protect you from yourself. This point reminds me of a wealthy private individual who made a considerable sum from the sale of his business. It wound up being something of a burden—he felt obligated to keep a tight watch on the markets and keep an eye on CNBC every day. If you are taking the long view you don't have to stay glued to small day-to-day changes. You also have to live your life. Even Keynes said, "In the long run, we are all dead."

Besides investing with a good manager, how can an individual simplify things so they don't have to spend so much time thinking about their investments?

It is possible to simplify. Start with liquidity. You need 10 percent to 15 percent in liquidity, which should cover your spending for two years. High-quality cash-equivalent, short duration, muni bonds, or even cash. You want two years of your spending in the bank so that you don't have to trade your higher returning, less liquid assets in a downturn. Each year after you spend a year's worth, you replenish. So, if you spend 5 percent a year, you have 10 percent in the liquidity bucket. You take out 5 percent to spend, you put 5 percent back in.

Where that 5 percent comes from is the "stay rich bucket." Now the stay rich bucket is 70–89 percent of your assets, which should be generating consistent returns.

Finally there is the remaining 10–15 percent. This piece is the "get rich bucket." The get rich bucket is that bucket that everybody shouldn't have, but everybody wants to have so they can do that stock tip, so they can do that friend's condo deal, and that brother-in-law's venture deal. Just assume you're going to lose all of that. That's why I tell people to make it very small, but everybody needs to have it. It's cocktail party conversation money. The get rich bucket probably allows the individual to satisfy that need to feel like they're doing something.

Taken together, this means that 70–80 percent of your money should be with an advisor who puts you in a strategy that's diversified, like an endowment style portfolio across nine asset classes with a disciplined balancing policy, and you should never even think about it. As the saying goes, "Don't just do something. Sit there." Patience is a virtue for the "stay rich" bucket. In his book, *More Than You Know*, Michael Mauboussin showed that the people who look at their portfolio every day underperform those that look once a year by something like 7 percent.

What should we learn from the market dislocation in 2008–2009? Does it change the endowment model or how we should be looking at investment management? There has been some talk that the endowment model is "dead."

No. I think endowments did relatively well last year. The large endowments outperformed by 1,300 basis points a year for the 10 previous years through June 2008. In 1999–2008, the 10-year period, endowments outperformed the diversified benchmark by 1,300 basis points compounded per year for 10 years. If you add 2009, so now it would be an 11-year period and you get a tie. It's not that the endowments did worse. They just did as badly as everybody else. So now over the 11-year period you outperform by 1,200 basis points per year.

As far as the bad press endowments got? Let's look at what actually happened. There are three ways that you can lose money. One, you can have it stolen. You can get a Madoff that comes along. That didn't happen to endowments. The bulk of the big endowments had no exposure to Madoff or any other fraud.

The second way you can lose money is you can buy an asset that disappears—a Washington Mutual common stock, Freddie and Fannie preferred, GM common stock. If you own a lot of those assets and made a mistake in judgment, those assets are now worthless. That's not what happened to endowments either.

The third thing is you can own assets that, because of accounting rules, have to be marked-to-market on a certain date and therefore you appear to have lost money. Over the six-week period from

September 19, 2009, to October 30, 2009, when the regulations changed and there was lots of de-leveraging and everybody had to sell what they could sell, not what they wanted to sell and mark-to-market accounting caused all kinds of distortions, everything correlated for one very short period of time.

Since that time it hasn't correlated at all. Emerging markets are up way more than U.S. markets. The bond markets are more than stocks. All the things that were supposed to happen—senior assets were supposed to outperform junior assets—they have. Emerging markets are supposed to outperform developed markets because they have less debt and more growth—they have. But just because the endowment hit one bad shot, do you think they really became bad golfers? Statistically, will their next shot be better, or worse?

You have seen nearly the worst scenario that could happen, and it was only a tie. Endowments won for 10 years running and tied in year 11. Sounds pretty good to me.

Any other lessons for institutional money managers coming from the crisis?

We aren't doing anything differently because we were satisfied with our process and that hasn't changed. The only change we have made is how we view cash. We all were taught that cash is not an asset and that it is the market timing thing. I am not sure I agree with this now.

Cash is an asset just like stocks, just like bonds, just like commodities or currencies. It's a form of a short-duration fixed income security. Warren Buffett looked at this and said something like, "If I look across all the assets out there, the only one that has a positive return that I can see is cash." And that was genius. It wasn't market timing. It was asset allocation. And because we have this disdain for cash in the investment management business, we all missed it. Buffett didn't, which is why Buffett is Buffett.

In 2009, cash positions let some investors make very good deals.

Yes. You get a unique chance to buy when things are at historical lows. It's peculiar if you think about it—investment is the only business, when things go on sale, people run out of the store.

How do you think about rebalancing?

If the majority of returns come from asset allocation, you have to get that right. So you better take a view on asset allocation themes, on sectors, on asset classes. The thing about investing is you can't make investments if you don't have conviction. If you don't have conviction about something, you won't do anything. That's why most people stay too much in cash for the wrong reasons. That's why they never change their portfolios, because they lack conviction and by actively managing a portfolio and constantly developing that conviction, they will put their money to work at the right time. A cash position plus conviction can let you take advantage of opportunities that present themselves.

This is hard to get right every time and that's why you have to risk management discipline of targets and ranges. So while I may have a target, a long-term target on an asset, like domestic equity or international equity natural resources, I am mostly looking for a range around that target. This allows me room to express a view on things.

For instance, if I have decided to have a 10 percent to 30 percent domestic equities range, today, I'm bringing it to the bottom end of the range because I feel very negative about domestic equities. I don't take it all the way down to 0 because I could be wrong. And then if equities go to the low end of the range, then I may add more because they are cheap. Conversely, when I want to get to the top end of the range like in 1999 when I got up to the 30-plus percent, then it is time to sell.

This is classic rebalancing. We're constantly selling into strength and buying into weakness. So it's a combination of having a view, having a conviction to be comfortable with that view, but then having the discipline to express that view positively or negatively, and then having the overlay discipline that says once I have achieved my goal, I don't fall in love with it and overstay my welcome.

What are the trends you are watching in the near to mid-term?

The long term is made up of a series of short terms and so long term, it's very hard to argue with a declining dollar, and rising Asian currencies just because of balance sheet differences between the Asian countries and the developed world. It is very hard to argue with rising commodity prices because of the supply, demand, and demographics. It is very hard to argue with rising equity values in emerging markets and declining equity values in the submerging markets—the United States, Europe, and Japan, just due to their demographics and debt.

One of our big themes is there's a massive wealth shift going on from the developed world to the developing world and it's just a de-leveraging. Capital flows to the people with the least amount of leverage. It happened in Europe to the United States when we were the emerging market. Now it is happening in the other direction as the United States is the biggest debtor nation in the world.

We think emerging markets will be important. They are paying, meaning full dividends now, they are actually growing at double-digit rates. Now they have good corporate governance because they went through a terrible period in the '90s where they didn't have good governance, and they didn't pay dividends, and they didn't have good growth, and they had too much leverage. Now they have clean balance sheets, spectacular growth, great upside, and that is when you want to own equities.

If you have a de-leveraging society, companies with overlevered balance sheets and a government prone to print money, which should be Europe and the United States, there will be deflation in equities. The United States was once the biggest creditor nation in the world. That's why we became the superpower. That's why China will become the next superpower.

We also believe there are some important demographics that will be coming from emerging markets. We believe that the Asian consumers can dwarf what happened in the United States and Europe because their baby boom is twice the size of ours—500 million people strong. This will affect things like leisure industries and travel and investments and finance and related things are going to just boom in Asia for the next two decades because they're going to have half a billion people turn age 40 over the next 20 years. It's extraordinary.

We think energy and natural resources will be important in emerging markets. There will be 3 billion new consumers. They all want scooters and cars and electricity, and so the demand for energy as commodity is going to rise.

In Western Europe and the United States there will be different trends. There is an aging population. That will mean lots more hip replacements and artificial lenses and cornea replacements and defibrillators and medical devices and biotechnology and new drugs. In developing nations, too, there will be demand for the health care basics.

How about shorter term themes?

In the near term, the fact that everybody thinks the dollar is going down means that we will see very sharp dollar rallies from time to time. It is likely that there will be one in the Q1 2010 because there always is in the first quarter. U.S. corporations with foreign earnings have to repatriate their earnings back to dollars to pay the taxes. This year, it will probably be bigger than average because so many people are short, and there will also be record overseas earnings because the dollar declined so much.

A big challenge we all face in investing is separating those long-term trends from the short-term trends. I am comfortable that long term we've got the portfolio positioned well to make 7 percent real in perpetuity with half the volatility. Our goal is very simple. We want to make the same return as equities, 7 percent real, 10 percent above inflation with half the volatility. If you can do that, you end up with twice as much wealth over five decades.

This is just simple math. If I can lose less, I have to go up less to get even, and the power of that is incredible, and it means you give up some of the upside in the bull markets. But that is okay. In fact, here's the amazing stat. If you could avoid all the downside, which is pretty tough to do, but if you actually could, you only have to capture 30 percent of the upside to win.

And our goal is to capture about 70 percent of the ups and about 40 percent of the downs. And if we do that over long periods of time, we will end up with twice the wealth for our clients.

Who is your ideal client that you all look for? Is it the moderate net worth?

We think individual investors of all types can benefit from the endowment investing style. The biggest part of our business, about 50 percent of our assets, is in The Endowment Fund. Our goal is very unabashedly to be the biggest pool of capital managed in the endowment style over the long term because we think it's the right way to manage capital. We have 21,000 investors. The range of investments in the Fund is pretty wide, but the average is about $250,000. So we have lots and lots of small investors and it's perfect for them. Our goal is to democratize investing and give investors access to asset classes and returns that are normally the province of institutional money.

What do you think will happen in CIO compensation at universities in the coming years?

This has always been a tricky area for universities. They need to find ways to compensate the staff appropriately. I think one important element is finding the right comparable. Comparing investment staff compensation to faculty may not be right. There are other examples of exceptions on a university campus, though. The football coach in a competitive school is one example. Or if the school has a hospital, there are exceptions for physicians. Universities are bureaucracies. Bureaucracies are typically not good at exception management, and the investment staff represents an exception. I think this is why there will be a continuing trend toward CIO and endowment management outsourcing.

Chapter 18

Rafe de la Gueronniere

Principal

New Providence Asset Management

"I think we are clearly in a new world. A lot of environmental variables are shifting, and rapidly."

New Providence Asset Management

Located in New York City, New Providence Asset Management dates back to 1996 as a long-short equity fund of funds with responsibility for sourcing, screening, hiring, and monitoring investment managers. In 2003, John L. Vogelstein and Rafe de la Gueronniere, who had worked together managing the endowment of the Taft School as chair of the board of trustees and chair of the investment committee, respectively, purchased the fund's management company.

The firm's mission was redefined to be a full-time investment office for tax-exempt organizations and select high-net-worth clients. In 2004, New Providence Asset Management became an SEC registered investment adviser. New Providence currently has an investment committee comprised of five seasoned professionals who collectively have over 150 years of direct experience investing money as principals and serving as trustees.

The firm works with clients to review their respective finances, objectives, and investment policies. Appropriate asset allocation parameters, risk profiles, and portfolio constructs are then agreed upon.

Thereafter, New Providence assumes responsibility and accountability for manager selection, asset allocation and portfolio performance. The firm manages all aspects of day-to-day investment decision making and execution. New Providence reports all portfolio-related activity to its clients on a real-time basis. The firm's partners believe that this model is more effective and sustainable than that of a traditional advisor who provides periodic advice but does not assume full responsibility for results. Direct accountability aligns New Providence's interests with those of its clients, as does the firm's partners and their families having the majority of their assets invested with the same managers and on the same terms as clients.

While the firm primarily manages separate accounts, it also has a partnership for smaller clients invested across asset classes.

Assets under management are approximately $2 billion and New Providence Asset Management serves over 25 investment office clients.

R afe de la Gueronniere is a partner and member of the investment committee of New Providence Asset Management. Previously, Rafe was a principal at the Mariner Investment Group, chair of the Discount Corporation of New York, a partner of William E. Simon's, and a member of the management committee and board at PaineWebber, Inc. He began his career at J.P. Morgan & Co. where he was a senior vice president responsible for the fixed income and precious metals businesses. Rafe served as a trustee and investment committee chair for the Taft School and was on the U.S. Treasury Debt Management Advisory Committee. He earned his BA from Brown University.

John L. Vogelstein served as president and CIO of Warburg Pincus for several decades before the founding of New Providence Asset Management.

Q: One of the biggest issues that endowments are thinking about coming through 2007–2009 is how to balance liquidity and return. Please tell how New Providence has historically and currently views the balance between liquidity and return.

Our fundamental approach has always been to capture a majority of the market's upside, protect capital on the downside, and maintain meaningful liquidity. This is not new for us. New Providence's long-standing view on this issue was shaped by our experience over many years in the asset management business; it predates the problems of 2008 by many years.

From January 1999 through the present we have almost always maintained a minimum of two years of clients' annual expenses in highly liquid assets such as Treasuries, cash, and other immediately liquefiable high-grade bonds. This has prevented New Providence from having to sell equities in bear markets. Fortunately, adhering to this philosophy allowed us to use the last two bear markets as buying opportunities. Thus, liquidity became an offensive weapon as well as providing other benefits. We believe that liquidity is underrated and misunderstood as an asset class.

New Providence is disciplined about what we consider a liquid asset: We do not consider junk bonds, emerging markets bonds, low-grade corporate bonds, or long-term corporate bonds to be liquid.

In years such as 2005 and 2006, when people made commitments to long-term lock-up investments such as oil and gas, private equity or real estate, there was an assumption, based on what was happening in the market at the time, that harvesting cash from these investments would be frequent and reliable. But since then, there has been a dramatic reduction in the pace and amount of cash that flowed back from these investments. Our approach toward private investments has never been to assume harvesting as a certainty. We have assumed that when commitments are made to a long-term partnership the money was then unavailable for other purposes whether or not the manager had yet called the capital. Only when capital is returned to us will we then redeploy the money elsewhere.

A lot changed from 2007 through 2009 with regard to endowment access to liquidity. Credit was harder to access and more expensive. New money coming in was likely to be down. Operating budgets were taxed. What were you advising clients during this time?

As early as 2006 we started to become concerned about the economy and financial markets. We saw a migration across a variety of investment pools, with endowment, foundation, pension fund, and individual money simultaneously going into a more diverse and global group of asset classes. As the global asset class migration occurred, we foresaw meaningful consequences.

First, the valuation levels of the assets being purchased were increasing as institutional money began chasing the same group of asset classes. For instance, many were investing in emerging market bonds and stocks in Europe and Asia and private equity. There was also a stampede into real estate, highly leveraged deals, and commodities. Due to this, we believed correlations would go up and that if a severe bear market developed, correlations across asset classes would move toward one as investors would simultaneously seek to increase liquidity and reduce risk.

Second, we also knew that the internal dynamics of tax-exempt institutions have a series of correlations, which coincide almost identically with the set of external circumstances described above. In a bear market several things happen: Fund-raising becomes more difficult, receivables increase, while the demand for pro-bono services and expenses also increases. In 2009, these conditions created the perfect storm for many tax-exempt organizations. We at New Providence think about the risks within an investment portfolio as well as those external to the portfolio. Our approach to liquidity was probably considered on the conservative side prior to the last 18 months, but it wound up being the right thing for our clients.

I think a summary of how we managed through the last two years provides a perspective on New Providence's thinking, asset allocation decision making, and risk management.

In 2007 our concerns about the economy and financial markets increased significantly; in the summer of 2007, we had our first significant stock market shock. By late 2007, we were sure that real trouble was coming, but we never imagined how bad it would get. We were worried specifically about the real estate markets, low risk premiums and massive leverage throughout the world, including derivatives.

Reflecting our concerns:

We steadily reduced the proportion of long-only equities in our portfolios, replacing them with long-short hedge funds and fixed income investments.

We chose our hedge funds carefully; we insisted on transparency and limited use of leverage. We emphasized those that we thought would outperform in difficult markets. In general, we chose well; for example, our in-house equity hedge fund of funds was down less than 13 percent in the 18 months from October 2007 to March 2009 compared to a 55 percent decline in the S&P 500.

We selected our fixed income investments to emphasize liquidity and safety, which meant that we avoided lower grade bonds; we owned government bonds and Treasury bills rather than money market funds.

We made a significant fixed income investment in Convexity, the spin-off from Harvard Management, which has been low to negatively correlated to equity markets and has generated good, positive returns since inception.

Understanding that there was a bubble, we did not invest in real estate.

We have not been investors in commodities, believing that one invests in companies that can grow because of human input and that ownership of commodities is nothing more than a bet on price.

We underweighted investments outside the United States generally and were not significantly involved in emerging markets because we didn't believe that these markets, as distinct from their economies, would be insulated from the United States and Europe.

As a result of all this, for the fiscal year that just ended in June 2009, our average portfolio declined by 13 percent compared to 26 percent for the S&P 500, and to percentages in the high 20s and low 30s for many leading institutional educational institutions.

What did we do after the financial markets collapsed?

New Providence began liquidating government bonds.

We bought very high-grade, intermediate-term corporate bonds at steep discounts, which had yields to maturity just under 10 percent.

We added meaningfully to investments with managers who invest in distressed securities throughout the capital structure.

We gradually began adding to investments with long-only equity managers who invest in emerging markets, with particular focus on China and India.

We also began to make commitments to secondary market private equity.

How do you approach target returns for endowment funds? How can endowments get the right mix of risk and return?

Regrettably, many institutions mentally extrapolated the double-digit returns generated in the 1990s and assumed they would continue into the 21st century. New Providence does not target returns. We make sound investment decisions and expect over time to cover our clients' annual operating expense and seek to maintain intergenerational equity.

We believe that the CIOs and investment committees of some foundations, endowments, and family offices should be trying to generate more consistent returns instead of seeking higher returns that inevitably come with too much risk and illiquidity. In 2001, 2002, and 2008, many institutions were forced to stop building programs, reduce personnel, and cut pro-bono services. We believe that tax-exempt institutions should consider continuity for their operations as well as long-term financial stability.

For 11 years we have achieved consistent returns for clients, outperforming equity and fixed income markets and relevant portfolio benchmarks by a wide margin. In the fiscal year just ended in June 2009, our average portfolio was down 13 percent. In strong markets our portfolios have also performed well. For instance, in calendar year 2009, our average portfolio was up 24 percent.

Clearly our strategy is to keep things simple. In good markets, we want to capture the majority of the upside. In years like 2003 and in 2009, we did just that. In bear markets we want to protect capital and to date have had reasonable success in doing so. If you do that over market cycles, you are going to outperform. In investing, if somebody's portfolio goes down 30 percent while you are down 10 percent, his ability to make up that ground becomes very unlikely.

How do you adhere to your liquidity model and still achieve consistent and high returns?

When you look at our historical asset class allocation for over a decade, one can visualize our strategy and understand our results (see Table 18.1).

Having already addressed asset allocation and portfolio changes from 2007 through 2009 in response to a previous question, we might review in a bit of detail how we came through the 2000–2002 bear market and subsequent recovery.

If you look at June of 2000, we had exited large capitalization growth stocks and taken our clients' equity holdings to the lowest levels in 15 years because valuation levels in certain sectors of the market were at unsustainably high levels. The stocks we did own were small cap and

Table 18.1 New Providence Asset Class Allocation

January 1999–December 2009

	1/99	12/99	6/00	6/02	6/09	12/06	12/07	12/08	12/09
Long Only Equity	52.2%	56.4%	45.1%	49.4%	55.2%	38.8%	39.0%	31.6%	34.4%
Equity Hedge Funds	5.6	7.3	5.7	10.4	12.0	24.2	25.1	34.7	37.2
Private Equity	0.7	2.0	3.3	4.6	4.8	5.7	6.9	7.7	7.4
Total Equity	*58.5*	*65.8*	*54.1*	*64.5*	*72.0*	*68.6*	*71.0*	*74.0*	*79.1*
Total Traditional Fixed Income	31.2	31.9	45.4	27.6	2.1	10.9	2.6	7.3	0.0
Fixed Income Hedge Funds & Alternatives	0.0	0.0	0.0	0.0	0.0	12.1	8.8	15.2	10.2
Total Fixed Income	*31.2*	*31.9*	*45.4*	*27.6*	*2.1*	*23.0*	*11.4*	*22.5*	*10.2*
Total Cash & Equivalents	*10.3*	*2.3*	*0.5*	*8.0*	*25.9*	*8.4*	*17.6*	*3.4*	*10.7*
Total Portfolio	*100.0%*	*100.0%*	*100.0%*	*100.0%*	*100.0%*	*100.0%*	*100.0%*	*100.0%*	*100.0%*

SOURCE: New Providence Asset Management

value oriented, which we viewed to be much more fairly priced than growth stocks.

We took high-grade bond holdings up to 45 percent of the overall portfolio. We were not speculators, but were of a strong conviction that bonds were at much more compelling valuation levels than stocks, both on an absolute and relative basis. We simply did what we believed was prudent.

Our asset allocation decisions and liquidity then put us in a position to be scaled down buyers of stocks from late 2001 through the first quarter of 2003. By mid-2003 we had reduced fixed income to 2 percent of the portfolio and had added meaningfully to equities.

In 2003, this portfolio returned +22.8 percent after we had actually generated positive returns on a cumulative basis in the prior three years when the S & P 500 was down −37.6 percent.

New Providence's strategy has been validated throughout market cycles because of numerous investment decisions related to asset allocation and manager selection. This has allowed us to achieve our objective of protecting capital in challenging markets and capturing meaningful upside in better times.

In sum, being liquid and protecting capital allowed us to think clearly and make rational, contrarian, and objective decisions during periods of market stress. Liquidity has also allowed us to take advantage of buying opportunities and was therefore an offensive weapon.

It seems that liquidity allows you to be nimble, especially in times like 2002 and 2008.

It allows you to take advantage of opportunities. You can be a buyer as we were in both those years when many others, regrettably, were forced sellers.

Has the approach to managing tail risk changed?

No. Tail risk is always present and becomes more dangerous the lower volatility and risk premiums get. We think that few clients should be meaningfully short volatility at the portfolio level. You should never allow investment decisions to jeopardize any client's program or viability.

At the individual manager level, some may have varying amounts of tail risk, but at the portfolio level we must manage that risk. We undertake scenario and correlation analysis to see how managers fare in good and bad markets and high and low volatility environments. At the portfolio level, you should never be short too much volatility or take excessive tail risk. We are quite mindful of our clients' responsibility to fulfill their duty of care as fiduciaries.

How do you think about asset allocation?

We work with our clients to evaluate their specific financial situation and agree on appropriate asset classes and parameters.

With the backdrop of our global macroeconomic views, we operate within those preapproved boundaries and if we ever want to operate outside those bands, we are required to get client approval to do so. Within those bands we go to wherever we think the most attractive opportunities are and we do not automatically rebalance to "target allocations."

We believe that automatic rebalancing to adhere to rigid targets can put a portfolio manager in the position of adding to losers and selling out of winners prematurely. Rather, we use our judgment before making any asset allocation change.

What is your stance on thematic investing and watching global trends to make decisions across and within asset classes?

We have always paid very careful attention to what was going on in the global financial markets across asset classes. The five members of our investment committee have spent over 150 years collectively as investors and trustees.

Our stance on investing and making decisions related to various asset classes are evident from a review of the asset allocation table.

We address this in considerable detail in response to your upcoming question, "What are the key trends near to mid-term?"

What can individuals learn from the way endowments invest?

In 2008, many endowments were invested with inappropriate levels of risk and illiquidity for them and for individuals.

There are also some important tactical and practical differences. Large and well-known endowments can invest in ways that individuals cannot. A large endowment has access to nearly any manager and often gets that access on favorable terms and with favorable fees. They may also get a degree of transparency and liquidity which individuals do not. We believe that some of the outperformance of large endowments is related to these advantages. In summary, the endowment model may not offer the best portfolio construct for individuals.

What else can an individual do?

New Providence Asset Management has constructed a portfolio balanced across asset classes where we take moderately sized individual accounts. This portfolio allows clients to invest through a partnership that gets access to top-tier managers. Managers and clients like this arrangement because of the efficiency of their having to deal only with New Providence. We often get scale pricing with long-only equity managers. We have figured out an effective way to provide smaller tax-exempt and taxable clients many of the tactical advantages which the large endowments have, and do so for modest fees.

What are the lessons of 2007–2009? Is this just another business cycle or has something fundamentally changed?

We believe we are in a new world. Many substantive and fundamental variables have changed. Everything from terrorism, to government budget deficits, state and local municipal budget deficits, higher tax rates in this country and other parts of the world are fundamental, long-lasting changes. There has been poor management in and oversight of the financial services industry and other sectors. The degree to which governments have chosen to intervene in economic affairs and businesses is unprecedented.

Yet New Providence is not changing how we operate because our management philosophy should continue to serve us well, because we are flexible, open-minded, and invest opportunistically as explained above. We will continue to invest in a contrarian fashion, adding to positions in asset classes that are out of favor and/or that can be invested in when valuation levels are attractive. By definition, we will also reduce or eliminate positions in asset classes when valuation levels reach excessive levels.

What are the key trends you see coming in the near to mid-term?

Perhaps the best way to answer this question is to share with you how we view the financial markets today.

In trying to project the stock market for 2010, the first question that must be answered is: Will the recovery carry through or will this be a "double dip" recession? In our opinion, the likelihood of a double dip recession is very low. There has not been one in the entire postwar period except for 1981–1982, when Paul Volcker intentionally engineered one by imposing 20 percent interest rates in a successful attempt to break the back of inflation that had become embedded at unacceptably high levels. Even in 1937, when recovery from the 1932 economic trough was aborted by a premature return to fiscal and monetary orthodoxy, the downturn lasted less than a year, and growth was reestablished in the second half of 1938. We do not believe that the Federal Reserve or the president's economic advisors will repeat the errors of 1937, or Japan's errors of 1997. The lessons of history are too well known and too obvious.

If we are not in for a double dip downturn, the question becomes: How rapidly will we grow and what will be the impact of growth on corporate profits? There is nothing scientific about predicting GDP growth rates, and economists who get paid to do this are all over the lot, with estimates generally ranging from 2 percent to 4 percent, and a few outliers above and below these levels. We are inclined to come out at between 3 percent and $3\frac{1}{2}$ percent, which is slightly above long-term trend (which we believe to be about $2\frac{3}{4}$ percent), and enough to make a small dent in the level of unemployment.

We think that growth initially will be driven by inventories and that there will be a modest recovery in automobile sales. We think that the impact of housing will be flat to slightly positive. We think that the consumer will continue to save more and spend less, but not to the draconian degree predicted by some observers, and that consumer spending will increase by 3 percent, or more, which will leave room for a measurable increase in savings. There is a lot of stimulus money yet to be spent, and most of it will impact the first half of the year. We think that the administration and Congress probably will take some further steps to buoy the economy—perhaps in housing or jobs—as midterm elections approach.

Of all of the factors listed above, inventories may be the most important. The mere cessation of liquidation will have a significant impact (first to be noted in 2009's last quarter), and we expect there to be moderate rebuilding on top of that. As business continues to improve, we believe that the credit crunch that is reflected primarily in bank lending will begin to dissipate. Credit quality will improve as the economy begins to grow, and bankers, who are flush with liquidity and very low-cost funds, will be unable to resist putting in place (and locking in) meaningful spreads, given the steep yield curve, now that the easy money from bond trading profits is a thing of the past.

If we are correct and the economy does grow at more than 3 percent, what will be the impact on corporate profits? In our opinion, it will be very positive. American industry is quite leveraged to volume; 2009 profits surprised all observers on the upside even though volumes were very sluggish (remember that for the first six months of the year the economy declined significantly). Many observers are calling for S&P 500 earnings per share of $75; some are beginning to talk about $80. We think that this is an appropriate range and are inclined to the higher end of it.

The $64,000 question when it comes to markets, however, is interest rates, and the $64,000 question when it comes to interest rates is inflation. We continue to believe that unless, and until, wages begin to increase considerably more rapidly than productivity, so that unit labor costs begin to increase significantly, inflation will not be a problem. With unemployment at more than 10 percent (and understated) and productivity increases high, we see no signs of this happening. We also expect the dollar to strengthen this year, as the United States outperforms Europe and Japan and the U.S. current account deficit continues a long-term decline; this is disinflationary. As a result, we do not expect that interest rates will be a serious problem; we do expect them to increase from today's abnormally low levels but we don't know when. However, if Fed Funds go from 0 percent to 2 percent; the 10-year bond from 3.75 percent to $4\frac{1}{2}$ percent; and the 30-year bond from 4.75 percent to $5\frac{1}{2}$ percent (which we do not necessarily expect in 2010), the bond market would suffer a lot, but we would hardly be suffering from tight money.

With the backdrop outlined above, what do we expect from the stock market?

We looked at market history after the severe market breaks of 1974, 1982, and 2002. What we saw was that:

In the market recoveries from both the 1974 and 1982 breaks most of the initial recovery took place in the first nine months, and all of it had taken place by the end of the second calendar year after the break. The second years also were positive, but not dramatically so. The 1974 market recovery stalled in 1977 (a 20 percent decline), and then went on to new highs before peaking in 1980. The 1982 market recovery reaccelerated in 1985 and continued on a tear until the 1987 crash.

After the 2002 decline, the recovery was slower, because of the overhang of the Iraq War, which started in March 2003, but once the war started a strong market developed and continued for more than four years, until the summer of 2007.

If history is any guide—and it very well may not be—and given our economic and interest rate outlook, here is what we think will happen in 2010:

The market will be generally positive and will finish the year higher than it started. Our guess would be 10 percent to 15 percent higher. This would bring the S&P 500 averages to between 1,275 and 1,280, which is somewhere in the range of 15 times to 17 times earnings of $75 to $80 per share, an entirely reasonable number given our expectation for interest rates.

We do expect a correction—10 percent or so—as the year progresses, if only because we haven't had one since March 9, 2009. The possibility is that this could happen as a knee-jerk reaction to the first signs that the Fed is prepared to let interest rates move up and will dissipate as it becomes clear that the move up is to a level of normal easy money, rather than to tight money. Of course, geopolitical events, positive or negative, could outweigh both economic and interest rate developments, and given the events of the past week, this may in fact be happening.

As to asset allocation, our thinking is as follows:

We are positive on U.S. equities. In the United States we continue to weight long/short hedge funds and distressed hedge fund specialists more heavily than long-only managers because we feel more comfortable with a hedged exposure. Within long only, we tend to prefer managers who emphasize large capitalization, dividend paying stocks.

Over the long term, we are positive on emerging markets, particularly China and India.

We are negative on bonds and fixed income generally, except for highly specialized niche managers.

We have generally chosen not to invest in Europe or Japan. With regard to Europe, we recognize the strength and soundness of Germany and the Benelux countries and that France is in better shape than we would have expected. However, the rest of Europe is in bad shape—in some cases very bad—and is faced with many years of stagnation. The euro, in our opinion, is overvalued. The euro block probably will survive, but the pressures on it will be enormous. In the case of Japan, although we recognize that the Japanese stock market is abnormally depressed, we remain seriously concerned about the country's fundamental economic, financial, political, and demographic problems.

We have not been owners of commodities, believing that these are not investments, but simply speculations on price. Our lack of interest in this area is reinforced by a belief that the dollar will be stronger rather than weaker (except against Asian currencies—ex Japan—which we expect to appreciate).

We continue to believe that, in a world where significant uncertainty is sure to be with us for some time, liquidity and reasonable conservatism will prove to be the hallmarks of good investing for the foreseeable future.

A lot of CIOs don't like leverage. What they have said almost universally is, "I'm not interested in leverage-oriented private equity investments because there are cheaper ways to get returns associated with leverage. I don't mind the use of leverage, but if I find out that that's where the preponderance of the return is coming from I don't like that." What do you think?

We believe that most proponents of leverage have generally changed their views post-2008. People wanted to beat the indexes. They wanted to generate alpha and take almost any steps to augment returns, still looking in the rear view mirror and chasing the returns of the 1990s.

Our view has always been that if you are a good investor, you do not need leverage to make money. If you are a bad investor, you do not dare use it because it is just going to magnify your losses.

We think the proof of the value of a nonleveraged approach can be seen in New Providence's performance and low volatility at the portfolio level.

We have selected equity managers and made asset allocations to equities for 11 years. Over that time, the equity part of our portfolio has outperformed the S&P 500 in every year and by 6.5 percent per annum on average. The fixed income component of our portfolio has outperformed the Barclay's Aggregate Bond Index by 2 percent per annum over the last 11 years.

One of the strategies endowments, the financial services industry, and consultants invented, used, and/or marketed was "portable alpha." This technique had managers investing in the following manner: If one had $100 million to invest, they would put $95 million in a "market neutral fund," and then take the remaining $5 million and use that as (initial) margin to purchase $100 million of S&P futures. Therefore they knew what they were going to get for their $100 million was the S&P return plus (or minus) whatever this market neutral or absolute return funded yielded. That's how they were trying to outperform the index . . . by leveraging 2 to 1.

There are basic problems with this approach. First, in a year like 2008, they lost a lot of their money in S&P futures and simultaneously lost money in market neutral and absolute return funds who were taking duration risk, credit risk, and were often leveraged as well. They could be down 20 percent even though they called themselves market neutral or absolute return. So portfolios lost money on both investments.

The investors in portable alpha also had another problem: The S&P futures they were long required mark-to-market margin calls, and so they had a liquidity problem.

Aside from our view that portable alpha is generally an imprudent way to invest in equities, we feel that many market neutral and absolute return managers have much more beta to the equity markets than the description of their strategies imply. The market does not hand you 9 percent for free when the fed funds rate is 1 percent without a manager incurring meaningful risk of some kind. To earn double-digit returns in almost any environment, these managers must be taking credit or duration risk and/or employing leverage.

While there seems to be widespread, stated distaste for leverage today, we believe if you analyze portfolios dating before the most recent downturn you would find the use of it to have been quite pervasive.

What do you do to understand the risks you have in your portfolio?

We stress test under diverse scenarios.

We run scenario analysis where we assume that very bad returns could be generated simultaneously in most asset classes where our portfolios are invested. We look at the results at the portfolio level and we try to make sure that our clients would not be in jeopardy even if that scenario came to pass.

What will happen with endowment portfolios in the coming few years?

We think that some institutions are in much worse shape than is currently understood and acknowledged. The market recovery in 2009 may have bailed out a number of institutions. To fully solve the problems of many others, the market needs to keep going up from here. We think there are reasonably widespread problems, which may come to light if we see another meaningful market downturn in the near future.

In the aftermath of 2008, endowments will make at least two major changes: They will be much more liquid and will meaningfully reduce commitments to investments that entail long-term lock-ups.

As far as trends go, we see more outsourcing of portfolios to firms like New Providence Asset Management. We believe that 10 years from now, the majority of endowments and foundations are going to outsource their investment management function. We think this will also apply to large endowments as well as small ones. Many issues for institutions and families are solved with outsourcing; finding, screening, and monitoring managers with comprehensive due diligence, compensation, and so on, while avoiding committee and family politics and assuring long-term continuity.

Many fiduciaries cannot fulfill their duty of care, meeting only sporadically as part-time volunteers. Investing at this level and as a fiduciary is a full-time job.

How should university endowments approach working capital management?

This is something we help all clients evaluate. We work with them to fully understand their current and prospective financial situations. This evaluation lets us determine their liquidity needs and help manage it appropriately.

Over the past few years some endowments got squeezed by investing working capital in what were in reality long-term, illiquid portfolio investments.

New Providence would never recommend that a client invest in any long-term lock-up that could not be comfortably funded out of the liquid portion of their portfolio, including high-grade fixed income.

How do you approach manager selection?

Rigorous fundamental analysis drives our process. Investment theses are built on our bottom-up work and our fundamental understanding of managers. Our fundamental analysis consists of:

- Multiple, documented on-site meetings prior to investing and on an ongoing basis.
- Focus on the history of success, managing the exact strategy in which we plan to invest.
- Managers must demonstrate distinctive and insightful investment theses.
- Strategy must be transparent: strengths, weaknesses and drivers of performance coherent and explicit.
- Quality of returns; out-performance must be generated by strategy without excessive leverage or concentration.
- Meetings and background checks must confirm the highest level of integrity throughout the organization.
- Each decision maker is held to the same high standards and must be directly aligned with investors.
- Managers must have substantial personal assets invested in the strategy/vehicle we invest in.
- Monthly questionnaires, reports, calls, and meetings must continue to substantiate our conclusions.

- Detailed quantitative analysis supports our investment decisions. Quantitative analysis is used to confirm fundamental conclusions as well as to monitor the strategy and risk profile of managers and portfolios.
- Statistical analysis: attribution, standard deviation, correlation, alpha, beta, risk metrics/ratios, and so on.
- Benchmark analysis: Managers are evaluated against benchmarks we determine are appropriate.
- Scenario analysis: Isolate performance during different market conditions.
- Market cap exposure, style, strategy, industry exposure, leverage, and AUM.

What differentiates New Providence Asset Management from other choices for portfolio management?

First, the length and type of experience our five-person investment committee team has is critical. The principals at our firm have over 150 years of experience operating as decision makers in the money management business across asset classes and as fiduciaries and trustees. We have been active in making specific investment decisions as well as selecting managers and are not academics. We believe our direct experience is a fundamental prerequisite to run an outsourced investment office successfully.

Second, interests should be aligned. We invest our own money with the same managers and on the same terms as our clients do. As a group we have the significant majority of our own liquid net worth invested through New Providence Asset Management.

In addition, we do not believe that outsourcing firms should charge incentive fees at the portfolio level because we believe it motivates additional risk taking that may be inappropriate.

Pre-crisis it seemed that fund-raising was considerably easier for managers. Is the balance shifting, and are investors now asking more from managers?

Absolutely. It has already happened. It is evident to New Providence that since 2007 there has been an enormous shift in the dynamic and the nature of the relationship and the give and take between the GP and LP. As a generalization, the LP has much more bargaining power than before and it is much easier to get capacity, transparency, and so on from managers.

Disclosures

The investment office results depicted for the period before fiscal year 2009 are those achieved for the endowment of New Providence's initial client. For calendar 2009 and the fiscal years 2008 and 2009 the results are the average of those investment office clients for which New Providence actively managed the entire portfolio during these time periods. The fund of funds performance returns have been presented net of fund expenses as well as the deduction of the highest management and incentive fees charged. The historical performance returns reflect all income, gains and losses, and the reinvestment of interest and other earnings.

The returns are compared to numerous indexes. The volatility and holdings of the New Providence accounts may differ significantly from the securities that comprise these indexes. The returns of the indexes are calculated on a total return basis with dividends reinvested if applicable. The indexes do not include the reinvestment of interest nor the deduction of advisory fees.

Past performance is not indicative of future results and all investments involve risk, including the loss of principal.

The performance results of New Providence's other clients may be different from the results presented.

Chapter 19

Bob Boldt

Chief Executive Officer

Boldt Ventures

"Diversification is the only real free lunch in the investment world."

Boldt Ventures

Boldt Ventures advises institutional investors, including academic endowments, foundations and sovereign wealth funds. The firm assists with fund strategy, structure and operations, risk assessment, asset allocation, manager and fund selection, competitive benchmarking and performance measurement.

B ob Boldt is the chief executive officer of Boldt Ventures. Prior to founding Boldt Ventures, he was executive chairman and chief investment officer of Agility Asset Management, a division of Perella Weinberg Partners which provides endowment investing approaches to institutions and high-net-worth individuals.

From 2002 to 2006, Bob served as the CEO and CIO of the University of Texas Investment Management Company, managing nearly $20 billion in assets. Previously, Bob was a managing director at Pivotal Asset Management, and also he served as senior investment officer for Global Public Markets Investments at CalPERS, where he oversaw the start of a hedge fund investment program.

Bob received a bachelor of science in engineering and a masters in business administration from the University of Texas. He has also earned the Chartered Financial Analyst (CFA) designation.

Q: Endowments seem more dynamic and have wider latitude to make investment decisions now than ever in the past. Would you agree?

They are certainly more dynamic now than they were 10 years ago. If your time frame is two years ago or one year ago, I'm not sure that is exactly true. One of the big advantages of the large endowment model is this flexibility, this willingness to be first movers into new asset categories, to invest with smaller money managers that may not have a 10-year track record like the large public pension funds always seem to want to have. Large endowments always seem to be a big part of a new manager's fund.

This flexibility has been one of the big advantages of the large endowment model and the reason it has performed so well over time. However, I think over the last couple of years, I detect retrenchment from this previous pushing of the envelope, particularly among the board members. The reason the large endowments have been able to be forward-thinking on manager selection is because they've had enlightened board members, wealthy individuals, leading-edge academics who have not only allowed the creativity but in fact have encouraged it and facilitated it by helping the endowment get into funds that have been historically difficult to get into. What I see now because of the market downturn is a reaction to the illiquidity that endowments got into. I think there is some pullback from that and we'll have to see if it's lasting or not.

The other big change in dynamism is the question of whether endowments will change their investing strategy as a result of the financial circumstances of the school themselves. Endowments have been very successful over the past decade or more. In turn, I think this encouraged rising expenses in university operating budgets and reliance on the endowment income to cover the increases.

Annual academic budgets are fragile things and schools don't well tolerate budget cuts. The idea that the same portfolio or even a more aggressive portfolio now supports 30 percent of the operating budget, when only 10 years prior maybe a more conservative portfolio supported 15 percent of the budget, is going too far. It goes against financial theory and common sense. You can relate this to an individual as they get older and as the income from their investments supports them their portfolio should get more conservative, not more aggressive.

That didn't happen in the endowment world, in fact it went in the opposite direction. While I was at UTIMCO, the income from the endowment only supported about 6 percent of the budget. So if anything, the UT endowment should have been more aggressive than other large endowments. However, it wasn't the case. UTIMCO was relatively conservative.

I think part of what's happened in the last couple of years is institutions are trying to determine if their goal is to build a portfolio that blows away peers in terms of performance or build a portfolio that is right for the institution's particular circumstance. I think you'll find more introspection going forward, which may lead to less dynamism.

Will this reduce the focus on a "Performance Derby" where institutions do annual peer group comparisons by relative performance?

You can still compare endowment performance to a peer group, but instead of comparing at the aggregate level you can compare at the subaggregate level. You can compare how you performed within an asset class, for example, how your private equity investments did versus theirs. The idea of comparing the aggregate portfolio across the whole universe of peers who have very different, varying needs and varying financial circumstances just doesn't make a lot of sense, never did, and makes less sense now.

So breaking the comparison down to the asset-class level may make sense, but looking at all endowments the same at the aggregate level turns out to be a poor mechanism for judging performance.

It really does. Other inaccuracy comes from trying to compare endowments to pension funds or even foundations. Foundations are a very different organism than endowments, which are very different from pension funds. For too long, we all collectively have thought of those as institutional portfolios and have compared performance and talked about them as though they are all the same, and they are really not. Sovereign wealth funds are different also.

A lot of people say that sovereign wealth funds are just big endowments. They are very different in some important ways. The industry needs to get more fine grained about how we evaluate the performance of these big pools of institutional capital. I think that will be one of the lasting lessons of what we just went through (the crisis). Unfortunately, I think that this and some of the other lessons from this latest downturn are going to be forgotten pretty quickly.

What are the models for endowment fund management?

There are two distinctively different models for managing endowments. One employs external managers only and does very little internally except asset allocation. They will conduct periodic aggressive rebalancing and perform excellent manager selection. The second model does all the things the first model does, but then goes further. It will internally manage money, make direct investments, and lever the endowment. It looks more like a multistrategy hedge fund than a typical endowment fund.

At University of Texas we leaned toward the second model. We managed some of our assets internally. In the future that is going to be an increasingly important facility to have internally at the larger endowments. You need internal trading strategies to facilitate your risk management system, the ability to put on hedges when you need them, the ability to amplify certain positions that your managers have when you think they should be amplified, and the ability to make asset allocation changes in more cost-effective ways using ETFs, options, and futures. All of that makes a lot of sense to have as an internal capability.

What this means for the endowment organization is that you have to have people on your staff that have managed money firsthand, and not just the ability to pick managers.

Is the probability of a tail event larger now and are the tails fatter?

I don't think the tails are fatter now than before. We just recently had a tail event. Human beings are subject to certain frailties that behavioral economists write about, and I think the recency is causing us to over-estimate the risk. For example, if you surveyed people right after any unusual event and you ask them what the probability of the event is, they will predict it higher than actual. So we think the tails are fatter now only because we had one very recent event. I'm not sure the tails are a higher probability now than they have been, but the industry was prob-ably underestimating it a few years ago, like they are overestimating it now. After a few years pass we will likely lapse back into underestimating the tails.

How should institutions and investors hedge tail risk?

I think this idea that we have to hedge tail risk is important. However, I am not sure CIOs have the tools to go about it effectively. Hedging tail risk is expensive in the short run. Almost everything you would do to manage tail risk has a cost to carry. You have to actually pay out money, like buying insurance. This kind of insurance is expensive because the cost of a loss is large and the probability is small and hard to estimate. Furthermore, because everyone is overestimating tail risk, the price gets driven up.

How are boards going to react when the investment staff come in and says, "We want to put this tail risk insurance on" and the cost is x and x is a large number? Then we go 4–5 years and there is no tail and we have this big cost for 4–5 years. If we go several years paying tail risk insurance and boards see they are consuming a lot of money for hedges, they are going to want to take them off. The tail risk hedges will fall into disfavor and they will take them off just about the time they are going to need them.

Another way to think about tail risk hedging is not necessarily put the hedges on right now, but changing the nature of the organization to be less brittle to tail events. The nature of a tail event is that you can't describe today what it is—it is unknowable. That means you can't know how to hedge it. What you can do, however, is create an organization that is less brittle to these events. An organization that has the capability to put on positions once a tail event appears, or appears imminent, may be the key. Even if you don't know what the event is going to look like exactly, you can see it forming. For example, there was plenty of time to put on hedging before the event we just went through. You didn't need to carry the hedges for 10 years. You could have put them on in the middle and still saved the endowment plenty of money. Endowments weren't structured to make these kind of moves, though.

Other things could have helped as well. Schools could have had standby letters of credit and other kinds of things to carry them through this situation instead of having to go out and do some of the difficult things we saw, like putting their private equity portfolios out to bid. There are things organizations can do to make themselves better responders to these kinds of events. This is what I would encourage institutions to do instead of actually putting on hedges so far ahead of time.

You would advocate building organization flexibility, process, and liquidity to carry out hedges instead of specifically putting one on now in anticipation of some unspecified event?

Absolutely. For instance, many people feel now that the largest tail risk we face is the loss of the dollar as the world currency standard. This would make for a complete fall in the dollar and a big inflation flare-up. Should we today short the dollar and do those things? If you did that over the last few months of 2009, you would have gotten hurt. Those are the things that in the short run debase the standing of the staff in the view of the board. The board would say, "Are we operating outside the capability of our staff and infrastructure?" "This is expensive." "Should we be doing this?" Then they would likely take the hedge off, instead of just being ready to do it when it is the right time to do it.

Related, I don't think cash is an asset class. Cash as an asset class is one of those things that will have an 18-month half-life. It is not a particularly good asset class. It doesn't hedge inflation. I don't think you will see people carrying large cash balances. But I think you will see people having liquidity facilities that can be tapped quickly. I don't think there is anything necessarily wrong with, instead of carrying cash, having the ability to tap credit markets quickly if needed. A large school that has a AAA credit rating can tap credit markets effectively and not have the drain of having a big cash position in their endowment. This is just something the CIO should prearrange.

A lot of liquidity-affecting events hit endowments simultaneously last year. Big donations slowed down, illiquid investments no longer generated cash, private investments began having capital calls, there was higher demand for operating cash, and so on. You are suggesting there are ways to ensure liquidity besides holding a lot of cash.

Yes. Having cash in the endowment didn't really help those schools with their payout anyway. Endowments have restricted funds that wouldn't allow them to dip into the endowment. I think you need to separate all the factors that affect liquidity requirements. Only a couple of them like the ability to fund private equity calls, and maybe the inability to move in on opportunistic investments are unique to the endowment. The others are unique to the school themselves. Liquidity is important. But you have to separate the liquidity needs of the endowment and the school. They are not necessarily the same.

What is your stance on how far schools should go in managing working capital through the endowment office?

At UT, we managed the working capital for the entire UT system. Endowment staffs are uniquely positioned to do a great job of managing the working capital. A lot of what universities call working capital is not working capital, it is permanent capital or "quasi-endowment."

Most people think of an endowment as a big pool of money in a holistic way. In fact, most endowments are actually 2–3 thousand smaller endowments that together create the endowment for the school. When a wealthy individual creates an endowment for the school, sometimes the donation has restrictions that dictate what it can do, what it can't do, what services or facilities it supports. That money gets lumped into the long-term endowment, but you can't think of it as one monolithic fund.

The timing of when the school wants to use money dedicated to a specific purpose complicates the matter further. If a donor earmarks funds, and funds are distributed through the annual payout, but the dean is not ready in a given year to use the money, then the money might be outside the endowment but also be a longer-term investment. If the money is to support a new chair in a department, it can take a while just to finish the faculty search. This happens frequently and with great volume, so there are pools of money outside the long-term endowment with long-term features and that are not really working capital.

These kind of funds need to be managed differently than working capital. This means that the university must be sophisticated in its handling of this. The chief financial officer of the university and the endowment head will need to work together. The endowment staff should play a large role in managing those funds, because they have access to the markets, expertise, and knowledge.

Endowment performance measurement is closely tied to CIO and staff compensation and the performance derby. Is this going to be an important issue for the industry to solve?

This was something I saw firsthand during my tenure at UT. UTIMCO was the first private separate investment firm founded by a public university. When I started there was a performance incentive plan in place, but it was relatively minimal. We wanted to orient the organization toward investment performance, which is how most external money management firms work.

One of the things we thought was central to that goal was putting in a more significant and structured variable compensation plan. The board and the investment team spent a lot of time evaluating how best to do this. The harder we looked, the more I felt there wasn't a perfect solution. There are a number of complicating factors. For instance, many of the investments an endowment will enter try to take advantage of the illiquidity premium. That means my private equity staff was making investments that weren't likely to pay off for 7–10 years. We wouldn't know the full performance for a long time, and a lot can change at the staff level over that much time as well.

This creates a challenge in short- to mid-term measurement, particularly for illiquid asset classes. You have to employ subjective judgment, since you can't use the performance numbers. The subjectivity is not very satisfying to the board or the staff. Nor is it satisfying to the many people who are watching the compensation structure at a public university.

One imperfect solution is to have performance be a part of compensation, but also to evaluate some qualitative things. For example, "are your due-diligence analyses well done?" Identifying qualitative performance is a difficult process, especially in the investment management field. This will be a continuing issue for the industry, and the whole compensation issue needs to have a lot more time spent on it than it has been given.

Do you think the compensation and performance measurement issues will lead to endowments just outsourcing, which eliminates the problem for the institution?

I think in time it's a nascent market. It is a market that's been around for a long time in very small endowments. That's why the Commonfund is the size it is and the TIFF has gathered foundation assets. I think you will see some of the middle-sized $100 million to $1 billion endowments realize that outsourcing is a better solution. It is getting increasingly hard for smaller organizations to hold on to good people on the staff and as CIOs. You can't get by with having a great CIO and not have the right structures in place that let them build and compensate a team. You need a solid staff at the top and the middle.

What is your thinking on thematic investing versus strict asset allocation?

This is a very interesting and important question. For example, up until the last three or four years the asset classes in most endowments were fairly standardized. You would see people have public equity, private equity, hedge funds, real assets, and then maybe another opportunistic category. Asset categories were the focus. The staff was organized around asset classes, and therefore tended to think about things in their own silos. Private equity guys went out and did private equity deals. Fixed income guys did fixed income.

One of the things we've learned from this crisis is that a lot of times there are opportunities that are present across asset categories. This means endowments will want to have people working as teams looking across asset categories to find the best way of implementing opportunities.

A good recent example is distressed credit. Credit markets became dislocated or dysfunctional. The bid ask spread was too wide to be bridged so the transactions were few. Transactions were only done by distressed investors. What were distressed in most cases were the investors and not necessarily the companies that issued the debt. So you had a situation where I would argue the right way to look at the whole distressed debt marketplace or the lock-up in credit markets was to look across the asset categories. Private equity people should have been looking at situations where distressed debt could be purchased to gain control. In fact, the worst way to play the locked up credit markets were in the public markets. While the spreads widened out, there was a lot more opportunity to buy distressed bank debt, for example, that was semiprivate rather than simply worrying about which corporate credits to buy. So I think the idea of themes is going to get a lot more important to people.

Another example of this might be the dollar losing its status as the reserve currency, which would cross many asset classes. The impact of inflation is another. If you have too much of a silo view you will miss some really important opportunities to implement large-scale investment themes as they come along.

It seems that a thematic investing orientation will change the way endowments organize their investment staff.

Yes. That is why I prefer people that have managed money. Everybody on our staff at UTIMCO and our staff here at Agility has managed money. They will have the skills required. For instance, they will have the background it takes to know how to do due diligence on a public market manager. You need to have people that look at the portfolio from an investment perspective, not just from a consultant perspective. Staff issues are at the heart of everything we do. What we worked to do at UTIMCO and Agility is try to find people that are willing and anxious to work together as a team looking across asset categories to implement a theme.

To orient to themes, it seems that they need to be experienced money managers, but they also need to be good at business and economics in general.

Yes. This goes back to my earlier comments on tail risk and endowment flexibility. This is important now more than ever, and it is why the staff must be good economic analysts. They have to answer the question: "Is the investment good from an economic point of view?" They have to make a primary decision.

For example, right now if we have cap-and-trade, and we start trading carbon credits, is that a market that makes sense? What is going to drive that market? Is there a way to make money in that market? We aren't going to own factories. Is there room in there for speculators similar to the commodities market who make money there? If so, how do you do it? That kind of analysis is what is needed. Answering these questions is a lot different than deciding whether you are going to hire manager A or B.

Why did you decide to found your new firm?

My time at UTIMCO was terrific. Being CIO at a major endowment fund is one of the best jobs around. It is fun, it is an investment job, and if you work for your alma mater, you get to be involved in the institution, you get involved in fund-raising, you get involved in planning for the university, and it has great personal meaning. The CIO role at a university is much more expansive than simply managing a pool of assets.

In my case, I had a satisfying and productive time at UT. We accomplished a lot. However, I decided I wanted to go back to the private sector. Managing a public university endowment also means satisfying a diverse set of constituencies both inside and outside the university. I was ready to focus solely on investment management. However, I enjoy working with endowment people and endowment boards, so I thought this was a way I could continue doing what I enjoy in terms of investing a large asset fund. I thought there was a market for bringing large-endowment expertise to smaller and mid-size endowments. This meant I could continue using my expertise and stay at the leading edge of looking at asset categories that are new and exciting and potentially very profitable for my clients.

The market has created some really good alternatives for medium and smaller sized endowments today that didn't exist before. For the reasons we discussed earlier, the outsourced endowment management business is going to build substantially over the next few years. I believe that the endowment style of managing also applies to other institutional assets such as sovereign wealth funds and for the private funds of high-net-worth individuals. The endowment style has a lot of flexibility and agility built into it and can be applied to many markets. I have very high expectations for not only what some people call the outsourced CIO market but also for growth in firms which provide this type of management (global multiasset management) into a number of large-end markets.

What, if anything, should individuals be learning from what endowment CIOs know how to do?

Diversification is the only real free lunch in the investment world. Take advantage of it. Second, don't outreach your capabilities. I think the most dangerous thing an individual can do is invest beyond their ability. If you can't identify the best manager in an asset category, you are better off not investing in it than picking at random. Finally, diversify across asset classes, not just within an asset class. Owning a broad set of U.S. public equities is not asset diversity.

What do you read that helps you stay informed?

I read a lot of nonfiction, strategic books. For instance, a good read prior to the crash was *A Demon of Our Own Design* by Richard Bookstaber (Wiley, 2007). It basically forecast everything that happened in this melt-down, and it did it before the meltdown occurred. The finance industry has created a web of derivative products that not even the people that designed them understand. This means that we don't know how this thing will react if something goes wrong. It was a great book. It's gotten more play now. It looks now like something you should have read before the crisis.

I also liked *Seven Deadly Scenarios* by Andrew F. Krepinevich, a military planner. I think we can learn from the military with regard to managing tail risk. That's what military planners try to do. This book explored how the military prepares their organization to handle a variety of scenarios. We talked about making your organization less brittle. This is one way to do that. I try to read a lot of books like these. Another example is *Against the Gods* by Peter Bernstein. I don't read a lot of pure investment books. I read intellectual strategy more than implementation-oriented books.

Any parting thoughts on trends?

It's almost impossible, statistically speaking, to be first to anticipate the event, but you don't need to be the first, you just need to identify it before it is too late and be able to react to it. For instance, when the subprime crisis hit, John Paulson made a fortune. He wasn't necessarily the first in the game. He just had himself and his organization set up in such a way that he could rapidly make the bets that he did and they really paid off.

There are a lot of opportunities in investments right now. We pretty much know that at some point something has to give with the dollar. The tax regime has to be changed—the current structure cannot pay for everything we have taken on as an obligation, and it is going to have to happen another way. I don't know precisely how it is going to happen at the moment, but I know that there will be some opportunities that will emerge from it. You don't have to be first, you just have to be ready to act when the time is right. Timing is important—if you look at when large fortunes are made, there could be numerous people that made the right decision but made it too early and got stopped out. Someone told them, "You have to take this bet off, it's costing too much money." The play that Paulson put on had a huge carrying cost to it and if the whole blowup had been delayed by a year or two, things might have been different.

Conclusion

Concepts for Individual Investors

"Individual investors are most comfortable when the stock market is going up."

—Endowment CIO

This journey started as a quest to understand how individual investors could benefit from endowment investment principles. We recommend reading the individual chapters for each endowment profiled in this book. However, we wanted to provide a closing summary for the reader in three key areas. First, what can individual investors take away from endowments and use to inform their own investment decision making. Second, a summary of the global macroeconomic trends that CIOs believed would be important in the coming few years and that the CIOs are using in planning their institution's midterm investment strategy. Finally, we have a few predictions about the future of the endowment business and the implications for the general partners in which they invest.

Lessons for Individual Investors

Individuals vs. Endowments

At the outset we wanted to determine if individuals would be able to implement the specific approaches used by endowments. We discovered that the number and magnitude of differences between the situations of an individual and an endowment make it difficult to mimic endowments closely. Here are the main differences we identified:

Access—Institutional money (foundations, endowments, pension funds, sovereign wealth funds) enjoy unique access to money managers, especially alternative privately managed funds. Institutional investors are attractive to private fund managers (hedge funds, private equity, venture capital) for a variety of reasons. Endowments are considered "smart" money—clients that will ask good questions and be helpful in the process. Institutions are long-term investors that will not redeem capital on a whim. Institutions can put considerable capital to work at once, typically much more than an individual can. If the fund goes well, institutions have the money to enter subsequent funds raised by the manager reducing the manager's future marketing costs. University endowments in particular also may help the manager with fund-raising, as it gives the manager the opportunity to add a well-known and respected brand name to their client list. Additionally, only the top decile of fund managers have beaten standard market indexes over long time periods. Therefore access to the top funds in any category is essential for outperformance, and typically these funds are only available to institutional investors. An individual can do more harm than good by trying to mimic the private investment strategy of an endowment and investing in underperforming private funds.

Expertise—Large endowments have as few as 3–4 and as many as several dozen investment professionals; some have one experienced person dedicated exclusively to each asset class. If they need additional information, endowments have easily-arranged access to the best economic and financial advisers across the globe. Contrast this with the expertise utilized by individual investors who usually do not have the investment expertise nor access to the best advice in making their decisions.

Bandwidth—The investment professionals we interviewed are dedicated to investment management full-time and spend the majority of their day evaluating different investment vehicles, understanding trends, and identifying new opportunities. This often entails considerable national and international travel. Once a trend is spotted, focused endowment staff work tirelessly to identify the best investment vehicle and execute quickly. It is difficult or impossible for an individual to devote this amount of time to their investing decisions.

Taxes—Endowments are most often nonprofit entities and can invest without the constraint of evaluating the tax consequences of their actions.

Time horizon—Endowments have a perpetual time frame; they are the ultimate long-term investor and are thinking about their strategy over a period of decades. Endowments have the time to recover bear market losses whereas an individual investor needing to liquidate due to an unexpected situation may be devastated. Individual investors typically think that a decade is a long time but it may take that long to weather a downturn in the public equity market.

Liquidity requirements/expense and cash needs—Endowments will have a range of spending policies and cash requirements, but generally will not have the higher liquidity requirements in a given year that a retired individual might.

Fees—Endowments have a large amount of money to invest and a brand name that fund managers can use in their own marketing. This often gives them access to lower fee schedules.

Tools—Endowments can afford to invest in custom tools and reports that give them the ability to understand and analyze their portfolio (e.g., allocations, risks, correlation).

Vintage year diversification—Endowments can afford to invest a material amount of money over a longer period of years, thus eliminating correlation due to investing only in a given year. They can put money to work in a given private fund over a string of subsequent years, while easily meeting the minimum investment for the fund in each year. This is important because asset valuations rise and fall. When investing in private funds it is critical to average out your investment across multiple years to reduce the potential of investing into a peak. Individual investors sometimes succumb to the herd mentality and invest in what's "hot" at exactly the time that valuations are at all time highs. One example is private real estate investments in 2006.

Taken together, it is easy to see that endowments have major architectural differences, which gives them advantages over options afforded individual investors. Only a few of these disadvantages can be overcome, and then only by the wealthiest of private investors.

Individuals do have one advantage, which is more control and speed in their decision making. Endowment spending and investment policies are geared to ensure good governance, but this also means that they have more procedures, policies, political considerations and formal decision making processes. Individuals can be more rapid and flexible than endowments. However, this may work out to be a disadvantage, since individuals may be too hasty and impatient in entering or exiting an investment.

There are still valuable lessons that individuals can learn from endowments. We asked each CIO what advice they had for the individual investor. Interestingly, they stressed a number of investing basics that individuals already know, but may not be practicing. The lesson is that there is considerable benefit to be realized from simply focusing on the basics and not trying to overcomplicate matters. In the conversations we had with CIOs a number of important ideas that individuals can use emerged.

Start with Your Objectives

We learned how heterogeneous endowments are. Every institution has its own unique operating budget requirements and culture, which have a large impact on how it will invest. Individuals have even more variation. CIOs agreed that individuals can mimic institutions by starting with an investment plan that clearly defines objectives. These will vary greatly depending on age, income, net worth, family situation, risk tolerance, retirement timing and income ambitions. To invest like an endowment you have to first understand what balance of wealth preservation, income generation, and asset growth will best fit your unique situation. No two endowments are alike and certainly no two individuals are. Are you looking to maximize the return of your investments for the next 10 years or next 30 years? Do you need the income generated from investments? What would happen if you lost 25 percent of the value of your portfolio tomorrow; could you afford to keep the portfolio invested and review 10 years from now? Determining your risk tolerance and your investment objectives are critical to understanding the return you should target.

Be Diversified

One CIO mentioned, "Diversification is really the only free lunch in the investment business." It was clear after our extensive interviews that CIOs think much more broadly about asset classes than the average individual investor. Individuals tend to look for diversification within U.S. public equities and various types of government fixed income instruments. Endowments go further—they evaluate U.S. public equities, but also want to have high- and low-risk corporate bonds, non-U.S. public equities, private equity, hedge funds, venture capital, real-estate, absolute return funds, real assets, and currency funds, to name a few. They further think about all of these in a time-phased way, or "vintage year" of the investment, so that they have diversification across time as well. They position these investments to carefully balance risks across market sectors, countries, currencies, debt and interest rates.

Finally, endowments told us they frequently observed a "home bias" in individual investment decision making. Investors can think globally about their assets and work to diversify away specific country risk. As one CIO put it, "A home bias plus a style box does not equal real diversification."

Endowments have significant advantage in terms of access, expertise, and bandwidth, which allow them to be precise in their diversification and asset classes. However, individuals can add ETFs and a variety of other investment vehicles that have emerged over the past few years to their portfolio. An individual investor can broaden their asset class horizon significantly, even without the advantages an endowment enjoys.

One thing that endowments had in common is three clearly defined "buckets" of money. The majority of the funds go into the core holdings, a diversified portfolio with target allocation and periodic rebalancing. The second, smaller portion goes into low-volatility, highly secure, low-return, highly liquid vehicles. This is "emergency" money. The final portion is invested in speculative, high-volatility, potentially high-return ventures or is used to "tilt" the portfolio without changing the allocation in the first portion. Individuals can put a portion of their own assets into these categories, and then focus their short-term and active management efforts on the third portion. This can satisfy the individual's need to feel that they are doing something proactive with their investments while minimizing the risk of damage to the overall portfolio and creating some potential upside.

Ask a Lot of Questions

Good investors don't make a leap of faith in their decision making. CIOs conduct extensive diligence even on managers they have previously used. They don't shrink from asking the tough questions. If they don't understand something, they keep asking questions until they do. If they can't get there, they don't invest.

Individual investors should be sure they clearly know what they own. Complex financial instruments can be difficult to comprehend and may not react as predicted under varying market conditions. Even large-cap public equities have diverse balance sheets. Know what you own. Also know what the fees are and how they will affect returns. Return net of fees is the most important benchmark.

Be Patient. Be Disciplined.

Another hallmark of good investors is patience and discipline. When an endowment develops a strategy, they know it may take 5, 10, or even 15 years to play out. They are constantly aware of taking a long view in their decision making and are not easily rattled by day-to-day or week-to-week changes in the markets. They develop a conviction on the state of affairs, act on it, and then patiently wait for events to unfold. They are disciplined in adhering to their policies—they are not emotional in their decision making. They will cut losers when they go over a predetermined threshold, and they will trim winners before they top out. As numerous financial sages have noted: "The stock doesn't know that you own it."

Endowments do not try to time the market. They may engage in opportunistic investments or they may try to hedge specific risks they see, but in both cases they move in a matter of weeks or months, not hours, and they rarely commit material portions of the core assets to the move.

Endowments also do not get carried away in their analysis of trends. They are skeptics by nature, and they know that it is easy to be wrong due to unanticipated circumstances. One CIO we interviewed put this well, saying:

> Good ideas on secular trends are seductive because it makes you seem wise. However, a lot has to go well. You have to be right. You have to select the right vehicle to invest in. You have to time it well, not too early, and you have to get in before it is too crowded. All this makes it difficult to manage to secular trends. Diversification is your ally here.

The virtues of patience and discipline in executing your investing strategy are readily available to the individual investor.

Read widely and constantly.

Endowment CIOs and investment professionals are voracious, omnivorous consumers of information. They read constantly. They read the business press for current events and because they know other investors will be working from the same information. They go further, seeking out industry-specific information. No level of detail is too deep because they will be committing significant resources to a theme or sector if they decide to invest.

CIOs seek out contrarian viewpoints. They are wary of consensus and they don't want to be unduly influenced by the inputs they are exposed to and keep those inputs diversified to prevent this. CIOs want to know where the herd is going but do not want to be in the midst of the herd. In spirit, CIOs adhere to the Warren Buffett aphorism, "Be cautious when others are greedy and be greedy when others are cautious."

Reading allows the individual investor to develop a conviction on what will transpire. The future is difficult to predict, but that doesn't mean it can be ignored. Good investors will do their best to gauge future events and their consequences. Without a conviction and a point of view, it is difficult to hedge losses or invest opportunistically for gains.

Parting Thoughts for Individuals

We've concluded that to avoid another "lost decade" individual investors must evaluate the endowment investment model and incorporate its concepts where appropriate for their risk tolerance and portfolio. There are two strategies for the long-term individual investor's core holdings—("bucket one") that emerged from our interviews. One strategy is to set investment objectives, determine an appropriate asset allocation, research and select a set of low-fee ETFs that match that asset allocation and then periodically rebalance. The second strategy is to select an investment adviser that provides investment management based on the university endowment model of investing or other widely diversified, long-term investing model. This strategy starts with developing a list of potential advisors in the space and performing appropriate due diligence. We are convinced that the individual investor will benefit from lower fees and higher returns.

CIOs mentioned a few other interesting things: First, the three decades have been mostly bullish. As one CIO put it, "There were unprecedented tailwinds." Regression to the mean says that returns in the coming decade may be lower. Looking for returns that equal 2002 through 2007 may lead to excessive risk taking or disappointment. CIOs say it is "time to get tough."

Be careful about whom you trust with your money. CIOs do thorough due diligence, even when they know the manager. They don't skimp on any steps, and they aren't influenced by who else is already in the pool. They get their own data, they draw their own conclusions, and they won't invest with someone who can't pass their qualitative and quantitative tests.

Prepare for investing in the coming years to be a slow, steady slog. In football terms, investing will generally be a running game. One CIO said, "Investors are most comfortable when everything is going up."

Trends

Endowments, it turns out, are much more interested in broad macroeconomic trends than we anticipated. While fundamentally conservative in outlook and philosophy, there is a conviction that the world is a rapidly changing place and that good governance entails a continuous intake of a wide variety of information, a frequent reevaluation of the portfolio strategy, and a small but material portion of the portfolio dedicated to investing in near to mid-term trends. As one interviewee noted, "The long run is just a series of short runs."

As part of our process, we quizzed CIOs on what they saw coming in the near future, defined as the coming 12 to 36 months. Due to publication time cycles, the trends will be clearer by the time our readers have this information. Most of our interviews were conducted in late 2009 and early 2010. Unexpected developments in geopolitics, technology, or the economy can disrupt anyone's forecast.

There was not unanimity among CIOs and advisors about the future, but they did identify some common themes. There was general consensus about what things would be important—inflation, the strength of the dollar, the importance of emerging and frontier markets. CIOs were consistent on what trends would be important, but less so on what specific actions they would take.

While CIOs did not necessarily consider themselves professional economists or statisticians, what they did have in common was a keen eye for what information would be relevant, how it would affect their existing portfolio, and where it might create advantage. We have aggregated some of their points here. For more detailed reading on these topics we direct you to the question on trends that we have included in nearly every interview chapter.

Emerging Markets

Emerging markets were the common and the most controversial trend mentioned. What was clear is that the developed economies—the United States, Canada, Western Europe, and Japan—are seen as economic growth laggards in the coming years. The emerging markets—particularly China—were the places where higher-than-average growth was anticipated. CIOs also saw demographics as an important driver important here—a large emerging middle class will create demand for energy, goods, services, and health care.

Two points of controversy came up on this topic. First, there are varying opinions about how best to implement the strategy. Although there is consensus on the importance of emerging markets, finding the best investable opportunities is something else, and each endowment we talked to had a different slant on it. All endowments (and advisors) seem to be in intense data-gathering mode, making numerous in-person visits to Asia in general and China specifically for diligence and on-site evaluation. The second point is that, as always, CIOs are wary of consensus. The fact that so much attention is being lavished on emerging markets at the moment suggested to some that there may be a near-term bubble forming, and at a minimum that investment prices would not be ideal. We heard the term "piling in" numerous times in reference to emerging markets. Investors are now trying to determine if there are other near-emerging markets that may have more attractive pricing. These "frontier markets" are in places like Eastern Europe and Africa. In some cases, CIOs believed that while China is attractive, if an investor had not already entered the market it was likely too late.

Deleveraging Process

CIOs consistently discussed the deleveraging process, across the globe but particularly in the U.S. economy. This involves consumers and businesses alike, as they draw down their debt levels. The implication is that the global economy cannot rely on the American consumer for recovery and growth, as in 2003–2007. CIOs believe that the consumer and corporate deleveraging process is not over, and that it will be a few more painful years before it is complete.

Inflation

CIOs predict that inflation is coming to developed countries in general and to the United States in particular. Massive government spending and debt, combined with the need to keep interest rates low, mean a likely wall of inflation. There was considerable debate about the timing. CIOs saw deflation in the short to mid term, followed by inflation. There was a belief that net-debtor countries will be more subject to inflation. From a tactical standpoint they were generally at consensus on hedging this risk, primarily using real assets and secondarily using inflation-protected Treasuries. Although commercial real estate has typically been considered a real asset, the high debt levels make it less attractive as an inflation hedge currently.

CIOs are not that concerned overall about inflation or deflation. They know that either one is going to simply be part of the environment. What they are concerned about is predicting the direction and magnitude of any major shifts in inflation. Several CIOs mentioned that a well-balanced portfolio with an appropriate amount of inflation and deflation hedges takes some of the pressure off needing to accurately forecast, at a small cost of return.

U.S. Dollar

CIOs are carefully watching the U.S. dollar and concerns about the dollar's status as the reserve currency. The dollar has gone through a period of weakening, and CIOs are considering ways to hedge this. The mitigating factor is that there is no strong contender for the dollar's replacement, making the U.S. dollar "the best of the worst."

Demographic Shifts

CIOs believe in evaluating large-scale demographic shifts to determine big changes in spending and investment. In developed countries, particularly the United States and Japan, a large contingent of aging population will drive preventative, diagnostic, pharmaceutical, therapeutic, and surgical health care.

In emerging markets, particularly high-population counties like India and China, CIOs are looking for opportunities to capitalize on a burgeoning youth and middle class. The size of the markets, combined with their growing purchasing power, make them attractive for both growth and a long-term investment over several decades.

Infrastructure

Infrastructure for delivering electricity, delivering water, managing sewage, as well as roads and bridges is a focus area. In Western countries the infrastructure is aging and has been underinvested for the past decade. Most capital flows in the 1990s and 2000s were going into the finance areas. CIOs believe there will be a large and ongoing reinvestment process in developed markets as the replacement for these items takes place. All are large projects that take years to complete.

Similarly, in emerging markets, increased demand for services and a more affluent population will drive new investment in infrastructure. CIOs are sometimes hindered by the difficulty of finding solid investable opportunities in this space, but they are continuing to carefully watch this trend.

Predictions for Endowments

The coming five year period will be a time of considerable change in the endowment business. The 2008–2009 downturn will drive detailed and comprehensive evaluations of tail risk. There will also be increased scrutiny of institutional liquidity requirements. Investment committees will rethink performance metrics and measures for endowments and will rebalance peer group ranking vs. absolute return and liability-driven investing concepts. Compensation for endowment investment staff will be an ongoing conversation, linked to both the rethinking of benchmarks as well as the disparity with market rates.

Smaller endowments in the $100-$650 million range will increasingly evaluate outsourcing to achieve scale and to simultaneously solve the performance management, benchmarking and compensation issues. They will turn to combined outsourcing advisory and asset management firms that provide a full-service model.

There will be increased external scrutiny of endowments overall and their spending policies. There will be a discussion and possible implementation of government policy which defines minimum payouts or a spending policy formula, similar to that of foundations.

Liquidity management will be a focus in the coming two to three years. This will manifest in changed policies on working capital management, increased scrutiny of private investment contract terms and lock-up periods, a focus on institutional creditworthiness and available credit. Investment committees and CIOs will re-evaluate asset allocation with an eye to increased liquidity at the cost of lower returns. CIOs will demand the deployment or return of unfunded private investment commitments with private equity and venture capital managers.

University budgets will continue to feel the events of 2008–2009 for some time, due to spending policies which use a rolling average over a number of years to determine endowment payouts. Some institutions will revise their policies in response, increasing the number of years in their averaging formula from three to five or seven, prolonging the pain but reducing the operating budget impact on the coming few years.

CIOs will look to managers and their own investment staff to produce frequent reviews of portfolio risk which cut across all asset classes to understand how macroeconomic factors will affect the portfolio as a whole. A view of total leverage, currency risk, economic sector, country and market exposure will be evaluated carefully and often. This will be a response by CIOs and investment committees to the 2008–2009 downturn in order to better understand correlations and tail risk.

This reporting will also facilitate university credit evaluation. Rating agencies such as Moody's and Standard & Poor's will demand increasingly detailed information from endowments as part of the rating process. The requirement for this detailed reporting will in turn be placed on fund managers wanting to invest endowment assets. Such reporting will be a minimum bar for entry for alternative investment groups such as hedge funds, private equity, venture capital, and real estate.

The market for private firms which specialize in the endowment model will strengthen. Existing firms will grow and new firms will enter the market. These groups will be led and staffed by endowment investment professionals. Three fund-raising models for these firms will emerge. They will focus on outsourcing for small-to-medium academic (non-profit) institutions, or provide a family-office investment vehicle for a small group of high-net-worth families, or provide retail-oriented access via low minimum investment requirements to large numbers of moderate net-worth individuals.

A number of these factors will combine to produce increased turnover in the endowment investment professional market, particularly in the CIO role. Private fund management will be an attractive option for investment pros with endowment experience, and the trend towards outsourcing will accelerate this. The trend will moderate after the performance measurement, compensation and outsourcing issues are addressed by investment committees in the coming three to five years.

Summary

Endowments have a superior investing model, as their consistent results over the past two decades and more demonstrate. Even in the face of the events of 2008–2009 the model proved durable. Endowments beat the general U.S. public market indexes handily and on a consistent basis. This is of concern to individuals whose investment returns are usually congruent with broad market indexes.

Replicating the precise investment strategies of leading endowments is a difficult task for the individual. The expertise, effort and access required are beyond what the individual can typically muster. However, there is a case for learning from endowment investment techniques, particularly in asset allocation and a view of asset classes in the broadest possible way. Individuals can also learn to identify macro-economic trends and work within "short" cycles of two to five years to position their portfolios appropriately. Our interviews produced two pieces of consistent advice from investment pros: think differently about asset classes and diversify across them, and second, eliminate home bias.

Much of what individuals can learn from endowment CIOs, however, is philosophical. Our conversations with the investing pros of the endowment world left us with a strong sense that individuals can do better in their investing lives with a focus on the basics and the specifics of their own situation. This is consistent with how endowment operates—their specific tactics and strategic goals are driven by their underlying asset management philosophy, which was shared throughout this book. It is clear that endowments have changed considerably over the last 20 years and will likely change again in the coming 20 years. Every endowment has a different situation, different constraints, and yet most manage to outperform. This is because they all share a common philosophical foundation that applies regardless of their unique situation and the most recent investing trends and strategies. Individuals can learn from this and incorporate it into their own decision making.

Second, the CIOs and investment professionals we interviewed were unanimous in emphasizing the basics for investors. We heard some of the classic investment advice that is conventional wisdom. The diverse market of financial products for individual investors seems to imply that there is a secret "trick" to investing. What we learned from top money managers is that, for the individual, sticking to the basics, reading for understanding and discipline in decision making should produce the best results over the long term.

Glossary

Concise and accurate definitions of the majority of investing terms in this book can be found on Investopedia (www.investopedia.com). For easy reference, we have included a number of terms used in the book here.

★ - indicates definitions courtesy of Investopedia; Granted permission for usage from Investopedia.com. A division of Forbes Media LLC. Copyright 2010.
★★ - indicates terms courtesy of the University of Texas Investment Management Company (UTIMCO) at http://www.utimco.org/funds/allfunds/2008annual/faq_terms.asp

Absolute return* The return that an asset achieves over a certain period of time. This measure looks at the appreciation or depreciation (expressed as a percentage) that an asset—usually a stock or a mutual fund—achieves over a given period of time. Absolute return differs from relative return because it is concerned with the return of a particular asset and does not compare it to any other measure or benchmark. "Absolute return" strategies aim to produce a positive return regardless of the direction of the market.

Active management*   The use of a manager or team of managers to actively manage a fund's portfolio. Active managers rely on analytical research, forecasts, and their own judgment and experience in making investment decisions on what securities to buy, hold, and sell. The opposite of active management is called passive management, also known as "indexing."

Alpha*   A measure of performance on a risk-adjusted basis. Alpha takes the volatility (price risk) of a fund and compares its risk-adjusted performance to a benchmark index. The excess return of the fund relative to the return of the benchmark index is a fund's alpha.

Alternative investment*   An investment that is not one of the three traditional asset types (stocks, bonds and cash). Most alternative investment assets are held by institutional investors or accredited, high-net-worth individuals because of their complex nature, limited regulations and relative lack of liquidity. Alternative investments include hedge funds, managed futures, real estate, commodities and derivatives contracts.

Asset allocation**   Asset allocation is the long-term strategy for investing funds into various asset classes based on investment goals, time horizon, and risk tolerance. It is the primary determinant of investment return and is defined by the investment policy for each fund.

Benchmark returns**   Benchmark returns are the returns for a specific index defined in the investment policy statement as the performance measurement standard for a particular asset class. The most commonly used benchmarks are market indexes such as the S&P 500 Index for common stocks and the Lehman Brothers Aggregate Index for bonds.

Beta*   A measure of the volatility, or systematic risk, of a security or a portfolio in comparison to the market as a whole. Beta is calculated using regression analysis, and you can think of beta as the tendency of a security's returns to respond to swings in the market. A beta of 1 indicates that the security's price will move with the market. A beta of less than 1 means that the security will be less volatile than the market. A beta of greater than 1 indicates that the security's price will be more volatile than the market.

BRIC   Brazil, Russia, India, China

Book value of an endowment** The book value of an endowment represents all contributions, reinvested income, and any realized gains or losses attributable to the sale of an investment held in the endowment.

Capital Asset Pricing Model (CAPM)* A model that describes the relationship between risk and expected return and that is used in the pricing of risky securities.

The general idea behind CAPM is that investors need to be compensated in two ways: time value of money and risk. The time value of money is represented by the risk-free (rf) rate in the formula and compensates the investors for placing money in any investment over a period of time. The other half of the formula represents risk and calculates the amount of compensation the investor needs for taking on additional risk. This is calculated by taking a risk measure (beta) that compares the returns of the asset to the market over a period of time and to the market premium (Rm-rf).

Chief Investment Officer (CIO) The investment professional in charge of an endowment (or other investment pool) assets. Responsibilities generally include selecting and managing staff, establishing endowment investment policy, asset allocation and rebalancing, fund manager selection, risk management, and reporting. In an academic endowment the CIO typically reports to the investment committee.

Corpus The main assets of an endowment or its principal.

Correlation* A statistical measure of how two securities move in relation to each other. Correlations are used in advanced portfolio management.

Correlation is computed into what is known as the correlation coefficient, which ranges between −1 and +1. Perfect positive correlation (a correlation coefficient of +1) implies that as one security moves, either up or down, the other security will move in lockstep, in the same direction. Alternatively, perfect negative correlation means that if one security moves in either direction, the security that is perfectly negatively correlated will move by an equal amount in the opposite direction. If the correlation is 0, the movements of the securities are said to have no correlation; they are completely random.

In real life, perfectly correlated securities are rare; rather, you will find securities with some degree of correlation.

Derivative* A security whose price is dependent upon or derived from one or more underlying assets. The derivative itself is merely a contract between two or more parties. Its value is determined by fluctuations in the underlying asset. The most common underlying assets include stocks, bonds, commodities, currencies, interest rates and market indexes. Most derivatives are characterized by high leverage.

Diversification* A risk management technique that mixes a wide variety of investments within a portfolio. The rationale behind this technique contends that a portfolio of different kinds of investments will, on average, yield higher returns and pose a lower risk than any individual investment found within the portfolio.

Diversification strives to smooth out unsystematic risk events in a portfolio so that the positive performance of some investments will neutralize the negative performance of others. Therefore, the benefits of diversification will hold only if the securities in the portfolio are not perfectly correlated.

Downside risk** A risk metric that distinguishes between "good" and "bad" returns by assigning risk only to those returns below a return specified by an investor. Downside risk is considered a more effective risk measure than standard deviation (volatility) for two important reasons: (1) It is investor specific, and (2) it identifies return distributions that have higher probabilities for negative ("left tail") market events. Downside risk is also referred to as downside deviation or target semideviation.

Endowment A long-term investment pool managed by a non-profit institution for the current and future benefit of the institution.

Endowment policy portfolio** The endowment policy portfolio is the hypothetical portfolio consisting of each asset category weighted at the neutral or target asset class allocation outlined in the investment policy of each fund.

Endowment policy portfolio return** The endowment policy portfolio return is the benchmark return for the endowment policy portfolio and is calculated by summing the neutrally weighted index return (percentage weight for the asset class multiplied by the benchmark return for the asset class) for the various asset classes in the endowment portfolio for the period.

Exchange Traded Fund (ETF)*   A security that tracks an index, a commodity or a basket of assets like an index fund, but trades like a stock on an exchange. ETFs experience price changes throughout the day as they are bought and sold.

Fund manager*   The person(s) responsible for implementing a fund's investing strategy and managing its portfolio trading activities.

General partner (GP)   A partner in a business who has unlimited liability. The GP typically has management control. In the investment industry, GPs are typically paid a management fee and a carried interest.

Growth investing*   A strategy whereby an investor seeks out stocks with what they deem good growth potential. In most cases a growth stock is defined as a company whose earnings are expected to grow at an above-average rate compared to its industry or the overall market.

Hedge funds**   Hedge fund investments are broadly defined to include nontraditional investment strategies whereby the majority of the underlying securities are traded on public exchanges or are otherwise readily marketable. These types of investments can include: (1) global long/short strategies that attempt to exploit profits from security selection skills by taking long positions in securities that are expected to advance and short positions in securities where returns are expected to lag or decline; (2) arbitrage strategies, which attempt to exploit pricing discrepancies between closely related securities, utilizing a variety of different tactics; and (3) event-driven strategies that attempt to exploit pricing discrepancies that often exist during discrete events such as bankruptcies, mergers, takeovers, spin-offs, and recapitalizations in equity and debt securities.

Illiquidity   A term used to indicate that an investment is not easily sold and converted to cash. For example, marketable securities like publicly traded stocks can be sold immediately on an exchange and converted to cash within a matter of days, whereas a piece of real estate would take months to sell. Illiquid assets are valued less frequently because market value is harder to ascertain.

Leverage* The use of various financial instruments or borrowed capital, such as margin, to increase the potential return of an investment.

Leveraged buyout (LBO)* The acquisition of another company using a significant amount of borrowed money (bonds or loans) to meet the cost of acquisition. Often, the assets of the company being acquired are used as collateral for the loans in addition to the assets of the acquiring company. The purpose of leveraged buyouts is to allow companies to make large acquisitions without having to commit a lot of capital.

Liability-Driven Investment (LDI)* A form of investing in which the main goal is to gain sufficient assets to meet all liabilities, both current and future. This form of investing is most prominent with defined-benefit pension plans, whose liabilities can often reach into the billions of dollars for the largest of plans.

Limited partner (LP)* A partner in a partnership whose liability is limited to the extent of the partner's share of ownership. Limited partners generally do not have any kind of management responsibility in the partnership in which they invest and are not responsible for its debt obligations. For this reason, limited partners are not considered to be material participants.

Liquidity* The degree to which an asset or security can be bought or sold in the market without affecting the asset's price; the ability to convert an asset to cash quickly, also known as "marketability." Liquidity is characterized by a high level of trading activity. Assets that can be easily bought or sold are known as liquid assets.

Lock-up period* Window of time in which investors of a hedge fund or other closely-held investment vehicle are not allowed to redeem or sell shares. The lock-up period helps portfolio managers avoid liquidity problems while capital is put to work in sometimes illiquid investments.

Manager see "Fund manager"

Mark to market* A measure of the fair value of accounts that can change over time, such as assets and liabilities. Mark to market aims to provide a realistic appraisal of an institution's or company's current financial situation. It reflects the value an asset would sell for if it was sold today.

Mean variance* A measure of the dispersion of a set of data points around their mean value. Variance is a mathematical expectation of the average squared deviations from the mean.

Modern Portfolio Theory (MPT)* A theory on how risk-averse investors can construct portfolios to optimize or maximize expected return based on a given level of market risk, emphasizing that risk is an inherent part of higher reward. There are four basic steps involved in portfolio construction: Security valuation, asset allocation, portfolio optimization, performance measurement.

Pension fund* A fund established by an employer to facilitate and organize the investment of employees' retirement funds contributed by the employer and employees. The pension fund is a common asset pool meant to generate stable growth over the long term, and provide pensions for employees when they reach the end of their working years and commence retirement.

Performance derby A term describing the phenomenon that chief investment officers are evaluated on the annual performance of their endowment returns versus peer endowments.

Private equity* Equity capital that is not quoted on a public exchange. Private equity consists of investors and funds that make investments directly into private companies or conduct buyouts of public companies that result in a delisting of public equity. Capital for private equity is raised from retail and institutional investors and can be used to fund new technologies, expand working capital within an owned company, make acquisitions, or strengthen a balance sheet.

The majority of private equity consists of institutional investors and accredited investors who can commit large sums of money for long periods of time. Private equity investments often demand long holding periods to allow for a turnaround of a distressed company or a liquidity event such as an IPO or sale to a public company.

Private investments**   Private investments consist of investments in the equity securities of private businesses including real estate. Private investments are held either through limited partnerships or as direct ownership interests. The private investment category also includes mezzanine and opportunistic investments.

Portable alpha*   The strategy of portfolio managers separating alpha from beta by investing in securities that differ from the market index from which their beta is derived. Alpha is the return achieved over and above the return that results from the correlation between the portfolio and the market (beta). In simple terms, this is a strategy that involves investing in areas that have little to no correlation with the market.

Purchasing power**   The primary objective of the endowment funds is to preserve the purchasing power of the endowment over the long term. This essentially means to increase the market value of the endowments over time at a rate at least equal to the rate of inflation after all expenses and distributions and to increase annual distributions at a rate at least equal to the rate of inflation.

Real assets*   Physical or identifiable assets such as gold, land, equipment, patents, and so on. They are the opposite of a financial asset. Real assets tend to be most desirable during periods of high inflation.

Side pocket*   A type of account used in hedge funds to separate illiquid assets from other more liquid investments. Once an investment enters a side pocket account, only the present participants in the hedge fund will be entitled to a share of it. Future investors will not receive a share of the proceeds in the event the asset's returns get realized.

Spending formula   Calculation used by an endowment to determine the amount to be provided to the institution's operating budget in a given year. Typically determined based on a rolling average of performance over 3, 5 or 7 year periods.

Style box investing*   Created by Morningstar, a style box is designed to visually represent the investment characteristics of fixed income (bond), domestic equity (stock), and international equity (stock) securities and their respective mutual funds. A style box is a valuable tool for investors to use to determine the asset allocation and risk-return structures of their portfolios and/or how a security fits into their investing criteria. There are slightly different style boxes used for equity and fixed income funds.

Tail risk* A form of portfolio risk that arises when the possibility that an investment will move more than three standard deviations from the mean is greater than what is shown by a normal distribution.

When a portfolio of investments is put together, it is assumed that the distribution of returns will follow a normal pattern. Under this assumption, the probability that returns will move between the mean and three standard deviations, either positive or negative, is 99.97 percent. This means that the probability of returns moving more than three standard deviations beyond the mean is 0.03 percent, or virtually nil. However, the concept of tail risk suggests that the distribution is not normal, but skewed, and has fatter tails. The fatter tails increase the probability that an investment will move beyond three standard deviations.

Distributions that are characterized by fat tails are often seen when looking at hedge fund returns.

Thematic investing The concept of developing macroeconomic themes to drive investment and asset allocation decisions.

Total return** The change in investment value during the period, including both realized and unrealized capital appreciation and income, expressed as a percentage of the market value at the beginning of the period. Total return is also known as investment return.

UMIFA Uniform Management of Institutional Funds Act; guidelines and standards established in 1972 determining how endowment investment decisions should be made.

UPMIFA Uniform Prudent Management of Institutional Funds Act; an update of the UMIFA standards from 2006.

Value investing* The strategy of selecting stocks that trade for less than their intrinsic values. Value investors actively seek stocks of companies that they believe the market has undervalued. They believe the market overreacts to good and bad news, resulting in stock price movements that do not correspond with the company's long-term fundamentals.

The result is an opportunity for value investors to profit by buying when the price is deflated.

Typically, value investors select stocks with lower-than-average price-to-book or price-to-earnings ratios and/or high dividend yields.

Venture capital* Money provided by investors to startup firms and small businesses with perceived, long-term growth potential. This is a very important source of funding for startups that do not have access to capital markets. It typically entails high risk for the investor, but it has the potential for above-average returns.

Vintage year* The year in which the first influx of investment capital is delivered to a project or company. This marks when capital is contributed by venture capital, private equity fund or a partnership drawing down from its investors.

VIX* The ticker symbol for the Chicago Board Options Exchange (CBOE) Volatility Index, which shows the market's expectation of 30-day volatility. It is constructed using the implied volatilities of a wide range of S&P 500 index options. This volatility is meant to be forward looking and is calculated from both calls and puts. The VIX is a widely used measure of market risk and is often referred to as the "investor fear gauge."

Working capital The operating capital of the university (i.e., those funds used to pay operating expenses and near-term financial commitments).

About the Authors

JOHN BASCHAB is Senior Vice President at Technisource, a leading technology services company and a division of SFN Group, Inc. He was a co-founder and president of consulting services at Impact Innovations Group before successfully selling the company to Technisource in 2005. After receiving his MBA with honors from the University of Chicago Graduate School of Business, Baschab worked as a technology consultant to Fortune 500 companies in the Chicago office of management consultancy Booz & Company. He began his IT career at AT&T and Intergraph following graduation from the University of Alabama. John is an adjunct professor at Southern Methodist University. He is also the co-author of three other books published by John Wiley & Sons, including the *Executive's Guide to Information Technology* and the *Professional Services Firm Bible*.

JON PIOT received a Bachelor of Science from Southern Methodist University and an MBA from Harvard Business School. Jon began his career at Andersen Consulting (now Accenture) and provided consulting services to Fortune 500 companies at management consultancy Booz-Allen & Hamilton. Jon is a successful entrepreneur. As co-founder and CEO of Impact Innovations Group, Jon led the sale of Impact

Innovations to Technisource in 2005, and was part of the executive team responsible for the sale of Technisource to Spherion Corp. He is currently the managing partner at Redpoint Capital, a private equity investment group, and an adjunct professor at Southern Methodist University. Jon is the co-author of three other books published by John Wiley & Sons, including the *Executive's Guide to Information Technology* and the *Professionals Services Firm Bible.*

Index